Managing
and Motivating
your Agents
and Distributors

Managing
and Motivating
your Agents
and Distributors

VINOO IYER

FINANCIAL TIMES

PITMAN PUBLISHING

Pitman Publishing
128 Long Acre, London WC2E 9AN

A Division of Longman Group UK Limited

First published in 1992

© Vinoo Iyer 1992

A CIP catalogue record for this book can be obtained from the
British Library.

ISBN 0 273 03956 3

Phototypeset in Linotron Times Roman
by Northern Phototypesetting Co. Ltd., Bolton
Printed and bound in Great Britain
by Biddles Ltd., Guildford

CONTENTS

FOREWORD

During the last few years the market environment has changed dramatically beyond every expectation. Trade borders and barriers are being removed; even in those countries whose markets were not accessible before, the expectations are high among new customers. In the war for market share, the manufacturer who quickly realizes an opportunity and establishes local distribution will often be the winner.

Working through distributors has often proved more advantageous compared to own subsidiaries because distributors:

- generally respond more quickly to market needs
- show greater flexibility to match local circumstances and solutions
- have a lower cost requirement.

In more mature markets, the distributors have proved to be as effective as own subsidiaries and where they co-exist with subsidiaries in multi-brand environments, they have proved to be a good competitive complement to the subsidiary.

If the manufacturer spends sufficient time to acquire market knowledge, supports the distributor with product education, good logistics and service training and is demanding about future targets and achievements, the distributor will regard himself as an integral part of the company and this will motivate him to reach new heights.

In our business we see a lot of manufacturers, products and brands which are continually looking for new consumers and market places. Good distributors are always in demand and they and the market expect much more than just a supply of products. In helping to add value through support in marketing, logistics, financial packages, etc., you are creating a competitive edge and developing leadership in the market-place with your partner, the distributor.

I think that all the topics I have referred to above are excellently covered in this comprehensive book by Vinoo Iyer.

Magnus Karlberg, President
Electrolux International Group, 11 June 1992

PREFACE

In today's world of rapidly changing technology and advancement in communication and in the face of severe competition, *Managing and Motivating your Distributors* as a subject is assuming great importance to many international businesses particularly those in growth industries; for example, businesses in high technology, information technology, pharmaceuticals, medicine and medical instrumentation, bioscience, and modern manufacturing (third and fourth generation) spring to mind. It is also relevant to many other businesses, especially in the context of:

- the creation of the Single European Market on 1 January 1993
- the moves to expand the European Community (EC), e.g. the recently negotiated European Economic Area linking the EC and EFTA
- the special 'Europe Agreements' for free trade with Eastern European markets
- the emergence of common European standards in many fields
- the opportunities for rationalisation of warehousing and distribution points within the enlarged Europe
- the increasing interest of Japanese and American companies in exploiting the European market
- the emergence of developing nations' markets
- the orientation of many economies towards a 'market' approach.

All these new trends demand that companies **review** their distribution strategies and the **available channel** options. One of the quickest routes to new markets for a company's product is through independent distributors who are already established and are known in the markets. Another quick route is through commercial agents appointed for the purpose of promotion and sales of products in territories where the firm is not represented.

There is also the pressure on companies to reduce costs and offer competitive products at attractive prices. A significant proportion of the ultimate sale price of a product is made up of the marketing, sales and distribution costs of the product, right across the channel. This can vary from 35 per cent to 60 per cent depending on the product and the industry. A regular updating of the distribution strategy and the management of the distribution channel are therefore assuming strategic significance.

The managers who have attended my seminars have often said to me that there exists a need for a comprehensive book that explains, in **practical** terms, the concepts, principles, good practices and pitfalls in distribution management, and that establishes guidelines for a European or an international manager to follow. Books which are available have been published mainly in the United States and may have been written with a domestic American market orientation. This book is intended to provide the 'missing link' for the European and international managers.

In writing the manuscript, I have drawn heavily on my own practical experience and that of my colleagues and those European managers who participated in my programmes on this subject over the last two decades. This book should serve as a reference point for all marketing and export managers, general managers and divisional heads responsible for distribution policy and management, marketing managers, and managers responsible for motivating distributors and getting the best out of them.

In preparing the manuscript, several of my colleagues and managers in industry across Europe have helped both my thinking and the development of my ideas considerably by sharing their practical problems and experiences, and I am grateful to them all. I would wish to thank specially my colleagues and friends: Phillip Day, Mike Eldon, John Freestone, Francisco Lafuente Bueno, Tony Garvey, Dick Handscombe, John Reynolds, Chris Steward, John Wellemin, Marie-Ann Rijs and Sally Green, and my publisher Soraya Romano of Pitman Professional Publishing.

In addition, I thank all those practising international managers who took the trouble to read the manuscript and offered suggestions for improvement. To my wife, Jay, a special note of thanks for assisting in the research, participating in the drafting and vetting of the manuscript, and getting it ready on time and meeting the publishers' requirements. This work would not have been possible without her help.

Vinoo Iyer
Berkshire, England

INTRODUCTION

Writing in the April 1962 issue of *Fortune* magazine, Peter Drucker, the well-known management guru, compared distribution to 'the dark continent'. That was thirty years ago and I find, in my discussions with companies in Europe, that this is still the case in many businesses, especially at the top levels of management. Many top managers delegate the responsibility for distribution; their lack of appreciation and control of the distribution function and marketing channels causes problems for their companies in the long run.

DISTRIBUTION AND MARKETING

No doubt everyone accepts the principle that when a product idea has been researched and the product designed, developed and produced, then it has to be marketed, sold, distributed and serviced profitably, and to the satisfaction of the customer. But in the practice of this principle, many things go wrong, particularly in

> *the movement of goods from the place of production to the place of the customer and in the satisfactory transference of title to goods from the producer to the eventual customer.*

that is, in the physical distribution process and the channel or route by which goods are distributed. This phrase also gives a practical definition of distribution. But this process cannot work satisfactorily without marketing. In my experience, marketing and distribution go hand in hand. So let me also define marketing, as it works in practice and according to my experience. The practice of 'marketing' is all about 'ensuring customer satisfaction through "values" while making satisfactory profits'.

Marketing is concerned with adding value through every stage of the distribution process including the channel. Value is added through features, branding, packaging, delivery at the right time at the right place at the right price, and merchandising at the point of sale and through promotion. If one or more intermediaries, such as distributors, are involved in getting the products to the final customer, it is often forgotten that they are also involved in helping to market the product. Many executives just treat them as traders or selling intermediaries. If the importance of their marketing role is not recognised, the money spent by the manufacturer, for example, in promoting the product, can be wasted.

DISTRIBUTOR

A distributor is

a business enterprise which buys or imports goods and services, stocks goods and perhaps adds value, resells and distributes or delivers to customers on its own account and at its own cost.

The intermediaries in general, if they are distributors, are entrepreneurs and as such are genuinely interested in furthering their own objectives. Manufacturers' executives responsible for this aspect of the business may be very good in managing and motivating their own employees, but when it comes to managing and motivating independent entrepreneurs a different set of skills and attitudes are required.

In essence, the task is similar to the one of managing different businesses and motivating several chief executives and sales forces of those businesses. The whole gamut of management principles, processes and practices is involved, especially the following:

- understanding of the environment and mapping out possible scenarios
- understanding of the market dynamics and competition
- evaluation of the opportunities
- critical examination of the various means of getting to the market
- designing the appropriate competitive response
- setting the mission and the objectives for the market
- selection of the most appropriate means
- selection of suitable partners
- ensuring that there is a common thread between the objectives of the firm and of the partners
- developing a relationship
- negotiating with the partners and agreeing a common set of objectives
- evaluating the performance of the business relationship
- managing the partners
- constantly motivating the partners
- deciding when to dissolve the partnership
- managing conflicts.

Although many of these aspects concern the general management discipline required for managing any business, they are of particular relevance when applied to distributors and independent intermediaries appointed to market the products of a company in international markets.

WHAT THIS BOOK IS ABOUT

This book deals with specific aspects of applying the essential principles and good practices for getting the most from the distributors and commercial agents. It is not a book on general management or management principles, neither is it a book about marketing in general nor is it a book about personnel management. It is essentially about distributors, particularly about managing and motivating distributors.

It is written from the manufacturer's point of view and not the distributor's. While the distributor is not a target, members of distributor organizations will also find it useful. They will be able to learn what a good manufacturer ought to be doing and, therefore, may be able to advance their own cause.

A reader will essentially learn the following:

- how distributors differ from other types of channels
- how to select and establish distributors
- how to measure a distributor's impact on the company's policies
- how to assess their strengths, weaknesses and positions in the market-place
- how to get the most out of distributors
- how to motivate distributors to major on the company's products
- how to evaluate the distributor's overall contribution
- how to maintain a competitive distribution network
- how to manage conflicts
- how to improve the position of the company in the chosen markets.

STRUCTURE OF THE BOOK

The book is divided into fourteen chapters each of which deals with a specific topic. An attempt has been made to provide several checklists so as to help the reader implement the main principles and good European practice.

Chapter 1 outlines the influence of distribution channels and how they affect company profits and identifies the importance of having a good distribution strategy.

Chapter 2 is about alternative channels which are available and developing a relevant distribution strategy for business expansion.

In Chapter 3, the selection of an appropriate type of channel is discussed.

As this book is essentially about distributors, Chapter 4 is concerned with effective marketing (not just selling) through the distributor.

Chapter 5 deals with the principles of a good logistics chain and the role of a distributor in this regard.

In Chapter 6, the comprehensive roles of the manufacturer/supplier and distributor are discussed and it is explained how these roles complement each other.

Chapter 7 outlines the legal aspects and the need for conformance with the local laws and the general principles of competitive policies adopted in various countries and in particular within the European Community.

In the context of the foregoing, Chapter 8 explains how to select a suitable distributor.

Chapters 9 and 10 deal with establishing a good relationship and managing and motivating the distributors. These chapters provide the vital ingredients in getting the best value from such business partnerships.

Chapter 11 discusses the role of the manufacturer's personnel dealing with the distributors and the characteristics and skills on which the futures of the company and its distributors depend for success.

Chapters 12 and 13 deal with unsatisfactory situations, how to remedy them and how to resolve conflicts.

Chapter 14 outlines the general trends in distribution.

A number of appendices, containing specimen contracts, additional information and a description of a technique for problem-solving have been included for the benefit of the international marketing and distribution managers.

At the end, you will find a list of useful references for those who wish to have further amplification.

1 THE INFLUENCE OF DISTRIBUTION CHANNELS ON COMPANY PROFITS

This chapter explains the influence of distribution channels, how they affect company profits, the importance of having a good distribution strategy and the role of the channel; it ends with a checklist.

DISTRIBUTION CHANNELS AND COMPANY PROFITS

The development of marketing and distribution channels can be attributed to two main factors:[1] the need for efficiency and competitiveness of delivery systems and the economic pressure. Rapidly changing technology, increasing competition, and the advancement of telecommunications and transport systems have all had a part in shaping this change.

An increasing proportion of the goods that we buy each year is made wholly or in part in another country. Today we live in a world of interdependent economies and no major country can boast that it is self-sufficient in manufacturing the goods it needs. The proportion of the world output which is traded each year shows a steadily upward trend.

The organization structure or system that enables a company to market, sell and deliver products either through wholesale and/or retail trade or directly to a customer is generally called the distribution channel. Distribution operates within the marketing system to effect the transfer of ownership of goods from the producer to the consumer. Moreover, any process of getting the products of a company to the end consumer or customer through a distribution channel involves a variety of activities such as:

1. First creating the need in the market-place through increasing awareness of the company's products and their benefits.
2. Actively promoting the products in the trade and/or retail outlets.
3. Having the products on the shelves at the appropriate locations, e.g. warehouses or stock-keeping units (SKUs).
4. Persuading the customers to buy the products.

5. Having the means, or access to the means, of transporting the products from where they are to where they are needed.
6. Delivering the products to the customers' named premises on time as promised.
7. Ensuring that the customer gets satisfaction from the use of the products.

Distribution consists of the agencies and the physical transfers necessary to perform all the activities involved in making the transfer to the ultimate user. Services can also utilize distribution activities, as in dry-cleaning of clothes or sewing machine repair services. A company's distribution system includes not only all of its own distribution facilities and personnel, but also those of the distributors and dealers who sell its products.

A producer company uses intermediaries or middlemen due to their efficiency in making the goods produced available to the target markets; they can manage this better than the producer alone, through their position in their markets, their experience, contacts, know-how, etc. From the point of view of an economist, the intermediaries can convert the portfolios of products offered by producers into assortments of products and services needed by consumers and final customers. Consumers and end customers, excepting the large ones, want the products in smaller quantities than the manufacturer can supply directly and economically. The intermediaries buy the products from many producers in larger quantities and break them down into smaller parcels required by the consumers. They perform the much needed service of matching 'supply and demand'.

A little thought will enable anyone to list all the tasks involved in getting a product to the final customer. A checklist of channel tasks, based upon a high technology product company, is provided at the end of this chapter. This can be modified to suit your own company.

All of these activities involve time, effort and investment, which cost money. Whether the company undertakes all of these tasks itself, or delegates the tasks to others involved in the process, such as distributors, licensees, commercial agents, brokers or other third parties, it all costs money. This means the ultimate profits of the company are affected by the process and the way in which the process is carried out. In other words, the distribution (and marketing) channels used affect the company's profits. If another party is involved, that party has to derive sufficient income to make the task a worthwhile one for that party to be interested in promoting the company's products. When a third independent party (the first party being the company, the second party being the customer) is involved, it does not need a lot of imagination to see why the management and motivation of the third party is vital to ensure that the company's profit is optimized.

Figure 1.1 illustrates the nature of a profit flow and how it is affected. The

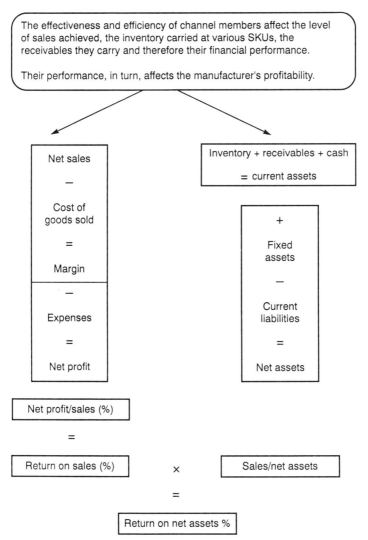

The effectiveness and efficiency of channel members affect the level of sales achieved, the inventory carried at various SKUs, the receivables they carry and therefore their financial performance.

Their performance, in turn, affects the manufacturer's profitability.

Net sales

−

Cost of goods sold

=

Margin

−

Expenses

=

Net profit

Inventory + receivables + cash

= current assets

+

Fixed assets

−

Current liabilities

=

Net assets

Net profit/sales (%)

=

Return on sales (%)   ×   Sales/net assets

=

Return on net assets %

Figure 1.1 Channels and profit flow

role of distribution management is to maximize profit through a favourable combination of service to the customers at minimum cost. Every element of distribution should be viewed as contributing to the profitability of the company in direct proportion to the degree of success with which these objectives are attained. Marketing/distribution managers and managers responsible for distributors must inform themselves fully of the impacts of distribution channel efficiencies (or inefficiencies as the case may be) on profit, competition and marketing. This will entail clear documentation describing the impacts, and this must be used for communicating and convincing top management.

DISTRIBUTION CHANNELS AND THE COMPANY'S OVERALL MARKETING STRATEGY

The overall marketing strategy of a company dictates the kind of distribution channels a company must decide upon. Decisions on marketing and distribution channels also affect every other marketing decision. For instance, the company's product pricing policy depends on whether it adopts a trade marketing policy or mass merchandising policy. A decision on advertising spend depends on the type of persuasive arguments, training of distributor/dealer sales force, motivation etc. which are needed. Many companies such as DHL and Federal Express have gained competitive advantage in the package delivery business through the adoption of imaginative distribution systems and promotional campaigns.

In an international context, a company's overall marketing strategy must be based on the knowledge of the external forces which shape the needs of the customers. The external forces generally include the competition, the market dynamics, the policies and the regulations of the governments concerned and the social, economic and political macro forces that affect the evolution of the markets.

As division of labour intensifies in an economy, the discrepancies between the requirements of the consumers and the extent to which the manufacturers can supply them widens more and more. For example, the consumers may wish to buy the product in small packages which the manufacturer may not be able to supply to all the retailers without a lot of inconvenience. It then becomes convenient for one or more intermediaries to step in in order to repackage the product in smaller amounts, as has happened in the case of food suppliers to airlines catering for their passengers.

In the transfer of goods from the original manufacturer to the end-user, the essential activities concerned are the transfer of title to the goods, their transport, their storage if needed, the finance of the goods in transit, in the inventory and on purchase as well as the transfer of information about the availability, qualities and price of the product. The importance attached to these activities depends on the characteristics of the product concerned and the relationships between the buyers and sellers. Industrial goods generally need personal selling whereas consumer goods require far more processing of information between channels.

Distribution channels participate in at least four important Ps of marketing: providing to the potential customer a convenient **place** at which the product or service is made available; a **price** at which it is available; further **product information** and answers to questions on how the product may be applied beneficially by the customer; and general **promotion** of the product. The channels may also provide the manufacturer/supplier with information on the market, the competition and the general market needs, depending on the motivation of the channel holders.

People, in particular the key individuals responsible within the channel organizations for performance, play an important part in the interpretation of agreed marketing strategies and policies. Appropriate motivation of such individuals and their positive involvement in the development of marketing strategies can go a long way towards the achievement of the marketing objectives, while its absence can have a detrimental effect.

It can therefore be readily seen how the channel decisions markedly affect all other marketing decisions; as they also imply the long term involvement of the company with the other channel partners, it is necessary to consider the future as well as the present when making such decisions. In essence, the overall marketing strategy must spell out the specific objectives to be achieved, the chosen market segments to be served, and the product and the marketing mixes to be deployed, including the chosen channels. Included in this should be a statement of the company's competitive advantages and the channels' contribution to them.

A marketing and distribution strategy should consider every existing and new product or service and assign a specific channel to it. It is easy to overlook new and better types of distribution channels which would serve changing needs or circumstances. It is possible to make major improvements on existing arrangements in some cases. In this process, consideration should be given to the following:

- relevant characteristics of the product/service
- the characteristics of the market
- needs of the specific target segments for which the product/service is appropriate
- available resources
- available channels and their costs.

The incentives the company can offer its channel partners, including the distributors, should be carefully considered. The smaller the company, the more difficult it is to interest good distributors in its products. The distribution strategies of the close competitors also merit consideration by the market planner. It might be worthwhile to try something different from them.

Everyone knows about the success of Swatch watches now. Yet the story is worth telling [1]. In the early 1980s, two famous watch companies with famous brands such as Omega, Tissot, Longines and Rado were experiencing bad times. Competition came in the form of copies of the Swiss watches and low priced watches from Japan. The lending bankers called in a successful entrepreneur by the name of Hayek, to merge the two companies and create SMH as a strong corporation with a clearly redefined strategy to move into high technology niche businesses. SMH diversified and invested in high technology machinery, systems and production facility. This was one of the planks on which the battle was fought and won. The industry expected SMH to come out attacking in the medium and high priced watch segments. But instead, in the words of Hayek,

> we hit them with a quality watch in the low priced segment, where the Japanese were strongest, where they would be hurt the most and where we had the highest risk. [He says] the Japanese price strategy worked as long as they were the cheapest. But they are so no longer and they are in trouble. So we have a new strategy – to open up a new front every eight months. Attack, attack, attack.

The marketing success of Swatch is a testimony to the epic part played by Hayek and his strategic thinking.

THE IMPORTANCE OF A ROBUST DISTRIBUTION CHANNEL STRATEGY

No distribution strategy can ignore the extent to which the chosen market needs to be covered to achieve the marketing objectives. This includes questions as to whether the products concerned should be allowed in all the relevant outlets in the market (intensive distribution) or whether the product should be placed in the hands of a single outlet (exclusive distribution) or whether the product should only be sold through a selected number of outlets (selective distribution). The distribution strategy must be consistent with the company's overall marketing objectives on the one hand and the competitive position in each of the chosen markets on the other. Coverage to achieve volume is one thing, but getting the required level of profits is another. These are considered again in the next chapter in the context of developing a strategy.

The strategy must be robust enough to withstand the marginal changes that may arise from time to time. Time may not be on the company's side for it to alter its strategy in the face of changing circumstances that may arise in the shorter term or the competition may be flexible in its response to the market situation and rob the company of its opportunity.

Economic development and channel development go hand in hand. So it is natural to expect the development of distribution systems in economically well developed countries. Distribution in a less developed country (LDC) is often one that has been tried and tested for a long time or has been adapted from those which have been well tried and tested in other countries. As marketing and distribution are intertwined and the development of marketing itself is highly differentiated in international markets, the distribution channels also are highly differentiated there.

In the development of a distribution strategy, due consideration must also be given to issues that raise trade-offs. Some examples are given below.

1. *Territories:* Disputes can arise in the way in which territories are allocated to the channel holders. If the customers served or the coverage of territories are restricted, the channel holder, whose interests are not served in a future situation, could challenge the decision in a court of law under certain competition or anti-trust laws.

2. *Customers:* Customers in a distributor territory may wish to buy directly from the manufacturer and the latter may also entertain that proposition. If the channel holder expects to operate an exclusive channel, this could cause friction. Such situations need to be resolved in the beginning.

3. *Products:* Is the channel holder responsible for the marketing of all the products of the company? What happens if a new product or a new brand requiring direct technical support from the manufacturer is to be launched?

4. *Prices:* Who is responsible for the market prices? What is the strategy of the manufacturer/supplier with regard to pricing? What policies would be followed in declining market conditions?

5. *Stocks/inventories:* How much of inventory is to be held and on what basis? What happens to the inventory in the event of a decline of the market? What happens to surplus inventory over market demand?

6. *Sales targets:* What if the channel holder considers the targets set by the manufacturer to be unrealistic? On what basis should sales targets be set?

A distribution strategy must take account not only of the channel structures that exist in the world but also the cultural and trade differences that differentiate them. In international distribution, people matter. It is all about relationships and the foundations upon which they are built. Good partners can help each other in adverse circumstances. Involvement in strategy development is a must – a way must be found to get inputs of your international partners in good time to shape your international distribution strategy. Some key principles have proved to be successful in the recent past for many companies:

1. Choose the type of channel that can navigate strange waters; but be prepared for shocks.
2. Cultivate personal relationships in international distribution.
3. Identify a distinctive market position for your product.
4. Select specific distribution approaches to satisfy specific service needs of market segments.
5. Do not sacrifice longer term benefits for short term expediency.
6. Do not put all your eggs in one basket. One channel alone may not be adequate or appropriate in a given market.
7. Do not forget that both you and the channel member have to reap adequate rewards.

THE VITAL ROLE OF A CHANNEL

The reader will be well aware of the following statements.

- Who is going to benefit from your product?
- Who is going to buy your product and why?
- How can you sell a product if you don't tell the prospective buyer about your product?
- Nothing happens until somebody has made a sale.
- Benefits claimed for a product during a promotion or the selling process can only be realised by a customer after the delivery of what is promised.
- Buying is one thing but being satisfied with what you bought is another thing altogether.

Your channel plays an important role in dealing with each and every one of the above aspects. There are nine key functions a channel performs: Fig. 1.2 illustrates this. Of course, these functions should be jointly tackled by the manufacturer/supplier and the channel holder. It would need a vast amount of resources to tackle them alone and it may take a long time on those terms.

A distributor's role in helping a company to increase its market penetration

As the locally established operation, a distributor can add weight and value to the manufacturer's campaign to penetrate the market, particularly through local knowledge, personal contacts and sales force, to gain mutual benefit. A distributor can offer an additional and independent point of view about how the product can be introduced/marketed/sold to the best advantage. On the basis that both parties benefit, the distributor should be able to utilize the sales and supporting resources to add value to the manufacturer's

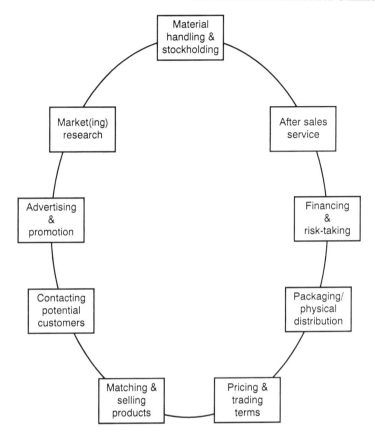

Figure 1.2 Key channel functions

effort in promoting the product and getting the interests of important customers focused on the company's offerings. Two parties, one with the market know-how and the other with the product know-how, have a better chance of penetrating the market than a single operation on its own, especially if the target market can be persuaded to see the benefits of the product offered and how it matches the target market's needs.

A CHECKLIST OF CHANNEL TASKS

1. As a stockist

    (a) fast moving high value items
    (b) slow moving high value items

(c) fast moving low value items
(d) slow moving low value items – critical
                                     – other
(e) stock reporting

2. As a promotion agent

(a) advertising copy creation
(b) trade promotion
(c) 'consumer' promotion
(d) trade journal articles
(e) learned journal articles
(f) company name promotion
(g) general brand promotion
(h) channel promotion
(i) participation in local exhibitions
(j) participation in international/national exhibitions/events
(k) participation in sponsorships
(l) public relations activity – image creation
                                    – corporate advertising
(m) product launch/promotion
(n) display advertising
(o) 'lobby' work

3. As an added-value provider

(a) additions to product features/facilities/applications
(b) packaging
(c) 'application' know-how
(d) 'benefit addition' by sales force
(e) 'benefit addition' by technical support/know-how/translation

4. As a sales resource

(a) face to face – channel links
                       – end-users/customers
(b) customer needs analysis/fact-find
(c) matching of product benefits versus customer needs
(d) order taking
(e) servicing of orders from customers
(f) obtaining market feedback from customers
(g) obtaining market feedback regarding competition
(h) obtaining market feedback regarding future needs

5. As an after-sales service resource

    (a) after-sales installation support
    (b) service under warranty cover
    (c) ongoing customer support
    (d) preventive maintenance
    (e) customer care programmes
    (f) quality audit
    (g) maintenance of parts inventory
    (h) parts sales
    (i) repairs service

6. As a distribution/delivery route

    (a) physical distribution
    (b) delivery control
    (c) returns management

7. As a test marketer
    (a) test marketing
    (b) reporting of test marketing result

8. As a safeguarder/protector of image

    (a) company image maintenance
    (b) brand reinforcement
    (c) protection of trade mark/name, registration
    (d) coverage of risk/insurance

Reference

[1] Swatch success story, *International Management*, January 1987, 18–19.

2 USING A DISTRIBUTION CHANNEL STRATEGY FOR BUSINESS EXPANSION

This chapter is about the alternative channels available to a business and developing a relevant distribution strategy for business expansion. It is assumed in this context that the business in question has the prime objectives of profitable growth and expansion into chosen markets including the domestic market. What sorts of channels are available to it?

CHANNEL STRUCTURES/SYSTEMS

This requires some definition. The channel structure consists of entities that are dependent on each other for the performance of mutually beneficial tasks. The manufacturer/producer depends on others to convey the product to its market, and ultimately to buy it and thereby provide returns; the consumers/end customers depend on others to produce what they buy and to deliver the goods.

The channel is bounded by its market area, the volume of products it can handle and its capability of response through its human resources. The channel structure is affected and partly determined by its industry environment as well as the national and international environmental considerations. It is a system which evolves continuously in response to changes in these environments.

Bucklin [1] has developed a theory that marketing channels which provide better service on four counts, namely, reduction of search time, the waiting time, the storage and product variety, will be preferred by the consumers, other things, especially price, being equal. These services are provided through the market flows and the amount of services available depends on the capability of the channel members to provide them and the strength of the consumer/end customer demand for them. Under low entry barriers and reasonably free competitive conditions, the channel should so evolve that it provides the greatest possible consumer satisfaction per unit of product cost.

The more the services required by the consumers, the more intermediaries will be necessary in the channel. For example, if the consumers wish to make their purchases in small lots, there will be a large number of intermediaries between the manufacturer and the consumer. The lower the level of service demanded, the greater the cost savings made by the channel members and the less the complexity of the channel necessary to provide the service.

Bucklin's theory postulates that the channel structure is a function of the desire of channel members to achieve scale economies relative to the market flows and the consumer demand for the various service outputs. The channel structure also depends to a large extent on where the inventory is held in order to provide adequate service levels, carry out the necessary sorting and provide the channel members with sufficient returns. To explain how these inventory locations are decided upon, Bucklin has developed the principle of **postponement-speculation**. This states that postponing the ultimate form and identity of a product to the latest possible point in the marketing chain and the inventory location to the latest possible point in time provides the most efficient channel structure.

For example, a manufacturer of wheelbarrows can hold a large inventory of wheelbarrow parts and assemble the finished products only on receiving definite orders. In this way, warehousing costs can be reduced considerably because the parts take up less space than an assembled wheelbarrow, and risks are reduced by only undertaking the final process on receipt of definite orders. A further step is taken by some mail order firms and other retailers when they supply the customer with the relevant parts and instructions for assembly at a cheaper price.

In addition to these explanations of channel structure through economic theory, channel structure is also influenced by geography and size of market area, location of production centres and population distribution; among other physical factors, technological, cultural, social and political factors also affect it.

TYPES OF DISTRIBUTION CHANNELS

Any combination of facilities and functions through which a product passes between the manufacturer/producer's plant and the user may be termed a 'channel of distribution'. One channel is usually considered to end and another to begin when the form of goods is changed by some manufacturing process. It could be part of a vertically integrated set-up or part of a horizontally integrated organization.

Vertical integration refers to the operation under single ownership of two or more stages of distribution. Thus, the manufacturer who owns or operates warehouses and retail outlets is said to be vertically integrated.

Horizontal integration is the ownership of a number of units at the same stage of distribution, e.g. the wholesaler who owns a number of warehouses in different locations.

A distribution channel is considered to have two dimensions, length and width. The length refers to the number of stages through which a product must pass to reach the customer. Width refers to the number of factors at the same stage of distribution. Thus a wide channel at the retail stage would result in placing a manufacturer/producer's DIY product in a large number of DIY stores in the market. The shortest channel length is when the manufacturer/producer sells directly to the consumer/end customer.

The same manufacturer may utilize a number of channels, using one channel for one product or part of the country and another for other parts. The width of a channel determines the selectivity of distribution. It is possible to sell to a broad market with many outlets or to restrict effort to selected areas, choosing outlets that can sell intensively within those areas and generate sufficient profit at the same time.

Levels of distribution

The levels of distribution are the number of intermediate stages between the producer and the consumer/customer. The number of levels generally increases with the difficulty in reaching the final consumer, for example, in countries where transport is difficult and the spread of consumers is over large distances. The options generally available are illustrated by Fig. 2.1 for consumer products and Fig. 2.2 for industrial products.

The important consideration is whether the manufacturer is going to be satisfied in selling to just one level or is interested in selling at other levels as well. In the latter case, there may be a clash of territories between the manufacturer and the distributors. There is also a choice between exclusive distribution in either case, where the sales are limited to a select group of distributors, and selling to any buyer who is interested. Exclusive distribution may contravene the law in some areas and it is necessary to ascertain the position before venturing in this field.

It is essential to have a positive trade distribution strategy to make sure that the product is getting sufficient exposure in the market-place. The information required concerns:

- the target market, its range and location
- the possible distribution channels for the product, their method of operation and composition
- the competition and its methods of operation
- a SWOT analysis for own business.

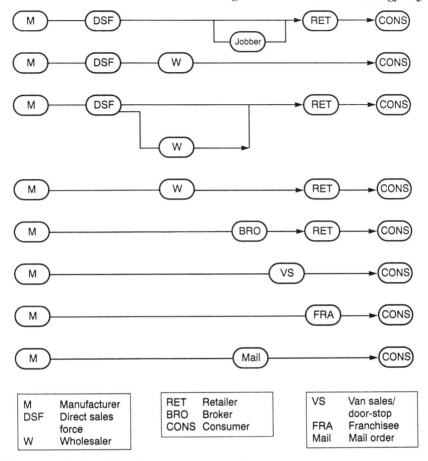

M	Manufacturer	RET	Retailer	VS	Van sales/
DSF	Direct sales	BRO	Broker		door-stop
	force	CONS	Consumer	FRA	Franchisee
W	Wholesaler			Mail	Mail order

Figure 2.1 Levels of distribution: consumer products

Domestic Market

The distribution of products within the domestic market may well vary according to the type of product in the following ways:

1. Consumer products: non-exclusive – open distribution, i.e. selling direct to retailers (shops, dealers, etc.) and wholesalers on a quantity discount basis.

2. Consumer durable products: as for consumer products but can have sales through franchised/authorized/accredited retailers and/or wholesalers – normally at lower discounts.

3. High technology products: direct to major users and original equipment manufacturers (OEMs) and through authorized distributors/dealers.

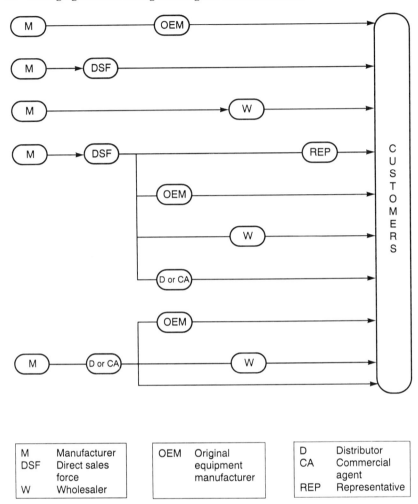

M	Manufacturer
DSF	Direct sales force
W	Wholesaler

OEM	Original equipment manufacturer

D	Distributor
CA	Commercial agent
REP	Representative

Figure 2.2 Levels of distribution: industrial products

4. Relative low cost capital plant: direct to major customers and OEMs and through authorized distributors/dealers.
5. Raw material and high cost capital plant: normally direct to user. The services of a commission representative may be used.
6. Industrial consumables/low cost capital plant: can be as for consumer durable products or could use one exclusive distributor, with branches/depots.

Independent stocking distributors enable a manufacturer to cover markets where it is not feasible, practical or profitable to do so through selling direct or with 'own sales company'; for example, in:

- overseas or distant markets (export)
- low volume – unsatisfactory profit margin markets
- limited development potential markets
- markets with traditional distributor pattern.

International markets

In contrast to the domestic market, products may be distributed in the following ways:

1. Consumer/consumer durable products: importer/distributor (wholesaler), generally exclusive by area/product line.
2. Industrial consumables: for customer/consumer durable products.
3. High technology products: as for the domestic market.
4. Relative low cost capital plant: as for the domestic market.
5. Raw materials and high cost capital plant: direct to user or using the services of a commission representative.

All the above products could be marketed through:

- import/export houses
- original equipment manufacturers (OEMs)
- trading houses
- co-operatives

PRINCIPAL METHODS OF DISTRIBUTION

It may be evident from the foregoing that there are three basic ways to distribute the product to the user:

1. Direct sales to the user by the manufacturer/producer.
2. Retail outlets, which may be:
    (a) the manufacturer's/producer's branch or store;
    (b) independent retail stores or retail chains or dealers;
    (c) others, e.g. direct mail or vending machines.

3. Through intermediaries, which fall into two broad classes:
   (a) wholesalers and jobbers (domestic appliances, toys);
   (b) distributors, for high value items such as cars, aircraft, machinery and components, representing and acting for the manufacturer/ producer in dealings with the user.

Any one or a combination of these methods may be used by a manufacturer/ producer to reach a consumer/end customer, depending on the specific distribution policies the company follows, and this combination will determine the distribution channel. Let us explore each main alternative in more detail (see Fig. 2.3).

Direct sales

Wholly owned subsidiary company with a direct sales force
A wholly owned subsidiary company is a business which is controlled by the parent company which owns all the shares or stock of the subsidiary company. In this case, the sales force employed by the subsidiary will be responsible for marketing and selling to the customers in the country and the subsidiary will also provide the full service to the customers. All the profits remain within the manufacturer/supplier company and that company retains full control over its marketing. As the subsidiary company is a corporation registered in the target country, subject to the corporate tax and other regulations in force in that country, profits would be shared between the parent company and the subsidiary, but for all intents and purposes the profits remain within the company.

PROS AND CONS OF SUBSIDIARY

Pros	*Cons*
1. Control of know-how and market.	1. Takes a long time for entry/ establishment.
2. Keeping customer contacts/ ownership.	2. Takes time to pull out.
3. Total profit retained within company.	3. Costly to enter and/or pull out.
4. Direct presence in the markets.	4. Cost of operation in terms of seasonality.
5. Ability to implement decisions rapidly following any re-adjustment to strategy.	5. Image affected if company pulls out.
6. Potential for pre-agreement on all issues.	6. Expense in staffing/retraining.
	7. Conflict with new channels.
	8. Might invite aggressive competition.

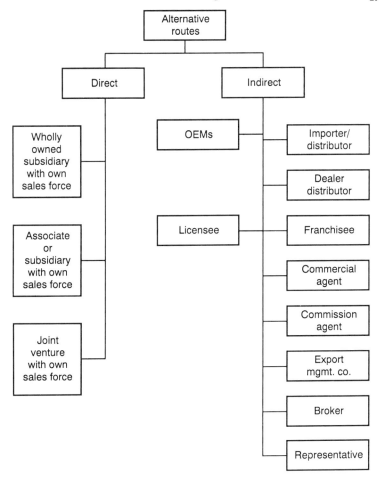

Figure 2.3 Channel alternatives

Associate or subsidiary under manufacturer control with direct sales force

In this instance, the main difference arises from the extent of the ownership of the subsidiary. If it is not wholly owned, then the profit share is dependent on the proportion owned; so is the control of the associate company.

Joint venture

Direct investment through the creation of a division within the country or a foreign subsidiary may not always be possible. The other primary method of investing in foreign jurisdictions is through joint ventures. This requires a reduced financial commitment and has the advantage of having the backing of the local people; however, there is a loss of control in having minority status. Usually it involves at least one other business enterprise. If the other enterprise happens to be much larger in size and has more experience in its markets and if its inherent (not the stated) need for the joint venture is not as great as that for your company, then obviously the real control could vest in the other company. 50/50 is no man's land. Many joint ventures of this type have ended in failures for want of common goals and effort on the part of the parent companies. However, for many small businesses, especially innovative companies, this may be the best option.

In all of the three possible routes mentioned above, it is possible to give the direct sales force employed by the subsidiary or the joint venture company the responsibility for sales to selected major accounts, while sales to other accounts are allocated to an indirect sales force by one or more of the means discussed later in this chapter.

PROS AND CONS OF A JOINT VENTURE

Pros	*Cons*
1. May be the only way of gaining access.	1. Problem of control.
	2. Lengthy decision-making.
2. Capability of handling both cultures.	3. Travelling costs.
	4. Management time.
3. Means of blocking competition in government controlled economies.	5. Insecurity of customer gains.
	6. Heavy investment of management time.
4. Potential for reciprocal trade.	
5. Reduction in risk-sharing and need for scarce resources.	
6. If the climate is right, full access to market and maybe later possibility of establishing a subsidiary.	

Indirect means

Distributor institutions

These fall into three broad categories: retailers/dealers, intermediaries, e.g. wholesalers; and facilitating agencies. Their prime purpose is to increase the efficiency of distribution by:

- reducing the relationship between the manufacturer/producer and the consumer/end customer

- providing credit/financing for the storage and movement of goods, which enables the manufacturer/producer to continue to operate and reduce the risks while the goods are being sold
- lowering of costs through routine transactions
- opening up a vast array of choices to the consumer/end customer.

RETAIL OUTLETS

A retailer is anyone who sells to the end-user, regardless of his prime function or trade name. Retail operations may be conducted through various physical means such as the following:

1. Retail stores which perform the functions of buying, storing and selling, as well as offering convenience and promotion.
2. Independent retailers which are not owned by the manufacturer/ producer; they can be either speciality stores, handling a complete assortment in a limited variety of goods or single-line stores.
3. Discount houses which operate at lower margins than usual.
4. General stores which handle a wide variety of goods, and are usually small and located in remote areas.
5. Chain stores, having four or more stores under single ownership, which can be local, national or international; they may consist of entire stores or leased departments in larger stores.
6. Voluntary chains, a group of independent retailers who have joined together to obtain the advantages of mass purchase.
7. Mail order selling which is carried out through catalogues, newspapers or direct mail advertising.
8. Vending machines which hold consumable products in specific physical channels and, on receipt of coins through specially designed slots, dispense the goods.
9. Door-to-door selling, which usually involves highly trained sales executives and is therefore expensive.
10. Product leasing which is often done through a leasing subsidiary, through which all agreements are transacted; a higher capital outlay for inventory and sales and service organizations is required of the manufacturer/producer than would otherwise be necessary.

INTERMEDIARIES

Intermediaries perform the specialized service of passing goods along to retail institutions and other wholesalers which is of great value for the efficient distribution of goods and services. They can be manufacturer-owned wholesalers, merchant wholesalers or third party agents. The last named do not own the goods that they sell or pass along. The services provided by all three types of intermediaries are:

- maintenance of sales force
- storage
- delivery
- assistance to the manufacturer
- credit to the buyer
- sales promotion
- product servicing
- collection and dissemination of market information.

FACILITATING AGENCIES FOR THE DISTRIBUTION OF SERVICES
In this context, services are defined as the performance of a function or business activity other than the buying and selling of goods. Finding of buyers for local services is analogous to retail distribution. In many cases, franchisees and other intermediaries are employed to widen distribution and find suitable outlets, handle licensing and the like. The distribution of services may be limited to a relatively small geographic area because of regulations, dispersion and dissipation of the product and the high costs involved in extending distribution. Specially selected agencies may be able to perform such functions.

Contract manufacturing and distribution/licensee company

A hybrid between exporting and investment in the local economy is contract manufacturing. When there is spare capacity in staff or machinery available in any overseas company's factory, then the management of a manufacturer could consider the possibility of utilizing this overseas company's facility to manufacture their own product under contract. This applies to both production and distribution facilities and to others possessing the technical and marketing know-how. Often done under a licensing arrangement, patent protection is usually a prerequisite. The approach represents a low commitment of financial resources and risk, a quick entry into the market and some control over marketing strategy; but there is increased risk of loss over quality control and loss of intellectual property rights.

Although licensing looks like an easy way to gain revenue, consideration of the long term risks has presented it as a moderate-risk approach. Licensing can result in a potential competitor; but it eliminates the investment and transportation cost risks, and minimizes the company's actual resource commitment to the project. Control is weakened and much care is necessary before this avenue is embarked upon.

When trying to enter the profitable Japanese market, Van Heusen, the shirt manufacturers, found direct export impracticable and opted for a licensing agreement with a Japanese company instead of a wholly owned subsidiary. The reason was that the majority of large retailers in Japan would accept their products only on a sale-or-return basis and the company could not cope with this on the basis of direct export. The licensing arrangement proved successful and the licensee had expanded to production of half-a-million of shirts per year by 1989. This helped to provide the support and market coverage which is necessary in the Japanese market.

PROS AND CONS OF LICENSING

Pros
1. A cheaper way of entering a market.
2. Quick entry.
3. Rapid exploitation of market opportunity if the licensee brings a substantial benefit to the equation.
4. Cash generating if licensees are selected correctly.
5. Access to markets which are otherwise unavailable

Cons
1. No control over volume or market coverage.
2. No control over quality but recovery partly through penalty clauses.
3. Limited revenue availability.
4. Limited exposure.
5. Risk associated with copyright and know-how.
6. Licensee deciding to go own way after the expiry of the licence.

PROS AND CONS OF TECHNOLOGY TRANSFER

Pros
1. A good way of making money quickly from old technology.
2. Released capacity for innovation.

Cons
1. Continuing support.
2. Licensee country can apply political pressure.
3. If the licensee is a notable, reputable or large or powerful organisation and if the licensee is upset because of a valid reason, your image and name could suffer damage.

The distributor based overseas or in another country

For a more direct penetration, export managements use a distributor based overseas or in another country, usually a wholesaler or local importer, as the sales funnel. Here the marketing involvement tends to be long term and total on both sides. The manufacturer supplies stock on a cash, credit or consignment basis. Distributors, given exclusive selling/service rights in a specific market, accept the local marketing and credit risk. They usually buy the merchandise on their own account, maintaining stock on hand, and sometimes installing and servicing the articles sold. They are generally independent and for all intents and purposes act as entrepreneurs. The manufacturer can gain a number of advantages in working through overseas distributors who:

- are already established in the market-place with the necessary contacts, thereby saving time and set-up cost to the manufacturer/producer;
- probably have the necessary sales coverage and exposure;
- have the necessary facilities for sales coverage;
- buy large quantities thereby making savings possible in costs of bank drafts, special invoicing, marketing and shipping, and optimizing the credit risk, if any, through concentration rather than diffusion;
- have every incentive to push sales in order to recover their total investment.

Of course, there could also be a number of disadvantages to the manufacturer in dealing through an overseas distributor, if manufacturers:

- gain no contact with the local customers;
- have no control exercised over marketing or selection of target markets;
- are not consulted on important marketing policies;
- get only limited control over price schedules and related matters.

Alternatively, problems arise if:

- the distributors dictate the advertising and promotion policy, select the media and have a large share in determining the budgetary appropriation, even though the advertising costs are shared between them and the manufacturers;
- the principal's company name is subordinated to that of the distributor, so that, in case of a break, if the distributor switches to a competitor, there is the loss of an established market;
- the 'sales quotient' conceals the fact that a few high yield lines are sold in large quantities, while the other lines languish;
- the commitment is for a longer period than normal and the business level is large and the distributors are difficult to change when the market conditions change so as to justify a new pattern which disrupts the old.

Having first listed a number of possible disadvantages, it is quite feasible to take appropriate and timely action either to avoid or to minimise many of the disadvantages. For example, although the overseas distributor's capital base may be relatively substantial, the working capital has to be adequate in terms of the principal's programme, and this has to be checked regularly. In general, commodities which lend themselves to bulk shipments and which require the maintenance of large stocks in foreign markets, for both supply and service, are usually handled through distributors. On the other hand, small scale, scattered operations tend to be handled by sales agents.

PROS AND CONS OF A DISTRIBUTOR

Pros	*Cons*
1. Ready presence in the market.	1. Loss of direct control over market.
2. The ability to meet stringent customer service requirements, if selected appropriately.	2. Possibly inadequate feedback from market.
3. Less company capital employed in distribution.	3. Increased costs of inventory due to higher stock levels.
4. Flexible use of capacity.	4. Lack of priority consideration.
5. Better geographical coverage.	5. Inability to respond to special demands.
6. Lower operating costs.	6. Higher direct costs.
7. Spread of risks.	7. Higher level of damage and stock losses.
8. Availability of specialist services, if selected appropriately.	8. No direct contact with customers.
9. Ability to redeploy management time.	
10. Overall risk reduction.	

The overseas-based sales agent

This agent can be either an individual or a concern, usually of local origin, operating in an overseas territory or the whole market, appointed by the company to obtain orders on a commission or salary basis, and carrying no inventory or credit responsibility. The agent contacts the local outlets and files the orders directly with the manufacturing principal and collects a commission after the bills are paid. The company checks and assumes all marketing and credit risks and shipments are usually made direct to the buyer. The sales agent is basically a salesperson.

The advantages of this arrangement are as follows:

1. Direct contact with local outlets.
2. Direct control of sales policies, prices and types of accounts selected.
3. Immediate market intelligence.
4. Unilateral control of advertising.
5. Establishment of company name and trade mark which is not affected by a change of agents.
6. The credit risk spread over many accounts, not concentrated in just a few.

The disadvantages are:

1. There is a need to handle many moderate sized accounts with the attendant expenses.

2. The range and the number of productive calls per agent are limited and for any one product, the space availability and exposure time are limited too.

3. Agents tend to carry many related, though non-competitive lines to optimize their time and increase their commission per call; they also tend towards sales of the lines with the least sales resistance.

4. If the agent gets orders for the manufacturing company, there is the question of where to keep the stock. If the stock is kept with another importer/distributor, the legal arrangement will have to be spelt out as far as the relationship between the agent and the importer/distributor is concerned.

5. If the products are shipped directly to the buyer, then it may become necessary to involve a shipping/forwarding agent in the overseas territory. Not only are the costs an issue but so also are the title to the goods, the storage and the transportation.

In summary, a distributor is generally an independent business enterprise whereas an agent is acting on behalf of the manufacturing/exporting company. To an exporter, the major difference between them is that far more control is retained over the pricing and disposition of the product when using an agent. On the other hand, distributors have a greater stake in the success of the venture and will often be more valuable allies in exporting.

Export management company

Export management companies are firms that can act as agents or distributors, that may or may not take title to the goods, and that may have one kind of arrangement with one manufacturer and a completely different arrangement with another.

Franchisee

A franchisee, under a licence granted by the manufacturer (in this instance, the franchisor), is permitted to carry on a particular business (in this instance, the distribution and service of products/services concerned) using a specified name belonging to the franchisor. In general, the franchisor will spell out how the business is to be conducted (a business format) and exercise control over the process which is the subject of the franchise. The franchisor is obliged to provide continuing assistance for the period of the franchise and the franchisee is obliged to pay during the period sums of money in consideration of the franchise arrangement or for the goods and services supplied by the franchisor to the franchisee. If the business is franchisable, then obviously this will enable the manufacturer to maintain the company/brand image in the market and tight control of the marketing of the product/service.

The franchisee gets a licence to use a logo trade mark or trade name and a proven business format in return for paying the franchisor a royalty besides an upfront or an initial fee for the know-how. The franchisor (the manufacturer) is obliged to keep the method up-to-date, provide continuing research and development (R&D), ensure that the franchisee has a secure business and contribute towards promoting the franchisee's business.

Notable examples of franchising are Coca Cola, Holiday Inn, Wimpy, Burger King, Pizza Hut and Kentucky Fried Chicken.

Pros	*Cons*
1. Sale benefits are the same as for a distributor.	Besides some of the points raised under 'distributor',
2. Majoring on franchisor-approved products only.	1. Manufacturer commitment to R&D is vital.
3. Continuing income.	2. A proven business format is needed.
	3. The franchisee has to be assured of ongoing business.
	4. Continuing advertising and promotion (A&P).
	5. Business must be transferable.

Commercial agent
The commercial agents are independent business people or business concerns who sell specific manufacturers' products for a commission based on the sales of the products and their primary role is to promote and sell the products and offer to the manufacturer/supplier advice regarding the market. It is important that they sell only non-competing product lines. In general, they do not purchase or stock the principals' goods.

Pros	*Cons*
1. The agent is paid on results.	1. An agent who is not hungry, may go on holiday.
2. In some countries, an agent is worthwhile because there is no need to maintain stocks.	2. No local marketing capability.
	3. Conflict in relationship.
3. Can claim access to customer.	4. Removing the agent could prove expensive.
4. Could be the only means of access.	

Broker

A broker's main role is to act as an introductory agent between the buyers and the suppliers. Over the years, largely in the commodity product areas such as the food industry, brokers have built up contacts with buyers and purchasing executives at the head office level and managers at the store level. These personal contacts enable them to sustain the roles of intermediaries in introducing suitable products and offering service on product information, availability and delivery issues. It takes a long time for a manufacturer to build this service capability. Their earnings are dependent on commissions, expressed usually as a percentage of sales, agreed with the manufacturers/suppliers with whom they enter into brokerage arrangements.

PROS AND CONS OF A BROKER

Pro	*Con*
1. Good for gaining initial introduction.	1. If the agent depends on you alone for a living, 'firing' him becomes expensive.

The overseas travelling representative

The travelling representative may be a freelance, per diem, or per contract representative or consultant, intermittently covering regions or handling specific assignments, or he may even be on the payroll. In that case, the representative is trained by the parent company and can be an extension of the overseas field force, which he periodically contacts to:

1. Update sales personnel on new developments.
2. Train foreign service personnel on improvements in mechanical or technical procedures.
3. Advise executive personnel in a broad spectrum of policy and operational revisions.

This person may be the export manager or director or a specialist in sales, service or management functions. The trend has been towards specialists, sending them where the scale of operations warrants the expense.

PROS AND CONS OF A REPRESENTATIVE

Pros	*Cons*
1. Fee-paying base.	1. Difficulty in motivating representatives.
2. Access to big names possible.	

Advantages and disadvantages of contracting-out distribution

As a summary, a number of studies appraising the costs and benefits of contracting-out distribution to a specialist service company have reported the following main advantages:

1. The ability to meet stringent customer service requirements at acceptable cost.
2. Reduction in the amount of capital employed in distribution.
3. Flexibility of capacity.
4. Increased geographical coverage.
5. Lower operating costs, both overall and in peripheral areas.
6. Spreading of industrial risks.
7. Availability of specialist services.
8. Ability to redeploy management resources.
9. Overall risk reduction.

Some of the potential disadvantages are:

1. Loss of direct control.
2. Inadequate feedback.
3. Stock rotation/product control reduced.
4. Increased costs of inventory due to higher stock levels.
5. Lack of priority consideration.
6. Problems of establishing accountability, e.g. for stock losses.
7. Inability to respond to special demands.
8. Higher direct costs.
9. Higher costs due to damage and stock losses.
10. Communications problems with customers.

The agent's agent

This comparatively new concept funnels new product lines through one local organization which recommends and then monitors the agent or distributor who is appointed. The agent's agent is responsible to the individual exporter or group of exporters, and receives a flat fee annual retainer or a small percentage from the principal. Ideally, he should assume the role of referee between the principal and the local representatives to resolve all marketing conflicts.

IDENTIFYING THE GAPS IN DISTRIBUTION

The most important thing is to make an audit of the current distribution objectives and the distribution operations and consider how they match the overall marketing objectives set for each chosen market. Any deviations indicate the absence of certain key factors which contribute to a successful distribution strategy. This analysis could be a starting point to establishing the gaps in distribution.

The following are some of the reasons why gaps could arise:

1. A basic flaw in the distribution objective (or even in certain circumstances a flaw in the marketing objective).
2. An ill-defined strategy.
3. An inadequate appreciation of the role of manufacturers and their obligations.
4. An inadequate definition of the role of the distributor and the necessary characteristics which they must possess.
5. A lack of motivation on the part of the manufacturer's staff dealing with the channel and/or on the part of the channel operators.
6. An inadequate profit margin for either or both parties.
7. A mismatch between the 'product' offered and the market's needs.
8. The absence of a committed action programme.

USING THE APPROPRIATE CHANNELS TO EXPAND CONSUMER BUSINESS

Retail trade – multiples/major accounts

It is usual for buying power to be concentrated in the hands of a few distributors or customers. Any person who gains a small advantage to begin with, is likely to grow more powerful, to spread out geographically into a multiple operation and to become a major account. This tendency is on the increase in the developed world. It becomes necessary for any manufacturer to win over such distributors before trying to reach the consumers. While such concentration of power is a disadvantage to the manufacturer in one way, it is counterbalanced by an increased efficiency in the total channel operation and better service to the end customers. The switch of even one key account can mean the difference between profit and loss. A business is considered vulnerable if there are fewer than twenty-five accounts in the first 50 per cent of the sales.

Such key accounts merit equal or more marketing attention than the product lines and may each rate a mini-strategy of its own. They cannot be considered as parts of homogenous trade sectors. It may be worthwhile to appoint account managers on the same lines as product managers to cope with major accounts and to ensure that all dealings with such an account will help to further the objectives of the mini-strategy for each such account and take into consideration:

1. The level of authority needed to conduct negotiations.
2. The necessary amount of time and effort required.
3. The area to be covered in dealing with the account.

The emphasis in negotiating with key customers who are distributors is on terms and conditions rather than on selling the products. It is better for each party to know what its final position is; for the seller, this is the price and terms below which either a loss is made or a better market will have to be found elsewhere; for the buyers, it is the price above which they lose by buying or can buy better elsewhere. It is necessary that each party works out this final position for the other party before starting the negotiations. If the two positions are separated by a gap, then negotiations are likely to be futile, unless one party can be persuaded to re-evaluate its position. Negotiation takes place in the overlap between the two final positions, the point being how far the terms can be made favourable to one or the other party. For this manoeuvre, the techniques of intimidation, bluff and outsmarting are used and the negotiators should be ready to counter them. As buyers are often in a stronger position than the sellers, it may be worthwhile discovering whether they are being offered any special rewards for any advantageous purchases they make and offer those concessions which will benefit them most.

It is essential that a detailed and up-to-date profile of the customer operations and dealings should be kept by the account manager so as to help with the preparation of a strategy and for discovering problems and opportunities in time. The volume sold, product mix, price and costs are considerations which should be constantly kept in mind. It is a fact of life that a major distributor is vital to the manufacturer, but the opposite is not true unless the manufacturer has a monopoly on their product. Therefore, manufacturers have to convince distributors that they provide something unique which the customers require. A distributor who is interested in transferring the customer's loyalty to the distributor instead of the product, may decide to get the product manufactured as an 'own brand', if it is profitable enough. In this instance, it may be necessary for the manufacturer to tailor the product to the particular market served by a large distributor in order to counter this threat.

Checklist for major accounts

1. Size and number of accounts
   (a) What is the total number of accounts and how are they ranked according to the annual sales made to them?
   (b) How many are there in the top 80 per cent of the sales? Does the 80/20 rule apply?

    (c) What percentage of sales does the largest account represent? How many accounts have sales of over 5 per cent?
2. Management of accounts
    (a) Who supervises the major account business and how many accounts is each responsible for? How does the position and status compare with that of the buyer(s)?
    (b) How are the accounts distributed geographically? If they spread across more than one sales region, are there arrangements for co-ordination across those regions?
    (c) Are advance preparations made for the sales negotiations?
3. Profiles
    (a) Is the planning done separately for each major account?
    (b) Are proper profiles of the accounts prepared and do they show up possibilities for new opportunities?
4. Trade co-operation: Is there an attitude of co-operation with the major accounts or otherwise? If the latter, is there any way of improving the situation?

Non-multiples

Speciality shops sell only one or two types of goods such as groceries or clothing, and operate in densely populated areas. They may carry only one kind of product such as sports goods. Even further specialization is possible, where a store may carry only bicycles and related equipment, for example. These businesses are comparatively inexpensive to start up if they are small and therefore the failure rate is high because many inexperienced people tend to start up such concerns. However, if they catch the right fashion at the right time, they can be very successful. In theory, this is one way to segment the retail market.

Discount shops such as cash and carry and DIY chains can sell branded goods at low prices because of:

- location in cheaper areas
- limited amount of upkeep and decor
- customer self-service
- charging for deliveries and demanding cash transactions
- no guarantees given or returns allowed
- obtaining profits mainly through large amount of sales despite low margins.

When department stores competed with discount shops by reducing prices on well-known brands of goods sold by them, many discount shops had to increase their facilities, thereby increasing their overheads. Consequently, many discount shops went out of business after the initial success of the concept.

Small stores which are open considerably longer than supermarkets and which mostly stock food for immediate consumption, are now common. Some of them are attached to petrol stations. The goods sold are mainly high turnover items such as confectionary, newspapers, packaged goods, cigarettes, refrigerated food and drinks, and quick meals/snacks. An example of these are CTNs (confectionery, tobacco and newspaper shops).

Merchandising

Merchandising means displaying the goods in a way to catch the eye in places where the consumers can see and purchase them. It can be considered the most important promotional activity. It is the joint responsibility of the sales and product management to see that the products are suitably packaged for such display. Most of the work should be done by the distributor who is paid for this service. This point should be stressed during the negotiations. The minimum of direct assistance should be provided by the manufacturer in the cheapest way possible. It should be remembered that once merchandising help is granted, it cannot be withdrawn without damage to the display itself. However, this kind of help may be needed in underdeveloped countries, where the distributor may not possess the right kind of facilities or skills and where the usual media make little or no impact.

Checklist for promotion and merchandising

PROMOTION

1. Does the marketing policy provide for consumer promotion and who controls the budget for it? Does it also provide for promotion aimed at the distributive trade?
2. Is the sales division consulted about these promotions and is the feedback from the distributors heeded?
3. Can the budget for both these promotions be combined? Do the distributors perceive these promotions as beneficial and is it possible to persuade them to contribute to them financially?
4. Are consumer promotions applied on a selective basis among the distributive trade and what control is there on the sharing of the benefits among the distributors?
5. Is the promotional work planned for in the sales force work-load and are schedules worked out in advance? If redemption coupons are to be used, does the sales force have to help out with spot checks for invalid redemptions?

6. Is it permitted both legally and by the trade to mark reduced price offers on the packaging?
7. When such offers are unmarked, how is it ensured that the reductions are passed on in full to the consumers, for the agreed quantity or for the agreed period?
8. Are the sales of promoted stock limited to a quota of normal sales per distributor?

MERCHANDISING

1. Is special staff employed for producing displays or is it part of the sales force work?
2. Do the distributors undertake a fair share of such work and is there a clear policy guideline on the amount of help to be offered?
3. Has the possibility and worth of direct consumer promotions been considered?

USING THE APPROPRIATE CHANNELS TO EXPAND INDUSTRIAL BUSINESS

Industrial goods usually belong to one of the following types: equipment, manufactured materials or supplies. The choice of distribution channels to suppliers of industrial goods is generally limited since the buyers are few in number and are usually concentrated within geographic areas. The costs of distribution may therefore be lower, but this is offset by the higher degree of technical training required of the salespeople.

Direct selling is most often employed to sell to industrial users as the resulting service and close touch with production are highly desirable. When the individual users are large, it becomes economical to service the accounts with full-time staff. The other popular method of industrial distribution is the use of wholesale intermediaries. Industrial distributors do not carry products of competing manufacturers but represent makers of related but non-competitive goods.

There exist various reasons why channels for industrial products include an intermediary less frequently:

- tailoring of products to purchasers' requirements
- extensive pre-sale contact between manufacturer and user
- need for after-sales maintenance
- need for applications assistance before and after the sale.

These reasons lead manufacturers to take responsibility for both the channel functions of exchange and physical distribution, though ancillary functions may be performed by facilitating institutions. Channel selection is affected by the elements in the following checklists:

1. Concerning customers

    (a) Number of potential buyers
    (b) Their locations
    (c) Frequency of purchase and average order size
    (d) The degree of need for the product
    (e) The requirement for technical assistance, if any
    (f) Credit standing
    (g) Pattern of purchases
    (h) Service requirements before and after purchase

2. Concerning intermediaries

    (a) Market coverage
    (b) Gross margin
    (c) Sales time available
    (d) Technical expertise
    (e) Financial stability
    (f) Warehouse capacity
    (g) Servicing capability
    (h) Number of competing products sold

3. Concerning the company

    (a) Size, both absolute and relative to its industry
    (b) Financial strength
    (c) Whether leader or follower
    (d) Location of plants and distribution service facilities in relation to major users
    (e) Technical skills
    (f) Degree of specialization
    (g) Range of products
    (h) Competence in provision of service

4. Concerning the environment and the competition

    (a) The shape of the demand curve over time
    (b) The extent of concentration among users
    (c) Characteristics of distribution channels
    (d) Legal constraints and regulations
    (e) The effects of taxation

(f) Government procurement policy

(g) The impact of changes in consumer/end customer demand on the demand for industrial goods

In direct channels, the manufacturers must perform all the functions which the customer cannot be persuaded to take on; in competitive markets, the customer may be unwilling to assume any functions incurring substantial costs, although by so doing the total costs to the customer may be reduced. Even in these circumstances, there may be opportunities for economising through functional specialization.

An example is a fuel distribution company which found that many of its customers were taking fortnightly delivery of quantities of fuel measured by their usage rate. These customers had much larger storage capacity and could have optimized their cost by taking fewer but larger deliveries of fuel, perhaps once every three weeks. The fuel distribution company found a way of consolidating the deliveries to its customers within a given area, thereby reducing its storage requirements, with a redistribution of deliveries to avoid a peak and achieving considerable savings for both customers and itself.

Other attempts to increase the cost efficiency of direct industrial channels have focused on cutting the costs of ownership and information flows. Compatible data processing techniques can reduce transaction costs for the purchasing and supplying companies. In other fields, manufacturers are aiming for greater standardization of product lines in order to reduce costs. At the same time, intermediaries able and willing to take over the maintenance and assistance functions are increasing in number. The problem of the cost of servicing small accounts can be satisfactorily solved in this way, if the manufacturer is willing to use a dual-channel system. The following are examples of merchant intermediaries in the industrial goods.

Electronic components

The market for these is widely diverse and, in order of size, consists of:

- production demands of major equipment manufacturers
- medium-sized and small manufacturers
- industrial R&D for prototype and small-batch work
- 'servicing' dealers for spare parts
- amateurs wanting spare parts.

Matching this variety and meeting the needs are the component stockists and distributors. They vary from those who catalogue many thousands of items to those who concentrate on fewer fast-moving lines. Some specialize in the needs of a particular type of customer. All emphasize customer service as their main business asset, though their interpretations may be different.

Builders' merchants

These are mainly wholesale merchants dealing in a variety of materials and sizes; their customers are mainly builders. The trade has specialized mainly along the lines of 'heavy' and 'light' goods.

MARKETING OF INDUSTRIAL PRODUCTS VERSUS CONSUMER GOODS AND SERVICES

It is a fact that one can build a unique definition of the marketing function which can well apply to any kind of business. However, it must be recognised that there are fundamental differences in the relative importance of the various aspects and factors of the function in the two large categories of business identification, i.e. industrial products and consumer goods. There are many other business categories, like public services, non-profit making organizations or the growing group of services such as banking, insurance, hotels, leisure industries, etc. However, most businesses fit into one of the two basic categories, industrial or consumer, so it is worth going through their major points of difference.

The fundamental basis of marketing is the same, either for an industrial business or for consumer goods. The content of the function, the terminology, the techniques and the resources are the same, as well as the importance of the marketing concept. As can be seen in Table 2.1, there are large differences in the relative weight of the key components and these should be kept in mind because:

- some products, like utilities, are sold simultaneously in both markets;
- some products move from an industrial approach to a consumer-style mass production;
- people who have been professional and successful as marketers and in sales in one category do not automatically succeed in the other.

ALTERNATIVE MEANS OF GETTING TO THE MARKET

The first step is to decide on possible ways in which the intended end-users can purchase the products. For example, a potter could open a stall on-site, try selling in weekly markets, craft fairs, etc., or sell to retailers.

The second step is to determine the channel paths which can reach those outlets. For example, a company considering the distribution of a new product may choose to use the present distributors or new ones or buy up a distributing company or sell in bulk to others already providing the product or try direct selling. Each method will have its strengths and weaknesses

	Industrial	*Consumer*
Number of accounts	few	many
Account identification	feasible (list)	impossible without the use of sophisticated statistical techniques
Buyer objective	production of further products	personal need
Buyer motivation	very complex = cost, reliability, service, comparatively objective	satisfaction = needs versus wants, psychological impact
Buyer loyalty	high	low
Impact of consumer demand	indirect or derived	direct
Scale of purchasing	generally greater in money terms	
Purchasing decision	formalised evaluation and decision procedures	informal
Market segmentation	important	imperative
Product mix	cost oriented	market oriented
Product life	rather long	rather short
Volume	possible control	low control
Price	cost plus	perceived value
Advertising and promotion	average/low	high
Marketing/sales cost ratio	low/medium	high
Selling forces	few professionals	many salesmen
Multi-level selling	high	low
Buyer/seller interdependence	high	low
Product presentation	minor value	critical
Degree of integration with other functions	high	low
Marketing style	'inside-out'	'outside-in'

Table 2.1   The major differences between the marketing of industrial products and consumer goods/services.

which have to be carefully considered in view of the company's requirements. It is possible to apply one of the decision techniques to this problem. The possible techniques include linear averaging, sequential elimination and simulation.

However, it is necessary to consider qualitative factors as well as economic criteria. The manufacturer/producer generally wishes to exert influence over the channel members and may be willing to forgo some monetary advantages in order to acquire such influence. There are constraints on entering new markets. There is also the ability of channel members to adapt to changing circumstances or to sudden change. All these should be taken into consideration when deciding on the possible alternative channel structures.

DISTRIBUTION CHANNEL STRATEGY

A strategy in this arena involves two decision areas, first the selection of distribution channels and the determination of strategy for the selected channels; second, the needs of physical distribution. They interact with each other and both relate to overall marketing strategy.

Channel selection is the choice of appropriate intermediaries/sales force to move goods closer to the ultimate consumer/end customer. Channels of distribution can be viewed as organizational structures through which goods and services move from manufacturer/producer to consumer/end customer, composed of a variety of intermediary-type operations. Channel decisions are made to some degree by all members of the channel. Manufacturer/producers choose among the alternative channels; intermediaries choose which market segments they want to reach; and the ultimate users choose which retailer they want to patronize.

Marketing channels represent a composite of activities essential to the efficient distribution of goods. When manufactured goods are produced by mass production methods involving minimum transportation cost, this is frequently accompanied by widely scattered consumption. Intermediaries serve as a low cost mechanism to distribute these products, because the economy of handling a number of different products results in fewer buyer–seller contacts than in direct selling. The functions performed by those who resell in the channels are as follows:

- Assembling over a period of time, in one place, similar commodities that meet standard specifications for the assortment.
- Assembling, as above, unlike supplies in accordance with some pattern determined by demand.
- Dividing large homogeneous lots into smaller lots.
- Breaking the assortment into various types of goods for resale.

Specialist intermediaries usually perform these activities more effectively than the manufacturer/producers.

As mentioned briefly in the previous chapter, the market executive has three basic alternatives with respect to overall channel strategy:

1. Exclusive distribution: when a single product outlet has exclusive coverage in a clearly defined territory. Products that require specialized efforts

and large investments in facilities and inventories are ordinarily marketed through exclusive dealers. This is essentially to allow the investor to have every chance of getting an adequate return.

2. Selective distribution: involves careful selection of a limited number of dealers to represent the manufacturer in a chosen market, often tightly defined. This is to give the manufacturer/producer a chance to match their product capabilities and benefits to the precise needs of the chosen market.

3. Intensive distribution: this is the policy of marketing a product in many different types of outlets and in as many of them as possible. Most products of low unit value and high frequency of purchase require intensive distribution.

THE DEVELOPMENT OF AN APPROPRIATE STRATEGY

Changes in demand, the required level of service, product characteristics, distribution costs or pricing policy should lead to a review of the existing distribution policies. Such a review is necessary for the creation of an appropriate strategy. Opportunities to gain lasting advantage through blockbuster strategic moves are rare in any business, according to Amar Bhide.[2] What mostly counts is vigour and rapid response, though these traits are largely ignored by strategic planning pundits.

Efficient physical distribution is a necessity for effective marketing. Physical distribution absorbs a surprising amount of resources and it is necessary to keep a strict watch on possible ways of cutting costs especially when demand is sluggish. The physical distribution concept aims at minimising the costs of distribution for a given level of customer service. This requires a co-ordinated system-wide physical distribution network.

The first decision is regarding the level of customer service to be provided. Market research will be needed for this, in order to find out what the customers expect from the service. The next step is to set standards for each factor concerned and check the service levels provided against these standards. Corrective action must be taken in case of significant divergence between them. After that, management have to develop physical distribution in terms of transport, warehousing, inventory levels and production policies, in order to adhere to the standards set. There are many possible ways of getting the products from one point to another. It is necessary to compare their advantages and disadvantages and match them with the company's expectations.

Warehouses can be privately owned by the company concerned or leased from another company or rented from the public sector. The considerations are the degree of managerial control over the facilities against the capital investment needed. There is also the decision regarding the number and the location of the warehouses. All these decisions are interdependent and affect the service level. For example, a large number of warehouses situated all over the country can make the products easily accessible to the customers but it is an expensive option.

Inventory management is very important in controlling costs and in avoiding shortages. It tries to minimize the inventory held, subject to demand and service constraints.

The ordering operation requires an accurate sales forecast. The forecasting model depends upon the nature of the demand, whether it is predictable or unpredictable, seasonal or otherwise, and so on. The model also depends on who needs the forecast. The nearer the channel member is to the end customer, the more volatile is the demand pattern. It is also necessary to take preventive measures to prevent stockouts occurring; demand can drop if they occur.

Production control has to be exercised in order that enough products are made available when needed. Physical distribution system management is a vital factor in the success of a firm's strategy. It is a complex task in which all the components have to be properly managed to obtain the end results.

Product, consumer and trade marketing strategy

Product and consumer marketing strategy defines the market segments being targeted, the range of products being promoted, and the market share and the targeted sales volume for each product plus an outline of the method of appealing to the targeted customers for each product. The only method of influencing end consumers which is independent of the distributive trade is media advertising. All other objectives require the co-operation of the trade to achieve them. First of all, the trade has to invest in buying the product, then to display it to advantage and to charge the correct price. The co-operation of the trade is also needed for any special promotion, because without it such promotion can be very expensive. Media advertising is used directly to influence end customers but it also indirectly influences the distributive trade through the effectiveness or otherwise of its appeal.

Trade marketing strategy takes decisions on how the available resources are to be used, in which trade sectors and through which channels in order to move the required amounts of the products to the consumers.

It seems obvious that the product sales targets in both the above strategies have to correspond in order for the process to work smoothly. The planning should therefore be jointly undertaken by both functions, to match expectations to available resources, both in terms of product volumes and distributive channels and outlets. The broad outline plan giving the product volumes by sector should first be agreed before the details, such as the amount of penetration and distribution needed to achieve that volume, are worked out. The possibility of stockouts through the fault of either the distributor or the manufacturer must be kept in mind and catered for, as also the existence of a percentage of distributors who will not have the product on their lists for various reasons. Market penetration and the availability of distributive facilities decide the level of achievement of trade marketing objectives. The sales function has the job first of selling the product to the trade and then selling it to the consumer to assist the trade. It is vital that both product management and distribution management try to plan in terms of each other's requirements and available resources. Their plans should be co-ordinated and committed to paper, for both the long and the short term.

Sales and services to the distributive trade

After a decision is made on which channels are to be used and what their rewards are going to be, the following issues have to be considered in the light of the objectives to be achieved:

- the level of support, help, services and supervision to be provided for the channels
- the amount of selling required for the channels which will also be cost effective.

The process of selling to the trade involves:

- negotiation for use of channel and terms and conditions
- getting the distributor to accept the product/new line
- ensuring the continuance of sales
- routine filling of orders
- physical distribution, involving service levels, delivery time, scheduled deliveries
- direct help in stock control, administration, staff training, organizing displays/demonstrations, customer calls

When a decision has been taken regarding the amount of selling and servicing to be undertaken, the required human resources and skills have to be determined. There may be different tasks involved in the selling process, requiring special skills. For example, the different product lines may need special selling techniques or their number may require extra resources; or the different types of trade customers may require a different kind of approach. It may be possible to delegate routine tasks involved in the selling process to junior staff.

In order to cost the selling requirements, it is necessary to estimate the amount of time required for the selling activities and the standard cost per activity. This requires the following:

1. Ensuring that the correct procedures are followed and then noting the time needed to perform the various sales activities through actual observation.
2. Finding out possible relationships between the types of calls on different kinds of customers and the observed time needed for them.
3. Calculating the average time required for the usual sales activities, including travel and possible interruptions.
4. Setting a norm for the sales executive's working day.

The need to intervene for sales support

Certain products may require direct sales to retailers in order to achieve the requisite amount of market penetration. This procedure should be amicably cleared with both the retailer and the normal distributive channel linking that retailer with the producer.

It should be realized that, generally speaking, retailers and distributors passively reflect the choices of their customers. The manufacturer must give thought to whether the free market choices would be sufficient to move enough of the products to the end customers or whether the company must aid the process and if so, to what extent and in what ways. The manufacturer can appeal directly to the end customers; it is also possible to influence and help the intermediate channels to gain their support in selling the products. The latter can be achieved by the manufacturer through:

1. Sales force visits to end customers where the distributor/retailer does not operate own sales force.
2. Sales force actually taking and transferring orders to the correct channel.
3. Running a van selling the products which are obtained from the distributors.
4. Assisting the distributor's sales force either through on-the-job training or extra visits to customers or actual selling from distributor owned premises.

The cost of support selling should be carefully calculated to make sure that the distributor is earning a share of the profits and that the support is earning sufficiently in addition to justify the extra costs.

THE CHANGING MARKETING CLIMATE AND THE IMPORTANT NEED FOR EXPANSION

The need for expansion into other markets could arise out of different pressures or their combinations. Several of the following have had an effect on businesses:

- environmental and other pressures
- changing employment patterns
- shortage of raw materials and food sources
- age distribution
- energy supply
- shifts in trade pattern
- increasing competition
- education standards/changes
- communication methods/technology
- geographic changes in population distribution
- increased leisure
- wealth distribution – between and within countries
- deficit financing by governments
- declining profits and government controls
- medical expenditure
- new disposable income
- new technologies
- international tension
- specialization of production
- inflation
- unstable currency exchange rates
- growth of multinational companies

The net effect of the new marketing climate has been to bring about changes:

1. Management, rightly or wrongly, have been forced to look for shorter term results, become accustomed to frequent forecasting, undertake additional contingency planning, adopt a hard line approach to budgeting, impose more controls and generally become defensive in setting strategy and policies. This has tended to increase overheads and reduce profits.
2. Markets have adopted cautious purchasing attitudes, lower receptivity to impulse buying and advertising, sought value for price in selection, become polarized into bigger segments and resorted to a critical examination of the potential of neighbouring markets. This has had the effect of squeezing margins.
3. In some industries, the trend has been towards less investment in R&D,

fewer 'new' product launches, reduction in service and removal of low margin, low turnover products. Some products have enjoyed longer life cycles and have been sold on the basis of value for economy offers. More and more firms have introduced detailed cost analyses.

There have also been marked changes in the promotional emphasis: lower levels of 'fixed' cost advertising, shorter term media commitments, more point-of-sale (POS) promotions. More incentives are on offer for the channels to obtain volume, and among the channels there has been a trend towards 'economy' outlets.

SELECTING A NEW MARKET

In selecting a new market, it is important to gather as much information as possible, analyse the data, and finally plan and take a trip to the most likely markets.

Information sources

Getting information from foreign markets can be very difficult and if obtained from secondary sources, it may prove inaccurate or out of date. The following sources should be tried.

1. Local
   (a) the government department for export assistance
   (b) bilateral chambers of commerce
   (c) foreign consulate(s)
   (d) banks
   (e) accounting firms
   (f) trade associations
   (g) suppliers
   (h) competitors
   (i) foreign forwarders/shippers
   (j) uncompetitive contacts
   (k) libraries
   (l) trade publications
   (m) lawyers

2. Foreign
   (a) embassies
   (b) trade associations
   (c) foreign chambers of commerce

  (d) banks
  (e) potential suppliers/agents
  (f) trade publications
  (g) directories
  (h) accounting firms
  (i) lawyers

Choosing the best new market for your product

In choosing which new market to enter, consider both the macro factors and market-specific factors. Try to understand the customer and to estimate the size of the market. A reliable estimate of the size as well as of the speed of growth is important. Consider as well taxes and duties, the size and effectiveness of the competition, the cost of market entry, the size and quality of the distribution system, and the level of effort required to have a material impact.

Data Limitations

Some of the most important questions may be the most difficult to answer and the available data would have to be analysed very carefully. If a direct estimate of the market size cannot be made, an indirect one might be developed on the basis of:

- national income statistics
- population
- hours of manpower in manufacturing
- production in the construction or agricultural fields
- international trade, imports and exports
- transportation
- wages
- prices
- consumption
- social statistics
- health statistics
- level of education

In developing indirect estimates, try to match your data with consumer profiles and to develop a secondary source standard of comparison with the known data. International market research can be expensive and the results less than meaningful. Great care must be taken both in the selection of the supplier and the development of the research problem.

Defining the problem
Define the problem carefully. Try to:

1. Establish clear research objectives.
2. Determine sources of information.
3. Gather the data.
4. Analyse the data, in the context of the local culture.
5. Keep in mind:
    (a) who collected the data
    (b) what methods were used
    (c) the purpose for which it was originally collected
    (d) who the respondents were
    (e) when it was collected

Try to use several sources of data. The keys to success in analysing market data are cultural understanding, creative ability, an attitude of scepticism, a good knowledge of the industry and actual experience in the country concerned.

Planning the first trip

This is important because it helps to confirm the preliminary findings and provides an opportunity to begin the process of selecting a suitable channel partner. It can be expensive and should be carefully planned, with the help of a good travel agency. Two to three weeks' duration is considered adequate in most cases. The first trip can involve a relatively short exposure to the market-place and minimal opportunity to discuss business with local people. It is better to leave decision-making till the second trip, so that first impulses do not affect the decisions. Make arrangements for communications with the home office before leaving and do not make decisions or attend important meetings till you have had some rest. Adapt to the local ways of operating but be careful to take time limitations into account when planning the trip. In deciding which strategy to use, consider the following issues, including the control required of the operation which can focus on:

• personnel
• pricing
• marketing strategies/programmes
• sales techniques
• delivery
• installation
• after-sales service
• spare parts

- confidential information
- patents and trade marks

A firm must decide how much control it requires over each of these facets of its marketing function. Knowing which critical factors have made a firm successful in its domestic marketing will aid greatly in identifying the factors over which the marketer requires high control. IBM, for example, did not enter into joint ventures and had wholly owned subsidiaries in order to maintain control over its intellectual property.

Profit contribution needs the consideration of the following factors:

- initial investment
- the time frame for an acceptable return on investment (ROI)
- landed price
- market size and growth
- expected market share
- estimated volume
- cost of the product including material, labour, selling and general and administrative costs
- the costs of capital
- taxes

Analysing all these factors will give a firm a realistic basis for evaluating a project. For long term projects, a discounted cash flow analysis can help determine the present value of profits. The following may constitute possible risks:

- political changes
- labour practices
- price controls
- contract and company laws
- local content requirements
- taxation
- repatriation restrictions
- currency fluctuations
- import restrictions
- export requirements
- the reversibility of decisions

Much has been made of political risks in recent years. For exporters, political changes usually mean limited loss of investment; but they can mean a complete loss. A useful approach takes the country in question and views it like a business, constructing a rough national income statement and balance sheet, and reviewing inflows and outflows in addition to liabilities and assets.

The stability of these factors is often an excellent indicator of the stability of the country's laws and policies. An additional consideration is the reversibility of decisions made. Other considerations are the market feedback for each entry strategy, the availability of necessary human resources and the fit of the particular strategy with the overall corporate objective, among others. All these have to be reviewed.

NEW MARKET ENTRY STRATEGY

There are many ways to enter new markets, especially overseas. To begin with, there is a choice between two alternatives: exporting or investing in a new market. Exports can be indirect, where goods are sold to an exporter in the country of manufacture, which is comparatively easy; or direct, where they are sold to an importer overseas, which involves shipping the goods to him. Exporting may be accomplished either by sales through a distributor/agent or by licensing know-how or technology to a party in the country. Sales through a distributor or agent can take many forms. In the case of exporting know-how, the 'export' is not the finished goods but technology, for which fees and royalties will be paid.

Investments may be made by establishing a manufacturing subsidiary, a division or a joint venture. Many firms, faced with the barriers to entry erected by foreign governments, may have to move immediately to a joint venture or opt for a licensing agreement as the only way to obtain revenue from that particular market. Indirect exporting requires no incremental investment, carries a low risk and can provide immediate additional volume and profits, plus a good initial learning experience, though the manufacturer will lose some control over market development strategy. Direct export makes it easier to maintain control over market development strategy and to get feedback from the market-place; it involves low risk and allows easier policing of the abuse of intellectual property.

Cadbury Schweppes possesses an asset in its international group purchasing system with its large resources. It used this to enter the Bulgarian market on the basis of barter. The British subsidiary accepted Bulgarian tomatoes in exchange for selling its drinks in Bulgaria; the tomatoes went to its Swedish subsidiary which made tomato puree. As a result of this successful deal, the company set up a special team to specialize in such deals, buying fruit pulp, juices, etc. from Bulgaria, which could be sold to other Schweppes subsidiaries in different countries. This type of barter helped them to penetrate the Bulgarian market far beyond the possibilities of ordinary export deals.

STRATEGIES FOR COMPETITIVE ADVANTAGE

The purpose of every strategy must be to 'create and sustain competitive advantage'. Achieving this purpose is an entrepreneurial activity. A strategy cannot be effective unless it:

1. Exploits unique aspects of the company and product features which can be termed as pluses/strengths/advantages when compared with competition.
2. Exploits relative strengths of the company *vis-à-vis* competition.
3. Attacks, if need be, the weaknesses of competitors and their vulnerable points.
4. Protects the weak flanks of the company from possible attacks from competition.
5. Exploits the specific opportunities and safeguards against possible threats.

In this context, the company and its channels form an integrated business complex and this must be taken into account when defining a strategy. The strategy must be acceptable to the key members in the channel and implementable by the key players, and it must confer benefits on all the parties involved. In this warfare, to gain business, profits and a share of the market means to win over customers to one side. Customers decide who wins and by how much – not the competitors. Creativity, flexibility and commitments are the three important attributes of a successful strategy. Strategy analysis requires insight and involvement of the key channel members – successful companies have evolved the principle of using 'strategy circles'.

A case history

This principle of strategy circles has been used in a major food manufacturing company.

(This case was prepared by John H. N. Freestone, a director of EMSA and a former managing director within Dairy Crest Limited. The substance of this case was delivered at a conference held at the City University Business School, London (1991).)

The case explores how the restricted markets historically available to the company were expanded. It shows how the use of IT enabled the company to develop a business strategy to bring about an association with other businesses, creating a venture to combine the skills of the company and the associates, rebalancing the business and expanding it, so that additional products could be sold to a wider range of customers. This also provided the opportunity for additional volume and improved margins. It outlines the analytical process adopted, the difficulties encountered by the manager and the team in developing the process that ultimately led to an innovative solution and the implementation process that enabled the cost objectives to be achieved. It also shows how this was accomplished without loss of control or interaction with the end purchaser and without any reduction in the standards of performance achieved by the company.

The case illustrates how the fundamental principles behind the creation of an innovative business concept were woven together with the business format franchise idea, the coupling of the skills of the company, the strengths of selected distributors and the adoption of IT, to underpin the solution into a successful business strategy. The development of an appropriate IT system solution was not accomplished without problems; the following sections describe how these were overcome.

The Business Situation in 1985

With an annual turnover of over £1 billion per annum, Dairy Crest Ltd is one of the top ten largest UK food manufacturers. They produce cheese and butter products, and their many brands are well known in the market-place. They also operate one of the largest transport fleets in the United Kingdom, collecting milk daily from over half of the country's farms, processing much of the milk collected and delivering it daily to the consumers' doorstep.

Dairy Crest inherited the information technology (IT) of the 1960s on many of its sites, through the acquisition of a competitor's factories in 1979. The prime objective then was to manage the business efficiently, while looking ahead, creating a strategy for the business and ensuring that the necessary data processing facilities were there to support the business. As a result, the company management primarily focused on the management of the business.

Total volume in the UK food industry had been static over many years. Growth had come from innovation and major brand development in the retail market, which was dominated by five or six major retailers. The available margins were small, and the cost of developing and launching any major new product was substantial and coupled with a high risk of failure. In the search for additional markets, the company identified an opportunity for increasing volumes and improved margins in the food services or catering industry. This sector had been growing consistently at over 6 per cent per annum and projections showed that this growth would continue.

The UK catering market has an annual turnover of £6 billion. Although comprising only 14 per cent of the retail market, it includes 300,000 delivery points, ten times the number in the retail market. Caterers have a requirement for more frequent and smaller deliveries than the traditional retail markets served by Dairy Crest. Like most chilled food manufacturers, Dairy Crest possessed a large drop distribution capability designed to serve the retail trade and deliver products to major wholesalers nation-wide. The drop size and the number of deliveries demanded by the catering market was totally outside its capability.

Not doing anything was not acceptable to the managers or to the company, so the available options were considered.

1. Organic expansion, involving the development of an in-house small-drop distribution capability through the expansion of the existing distribution operation, was too expensive and was associated with high operating costs and high risk.

2. It might have been possible to acquire another business capable of performing the required tasks or to enter into a joint venture or a co-operative relationship with another business capable of undertaking these activities, but the available margin was not sufficient for two participants.
3. In contracting the required tasks to a third party, the available margin was too small to cover the operating costs and there was no third party available anyway!

All three options were discounted, but the requirement to serve the market remained. The search was now on for some other means of meeting the catering market requirements. A structured strategic analysis was undertaken to define the opportunity in detail, determine the requirements, identify the means by which they could be met, the resources and investment needed, and the payback from the investment and consider the risks. Time was taken to identify the lowest risk approach and the least capital-intensive method of serving this customer base.

The need for a structured approach was clear and Dairy Crest used the EMSTAR Problem Manager for this task.

(EMSTAR Problem Manager is a problem-solving methodology developed by the author and EMSA; see Appendix 9.)

This approach is based on a systematic, step-by-step process which enables managers and their teams to scope and define a problem, pin down the root causes and establish alternative ways of resolving the key issues/root causes. It helps to resolve such issues in a creative manner using the team's resources, undertake an option analysis in a methodical manner; evaluate rewards and risks, select the most productive, feasible, viable and cost effective solution, and thus gain the management's commitment to the proposed solution.

Using this approach, the core objectives were identified and the alternatives evaluated. Franchising has long been an established way of delivering fast food to consumers. Successful companies such as McDonalds and Wimpy have operated franchises for many years. They provide the consumer with an identified brand and uniform standards of quality and service, which are indistinguishable from company-owned operations. In this way, franchiser and franchisees have expanded their business and increased their profits in a way that would not otherwise have been possible. For many of these businesses, the risk capital and management would not have been available for other traditional methods, and the costs of controlling such a vast and rapidly expanding international operation would have been prohibitive in the formative years.

The solution identified involved the following:

1. The idea of putting together a 'comprehensive service package'.
2. A novel creative concept of triangular relationship between customers, distributors and Dairy Crest.
3. The franchising/licensing concept.
4. IT as a basis for implementing the concept.
5. A suitable organization with appropriate control mechanisms.

Dairy Crest had traditionally enjoyed good relationships with a number of independent small wholesalers or distributors located throughout the country. The strategic analysis showed that individually they possessed local capabilities that were required, but they lacked the broader competencies which were available within Dairy Crest. By combining the skills of the two parties, in particular the product competencies and procedures in Dairy Crest, with the local care and attention found among the distributors, it was considered possible to meet the needs of the major catering customers and obtain competitive advantage.

Under the scheme envisaged, the 'concept and the method of working, including the IT system software' created by Dairy Crest would be licensed by Dairy Crest to selected distributors who would become the scheme licensees. These distributors would continue, under normal arrangements, to buy dairy and other products from Dairy Crest. Dairy Crest would find major customers in the catering industry and negotiate with them, on behalf of the scheme, to list agreed products at agreed prices so that the licensee distributors could take orders from the branches of these customers and supply them with agreed products, making small drop deliveries as necessary and issuing priced delivery notes to the branches ordering the listed products. Orders would be captured by the licensee distributors using the licensed software. They would periodically transmit copies of the order and invoice data in an approved IT media to Dairy Crest so that the required monthly collation, statement submission and money collection from the customers' head offices could be processed at the centre. In turn, the licensee distributors would get the payment for their invoices from Dairy Crest. In essence, the scheme strategy, from a business and commercial point of view, was to offer precisely what the target market required in the following way:

1. A link was established between the wholesalers i.e. the distributors, Dairy Crest and the major customers, and central negotiation was planned to be undertaken by Dairy Crest with the major customers' head offices.
2. The distributors took responsibility for local order capture, distribution and deliveries to the branch offices of the major customers, and invoiced to all the delivery points with notification to Dairy Crest.
3. Dairy Crest presented statements to and obtained payment from the head offices of major customers and developed the necessary computer link and software for the co-ordination of the entire operation of this venture.

It can be seen that this scheme depended on the licensee distributors performing certain functions and Dairy Crest performing certain complementary roles besides the normal supplier/distributor relationships. It was vital that all parties performed to agreed standards of performance – otherwise the risk of failure of the whole scheme would become prohibitive. A special purpose-built IT solution/software formed an integral part of the scheme and this had to fit in with the procedures/practices not only of Dairy Crest, but also the selected distributors.

Dairy Crest saw this as a way of creating a national delivery capability that would meet the needs of all the parties. It could be up and running within one year and, most importantly, it could be developed and controlled to meet the needs of the target customers. After some deliberations, the decision was taken to 'go for it'. Dairy Crest adopted the solution based on the franchising/licensing coupled with IT to develop its strategic response to this challenge.

To meet its objective, the new Caterlink operation had to have the ability to handle over 4000 transactions per week from its first day of operation, almost as many as Dairy Crest with its multimillion pound turnover! To achieve these objectives, strong procedures had to be implemented. Account registration on the product catalogue and nationally agreed prices had to be automatically and strictly controlled. All participants had to focus on the end-user requirement of a good, controlled and regular service. Invoices and other administration had to provide the data that was required by major customers, they had to be accurate and, most importantly, this documentation had to be provided with the goods at the time of delivery, so that it created a competitive advantage by simplifying the administration and control for major purchasers. As all this had to be achieved with participating distributors spread across the country, each holding stocks of some 1200 line options, there was a very clear need for automatic controls.

The scheme had to be costed and draft business plans developed to show how a licensee distributor would benefit under various local conditions with different drop sizes and volumes of business in the initial period and also subsequently. The proposal had to be presented to the distributors collectively, individually and severally according to the particular preferences of the potential distributors. This is an obvious requirement of any scheme of a franchising type.

The initial pilot involving two licensee distributors helped to iron out many problems. The two distributors chosen were very helpful. Much care had been taken in the choice of these pilot partners. The one significant competitor did not have the unique combination of competitive advantages which Caterlink had. Dairy Crest was conscious of possible competitive reactions, therefore much care was taken always to keep a step ahead of the competition. Eventually a decision had to be made to take on other distributors as the business demanded.

The concept and capability had by then been installed with over twelve distributors. Caterlink operated nation-wide, it supplied some 3600 delivery points with products from several manufacturers each week. It had a £15 million turnover after only three years of operation and had achieved every one of its goals; and it was expanding its turnover at 30 per cent per month. Operational accuracy levels in the fields of invoicing and reporting were quite significantly ahead of those achieved by its prime competitors. It had paid back handsomely.

A CHECKLIST FOR EFFECTIVE DISTRIBUTION STRATEGY

An effective distribution strategy often is based on the following:

1. A clear mission with a set of goals which are consistent with the company's business and its marketing strategies.
2. The specific characteristics of the product in question, in particular its life span, the technology upon which the product itself is based, the production process, the physical handling such as packaging.

3. The specific channels through which the product is marketed and the marketing mix aspects including channel margins.
4. The outlets through which the customer gains access to the product.
5. The customer service requirements, including the delivery, after-sales service, training, etc.

Some of the critical success factors are:

1. Service output levels, e.g. timeliness of delivery, accuracy of delivery (amounts actually delivered against what was needed).
2. Market coverage.
3. Perceived effectiveness of the co-ordination between internal and external marketing organizations engaged in the marketing channel.
4. Profit performance – manufacturer and channel members.
5. Customer satisfaction.

References

[1] Bucklin, Louis P., *A Theory of Distribution Channel Structure*, IBER Special Publications, Berkeley, Calif., 1966.
[2] Bhide, Amar, 'Hustle as strategy', *Harvard Business Review*, Volume 64 September–October, 1986.

3 SELECTING APPROPRIATE CHANNELS

Having considered the role of a good distribution strategy and the part played by a channel, let us examine the selection of appropriate channels in this chapter. First of all we will explore the basic trends.

TRENDS IN RETAILING

The concept of retailing includes all transactions directed towards selling goods or services to the end-users. It does not include purchases for resale activities or for business, industrial or any other kind of institutional use. The ultimate consumer is the buyer who makes the purchase for their own or family consumption.

Although small stores still make up a major part of the retailing scene, the future could be different. The future of retailing as a whole appears uncertain, with slow growth and low investment returns. The percentage growth has been fairly low for many years. The sector is oversupplied with retailers compared to the existing demand. This state of things is likely to continue until a major re-organization takes place. Some specialized types in retailing may continue to enjoy growth, particularly mail order ventures and direct mail companies.

Despite this forecast, some retailers who cater meticulously to consumer demand and provide good service with reasonable prices will continue to prosper, as will efficiently managed stores which also provide them. The losers will be those who continue in the conventional paths. The costs associated with property/sites will be a major issue in the face of high interest rates and inflation.

The retail revolution has been mainly concerned with changing the pattern of services available to the consumers. This is because retailing is one of the most labour-intensive industries. By finding out what level of service the customers can be happy with, the retail operation can be designed around that level. The growth of the suburbs and the number of cars has made it possible to site large stores in comparatively cheap localities with free car-parking facilities. In turn, this has slowed the growth of city centre shopping precincts. The shortage of time available for shopping and cooking, etc., has caused the development of mail order and similar shopping facilities as well as that of convenience foods. Demographic trends also play a part in retailing. An ageing population requires different varieties of retail goods than a young population; a wealthier society needs more luxury goods; and so on. There is also more competition between different types of retail establishments than before. For example, some drug stores are now selling foodstuffs.

The retailer's strategy mix is made up of product mix, location, service level, shelf stock/inventory and margins.

Retailing in the EC

There are a large number of similarities in the retailing businesses in the European Community. The special features of the retail market in some of the countries is given below:

- France: Despite very large department stores and hypermarkets, the French retail scene is still dominated by small traditional shops because the customers prefer products and services tailored to their needs. The number of intermediaries is large at each stage of distribution, and the selling and distribution costs are high. Things are changing slowly but high margins on relatively low turnovers are still preferred by the shopkeepers.
- Germany: Low margin and high turnover shops are well established, although there are fewer very large multiples compared to the United Kingdom and the distribution structure is more fragmented.
- Italy: Consumers prefer tailored products and goods, so a large number of intermediaries perform the processing and finishing of the goods. The number of shops is large and the average size small. Selling and distribution costs are heavy.
- Belgium: Although the number of total retail outlets is very high compared to its population, it also has some large retail multiples. There has been a lot of growth in self-service and specialized non-food outlets.
- Netherlands: There are retailers of all sizes, most of them organized into co-operatives or multiples or voluntary chains. Priority has been given to the integration of retail outlets into populated areas.
- Eire: Low urban concentration means that mobile traders are still important. Large retail shops are common in cities.
- Denmark: The consumer co-operative movement is active and competes strongly with multiples. The retail business is concentrated in Copenhagen.
- Greece: The population is concentrated in and around Athens. Transport

facilities are poor in the rest of the country. Retailing is still mainly done through small businesses.

TRENDS IN WHOLESALING

The main function of a wholesaler in distribution is to obtain supplies from a variety of sources and distribute the wide variety of goods to different buyers according to their needs. The more efficiently this function is performed, the more success is achieved. For the manufacturer, selling to a wholesaler removes the difficulties and costs of selling in small quantities and to varying locations and holding inventory for that purpose. The wholesaler deals in a wide variety of goods and can spread costs over goods from many sources. Wholesalers can also maintain better contacts with their retail customers. They are naturally more concerned with their customers than their suppliers and often offer them assistance, such as credit extension.

The average size of wholesaling distribution companies is expected to rise significantly, aided by acquisitions and mergers. New technology will help these businesses to reach new market areas at reasonable costs. The areas covered by wholesale organizations are expected to increase considerably. The role as well as the size of the sales force in wholesale distribution companies is expected to change; there will be a much bigger emphasis on marketing, promotion, merchandising and space management. The use of computer technology will mean significant changes in marketing and sales strategies, with the use of on-line order entry systems and other systems for analyses of marketing and sales.

The proportion of goods carried by outside carriers is expected to rise significantly, while that carried by internal delivery vehicles is expected to drop. The proportion of businesses using on-line information systems for inventory and purchase is expected to rise dramatically. On the whole, the future of wholesaling is bright for those willing to change and to make full use of the new technology which is available. It may be possible to remove a wholesaling firm from a channel of distribution, but only if some other member of the channel is willing to perform the same functions.

In the consumer goods trade, wholesaling businesses are on average larger in the United Kingdom than in other EC states, although they play a less important part in distribution in the UK than they do elsewhere in the EC. The wholesalers in the rest of the EC are not so well organized in their buying, and the scale of production and marketing is smaller in general; the retail market is also more fragmented there.

CONSUMER GOODS INDUSTRY

For consumer goods, retailers are the end of the chain, which can be quite lengthy in some cases. Between them the various channel members perform the services of transporting and storing the goods, transferring the title to the goods, supplying the necessary information regarding the goods, standardizing, grading and processing them, avoiding stockouts, running the risks associated with volatile demand and fulfilling the financial requirements for credit, etc.

Distribution has become more complex in the consumer goods area. The number of ways of marketing a product as well as the number of potential customers is increasing all the time. While the goal must be to satisfy consumer demand, discovering the size of the consumer demand is extremely difficult. There may be one to three links in the distribution chain reaching from the manufacturer to the consumer. It is not feasible for a manufacturer of consumer goods to sell through their own outlets because of high costs and limited distribution. The retailer chooses which products to sell and manufacturers can only try to persuade the retailer to stock their products.

Consumers choose the shops they shop at, as much as they choose the items they buy, on the basis of certain criteria. Market research to find out the reasons for the choice of retail outlets by consumers has not proved very successful. However, the saving of time and general convenience are definitely factors in favour and so is accessibility. Parking facilities may be important in some localities. Other factors may be store design, display, number of products available, service, personnel, advertising and promotion, and, of course, price levels.

The packaging, advertising and promotion, and brand name may be more important to a sale than the product itself. It is necessary to give some thought to the effects of a manufacturer's actions on each of these links. The following factors are important in motivating consumers to buy and motivating retail personnel to sell:

- informative packaging
- good quality manuals, catalogues and literature
- displays
- training
- audio-visual materials
- incentives in various forms

The manufacturers of consumer goods are generally concerned that the image they are trying to project should tally with the image of the outlets which sell their goods. This matters more if the distribution is limited or selective. The pricing of the goods, their shelf location, displays and availability also influence the image of the goods in the minds of consumers. It has to be remembered that the relationship between the retailer and the manufacturer is forced upon them because of their interest in selling to the end-user. Otherwise their interests diverge considerably. The manufacturers are interested in distributing their products widely, displaying and selling their own products, maximizing their own profits, low retail margins and consumer loyalty to their brands. The retailers are interested in being exclusive distributors, selling from their shops, retail profits and high margins, display of the most profitable items and consumer loyalty to their shops.

INDUSTRIAL GOODS

The functions of an industrial intermediary include buying and selling, transport, credit, feedback of information, technical support and service. The activities of a third party 'add value' to the products through repackaging, product modification or addition of extras, and assembly of products from different sources into packages, among others. A distributor of computers may combine a central processor from one manufacturer with a screen from another and software from a third and sell them as a package. The salesforce have to be technically trained in order to sell the products. The manufacturers of many types of industrial goods are often technical types who prefer to leave marketing to a specialist distributor. Industrial distribution has been expanding as the number of companies decreases, making it viable for the larger firms to invest in electronic data processing devices, inventory management packages, etc. The importance of industrial distributors is tending to increase as manufacturers shed their marketing responsibilities as cost-cutting exercises, and the distributors take upon themselves services such as assembly of the manufacturer's products. It is much easier for an industrial manufacturer to sell direct to the customers than for a consumer goods manufacturer. Industrial distributors have also tended to specialize in their products, reducing the breadth of their product lines but increasing the depth of the inventory and sometimes employing highly trained personnel. Despite these improvements, manufacturers still feel that industrial distributors need to improve their management skills, market research and information feedback.

THE SPECIAL CHARACTERISTICS OF HIGH TECHNOLOGY MARKETING CHANNELS

In this context, a high technology marketing channel means a sales and service organization concerned with:

1. Identifying prospective markets/customers in a territory in need of the benefits of the applications of a high technology product.
2. Promotion by a variety of means which include at least one channel concerned with direct face-to-face communication with the customer, presenting the latter with arguments and reasons to show how they will benefit and persuading them to buy the product.
3. Offering satisfactory after-sale technical service.

The channel members need to be fully conversant with the changing technology and its applications and also technically competent to make what in effect is a technical sale. The products themselves may not be different in appearance or performance from what is generally available in the market – in such situations, the sale of the product is effected through competence, confidence, comprehension of customer needs, relationship, communication and professional application, counselling and consultancy.

The background, training, experience, know-how and technical skills of the staff members engaged by the channel often make the important difference between a good high technology channel and a bad one. The technical competence resident in the channel is one of the most critical factors to the success of high technology marketing.

STRATEGIES AND TACTICS FOR EXPORT CAMPAIGNS

There are two main strategies that can be adopted in planning an export campaign. The military analogies are the theories of the broad front and the narrow thrust. The first approach consists of trying to open up as many markets as possible, all at the same time. It saves the expense of detailed and sometimes unproductive market research, because a simultaneous attack quickly shows up the unprofitable areas and the efforts can be switched to the profitable ones. This can work for some organizations, but it is very extravagant in staffing and other resources, which tend to be so thinly spread that the marketing impact is slight.

The narrow thrust strategy consists of a careful survey being made of all possible markets as a first step. Seven or so likely prospects are investigated in greater detail and a final choice of one to three is made, depending on the available resources. The risk is that the research may be inaccurate or the conditions may change in the development stage. Apart from this risk, this strategy is successful on the whole, provided the research is properly conducted and a lot of work is put into the development.

The Timex Watch Corporation researched the German market carefully before finalizing its marketing strategy there. The German jewellers sold high and medium priced watches in the main with some low priced and low quality items also being sold without guarantee. The Timex products filled the gap between these two types, as to price. By giving a one-year guarantee for their watches and providing repairs for reasonable prices thereafter, Timex also could compete against both ends of the market. The Timex guarantee was comparable to that provided for far more expensive watches. Retailers were enticed by the offer of a margin equal to that on high priced watches while a decision was taken to maintain price levels, so as to help establish Timex in the German market. Timex were also successful in getting their watches distributed to department stores and mail order houses as well as the jewellers. The jewellers were kept happy by a large margin, saving in repair work as the watches were sent back to Timex for repairs and a heavy advertising and promotion campaign which made the name well known in the country.

If a distributor is chosen, the management of the distributor company is the most important factor in the success of the venture. It is better to have just one distributor in one country, if it is small enough for them to handle. If this is not possible, a company in one part of the country, with branches in the other parts, is ideal. This saves useless in-fighting among the distributors. The following case illustrates this point. A company, which had grown out of a number of mergers, had three distributors in a small country, with just one large industrial town. For years, the export manager had to fulfil the role of a United Nations peace-making mission.

Having selected the distributor, it is necessary to do everything to back them; regular visits and ensuring that their correspondence and queries are dealt with promptly, help in this area. This usually stops problems from blowing up into a crisis. The narrow thrust has the virtue of minimizing these problems. It is possible to study in depth the conditions prevailing in one country, its customs, geography, etc., and even to pick up a working knowledge of the language. When the local turnover is high enough, a full-time sales executive may be appointed, a local inhabitant if possible. This increases the sales effectiveness and gives users confidence in the stability of the company.

The next logical step is to open a small subsidiary company, to provide office and warehousing services, staffed again by local people. This means the bulk of the business is carried out in the local language and the complications of international payments are avoided. This company can then sell to the smallest dealer in the most remote parts of the country.

There is an old saying that the most important asset of any company, is not shown in the balance sheet – it is the people who work for the company. This is particularly true of a foreign subsidiary where they have to manage for themselves sooner or later. Naturally the key personnel are trained by the parent company in their methods and the company is set up and organized to meet its requirements; but regular and vigorous inspections are necessary to keep them in line at all times.

Recruiting is a difficult business at its best and before embarking on it in a foreign country, it is a good idea to build up a picture of the national characteristics by reading up on the subject. Finding suitable premises is another difficult job. Expert advice is needed to negotiate leases and contracts of sale and a good local lawyer is of great help in these matters.

A British export manager in Scandinavia learnt a lesson in manners from his lawyer. Regarding the wearing of galoshes (protective footwear worn over shoes in wet or dirty conditions) as unmanly, he tramped into beautifully carpeted offices in his dirty boots, straight from the mud and slush of the streets, while his local colleagues carefully removed their galoshes and hung up their coats in the foyer. Thus, as his legal friend pointed out, he literally 'left his mark' in Swedish business circles.

EVALUATION OF OPPORTUNITIES AND THREATS

Introduction

After twenty years of business boom, the mid-1970s could be considered as a milestone and a bleak one at that. All kinds of changes, crises and new forces have appeared since then; some may be temporary, but many are likely to be permanent, leading to a new business world whose final features are not yet clear. The years after that can be considered as a time of transition, characterised by confusion and discontinuity, and adding to the difficulty of decision-making in business.

This difficulty can be illustrated by the several new business approaches, such as 'Strategic business planning', 'Planning under uncertainty', 'Strategic windows', 'Planning without forecasting', probably followed by many others. Whatever the approach, it is important to identify the changes, evaluate the degree of their impact on each specific business (positive or negative, i.e. resulting in an opportunity or a threat) and to do something about it.

The new business environment

Conditions are changing simultaneously in different fields, social, political, economic and technological, and they are often in conflict. It is difficult to forecast the area where changes will most affect business. For each specific business, it is important to keep in touch with the key changes in each area of the business environment and to update the forecast.

Technological environment
This is probably the easiest to identify:

- Accumulated technical knowledge (general exponential curve)
- World-wide communications system (transport, satellites, etc.)
- Data processing (mini-computers, data banks, office systems, electronic mail (E-mail))
- New processes aimed at lower energy consumption and higher feed/raw material utilization, new energy sources
- High investment cost
- New technology for basic human needs (biotechnology, synthetic food, genetic engineering)
- Hybrid electromechanical cars

Economic environment
This changes in the following areas:

- Obsolescence of all past theories
- Irrelevance of past extrapolation
- World-wide population growth, but concentrated in certain areas
- High energy/raw material costs
- Inflation coupled with lower economic growth (stagflation)
- Monetary instability and disparity between developed countries (DC)/Organization of Petroleum-Exporting Countries (OPEC) and LDC
- Shortage of capital, credit squeeze, very selective investments
- Shortage of people able to understand the new environment
- Potential shortage of food world-wide

Social environment
Changes occur in:

- Collapse of tradition and structures
- New education, new expectations, new motivations
- New life styles, mobility, quality of life, health care
- Consumerism/ecology/anti-business attitudes
- Unemployment and shorter working time
- Crime/terrorism
- Participative working conditions

Political environment
The political environment is subject to

- Nationalism versus grouping of industries
- Higher government intervention/trade and job protection
- Price control and income equalisation
- Political instability/wars
- LDC solidarity

Relative importance of the external factors
Generally speaking, the changes in social environment and to some extent the political factors will play a much larger part in shaping the business environment than they did in the past.

General impact of environmental changes on business

Coping with the changing environment is already a difficult task; the difficulty appears larger when it is realised that not only is the number of changes high, but the difference in 'quality' is even more striking. Most conditions show fundamental differences with past history and knowledge, as well as the past and even the current approach to business theories and management. Things are not only drastically different, they change quickly, much faster than they did in the industrial revolution during the 19th century. These fast changes are therefore very difficult, if not impossible, to foresee; they create business turbulence and unexpected crises at short notice; instability, discontinuity and uncertainty seem to characterise the present years and this situation will continue until the world reaches a new period of stability in all these respects.

During this period of change, which started in the mid-1970s and may continue for many years, a few general business trends can still be clearly identified, such as:

1. Acceleration in a world-wide approach.
2. Continued growth in international trade.
3. Faster growth of large internationals. By the year 2000, 300 Multi-national Corporations (MNCs) could control half of the world's commercial transactions in the world and own three-quarters of the assets there; but they will be faced with major external and internal constraints to their growth.
4. High product development costs and very high risks in case of failure.
5. The growing size of the service sector and the emergence of the post-industrial society in the 'developed' world, so that income and work may no longer be related.

Evaluation

All these changes can be frightening and leave one wondering whether the ordinary business executive can cope with them; whether the 'human gap' is not too great. However, there is no choice, so one might as well adopt a responsible and positive attitude instead of a passive and negative one.

The 'serenity prayer' says:

> *God grant us serenity to accept the things we cannot change, courage to change the things we can and wisdom to know the difference.*

In most businesses, a change in environment can be considered either as a threat or as a new opportunity depending on the point of view. A newly industrialised nation can be considered as a threat (cheap competition) or an opportunity (new market). While excessive inflation is a nightmare for most governments, it is viewed as an opportunity by many businesses. Increasing crime is a frightening trend to most people; but security companies consider it as an opportunity for more business.

It is important to conduct a rational and systematic analysis of the future impact of each environmental factor on a specific business; and to avoid being trapped in a last minute crisis, under the pressure of events, when it may be too late to adjust to them. This analysis can be set out in the following manner.

1. Environmental factor: technological
   (a) Degree of change: high/low
   (b) Probability of occurrence: high/low
   (c) Implication: opportunity or threat
2. Environmental factor: economic etc.
   The probability level associated with each factor is a basic ingredient of any potential 'environment scenario' and concerns the risk evaluation of each future business strategy. Thus the systematic evaluation of opportunities and threats is a key part of the overall process of strategic business planning.

THE IMPORTANCE OF SWOT ANALYSES

Answers to the following five essential questions, asked periodically, will provide clues to gaining advantage over competitors:

- What are our company's **unique strengths or aspects** which give us competitive advantage over our close competitors?
- What are our **relative strengths** in comparison to our nearest competitors?
- What are our **weak flanks** which we have to guard?

- What are the **weak points** of our competitors which we can attack?
- What **ideas** do the foregoing give us in terms of opportunities?

To do this, it is necessary to make an analysis of the strengths, weaknesses, opportunities and threats (SWOTs) faced by the company and the distributor. Since the market-place, the conditions and the competitors may be different as far as each distributor is concerned, it is important to start afresh in each case. This analysis must be undertaken at least once a year. Use a diagram such as that shown in Fig. 3.1 and identify the main items under each heading.

MARKETING AND CHANNEL FLOWS

The above analysis of a company's SWOTs must be augmented by similar analyses of the other channel members. The number of members in a particular channel can vary according to the length and width of the channel strategy a company adopts. The types of channel flows can be illustrated as in Fig. 3.2.

A CHECKLIST FOR SELECTING THE MOST APPROPRIATE CHANNELS

Product factors

Four product variables must be weighed in channel selection.

1. Physical nature: the variations that influence the decision are:
   (a) perishability of the product, whether physical or due to fashion;
   (b) seasonal variation, causing inventory problems;
   (c) unit value of the product;
   (d) inventory investment required; and
   (e) customer service requirements.
2. Technical nature: whether
   (a) a simple or complex product;
   (b) advice is needed on product use;
   (c) installation is needed or
   (d) special training is needed.
3. Length of product line: This consists of a group of products related either from a production or a marketing standpoint. Intermediaries are preferable to own sales force when the line is short. Decisions must be made whether to use a single channel for the entire line or split the line and use multiple channels.

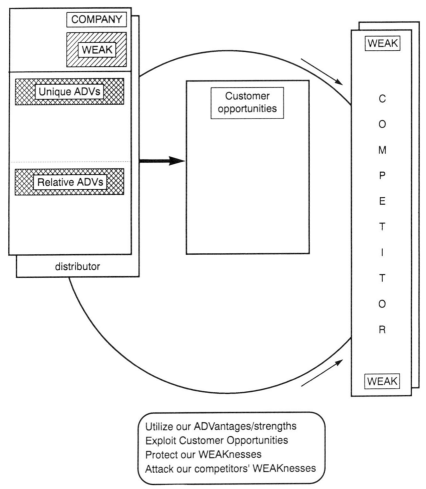

Figure 3.1 Competitive advantage: SWOTs

4. Market position: An established product made and promoted by a reputable manufacturer may have a high degree of market acceptance and can be readily sold through more channels than a lesser known product.

Market factors

1. Existing market structure: This includes traditional modes of operation, geographical factors, size and placement of the population, etc.
2. Nature of the purchase deliberation: The amount of deliberation by the buyer before purchase differs from product to product. Frequent

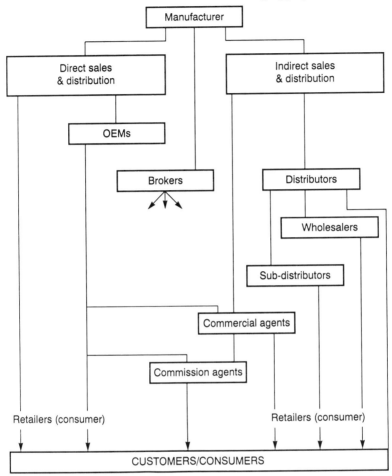

Figure 3.2   Channel flows

purchases need more buyer–seller contacts and intermediaries are indicated. Formal specifications and competitive bids may be used in purchasing certain industrial products.
3. Availability of the channel: Existing channels may not be interested in new products. The promoter can either persuade them or use aggressive promotion to stimulate consumer demand on the theory that this will force the intermediaries to carry the product in order to satisfy the customers.

Institutional factors

1. Financial ability of channel members: Manufacturers may find it neces-

sary to aid their retailers through direct financing; willingness to extend credit can influence channel acceptance. Conversely, mass retailers sometimes finance their suppliers.

2. Promotional ability of channel members: Wholesalers cannot aggressively promote particular products, but exclusive distributors usually join the manufacturer in doing so. Manufacturers assume this function in the case of national brands, while the promotion of private brands usually rests on the mass retailer or wholesaler who establishes the brand name.

3. Post-sales service ability: The after-sales service, with or without a warranty, may be performed by the manufacturer, the retail distributor or an independent service organization. This ability affects channel selection.

The channel decision

This is made by a combination of intuition and analysis, and the exercise of judgement. The decision is complicated by the interdependencies existing between relevant factors. While it is difficult to quantify the many trade-offs associated with channel decisions, certain tools can be applied to them. Cost analysis techniques will give reasonable estimates of each channel cost. System analysis involves trade-offs in time, service and costs in order to maximize profits in the long run. Quantitative comparisons are made between alternative production runs, inventory holding levels, transport modes, customer service standards, order transmission, processing systems, etc. This must involve computer-oriented modelling techniques owing to the large number of variables to be considered.

In recent years, significant environmental changes have taken place:

1. Trend towards a short-order economy – the increase in inventory has meant that the best decision is to order frequently, forcing the primary supplier to carry the necessary inventory.

2. Rapid expansion of product lines – this generates obsolescence and stock availability problems as well as inventory imbalance.

3. Price differentials and discounts – legally speaking, these have to be cost-justified.

4. Competitive strategies – at one time they centred on product features and price; now the emphasis is on indirect competition such as outperforming competitors on logistic planning and customer service.

The members of a marketing channel are interconnected by several different factors:

1. The product line from manufacturer to end-user
2. The flow of ownership from member to member
3. The cash flow as payments are made by one member to another

4. The exchange of information between channel members
5. The advertising and sales promotion directed by channel members towards other members or end-users.

According to Kotler[1], 'a physical distribution system can be said to be efficient if no re-organization of logistical inputs could reduce the costs **while maintaining the present service level**'.

The distribution manager must consider the inter-related functions and their costs as a total entity when costs are being cut. Otherwise, cost-cutting by one function can end up with higher total costs. For example, capital costs of investing in new transport may be reduced by keeping the old trucks in use but their repair costs and lost orders due to delays in deliveries may end up by costing the company far more in the end. The number of possible distribution strategies increases as the complexity of the manufacturing company increases, from the simple options available to the single plant supplying a single market to the large number of possible choices faced by the company with many factories and a large number of markets.

Inventory decisions form an important part of the strategy because of the costs involved and the effect they have on many functions, especially the marketing function. The inventory decisions consist of deciding when to order and the amount to be ordered. The inventory maintenance costs can be as high as 30 per cent of the actual value of the inventory. It is possible to determine the optimal order quantity by using mathematical methods.

The location of warehouses and retail outlets is also an important part of physical distribution strategy in which the marketing function has a keen interest. They affect the speed and cost of delivery to customers and the number of potential customers.

The channel decisions depend upon the characteristics of:

- customers
- products
- company
- intermediaries
- competitors
- industrial/legal environment

The alternatives available differ according to:

- the types of channel members involved in the industry
- the number of channel members to be used at each stage of distribution
- the functions performed by these channel members
- the mutually agreed terms and conditions and responsibilities of the company and its channel members.

The following criteria should be considered in the selection of the best possible channel:

1. Economically, the channel chosen should yield the most profit.
2. If the role of marketing is important in a channel, the relevant skills and enthusiasm for the role must be present in the channel.
3. If there exist significant marketing objectives for the company, then the channel members' goals must be compatible with those objectives.
4. In respect of the control exercised over the channel and the vertical and horizontal interaction, possible conflict between different channels and legal difficulties should be considered.
5. There must exist the requisite management capability to make the business and trading relationship work for the success of both parties.
6. With regard to the future relationship, the adaptability of the system is also important.

References

[1] Kotler, Philip. *Marketing Management*, Prentice Hall International Inc. London and Englewood Cliffs, p. 306, 1976.

4 EFFECTIVE MARKETING THROUGH THE DISTRIBUTOR

As this book is essentially about distributors, this chapter explains why and how the role of the distributor is concerned with effective marketing (not just selling as is commonly assumed).

THE MARKETING CONCEPT (MARKETING NOT JUST SELLING)

Companies adopt different approaches to conducting their business; size and origin, market tradition and present structure are specific in each case, and so are business concepts. The importance of the market and of the customers is recognized by all businesses. The management styles begin to differ where the degree of recognition of this importance is concerned. When the whole company focuses on the needs of the customers and their satisfaction, the style is described as market-oriented and follows the marketing concept. This concept implies that the starting basis, the core of the activity, is the customer and so the management philosophy, the company organization and responsibility of marketing, including the channels of distribution, are derived from this concept.

The profit objective is even more important here than in other management styles. A business cannot be profitable if it does not provide the right product or the right service, if it is not built on the needs of the market or the needs of the customers, and if it does not achieve customer satisfaction. When intermediaries such as distributors or dealers are also involved between the manufacturer and the final customer, everybody has to make profit without sacrificing the marketing aspects.

There are still many companies who conduct their business by applying not the marketing concept but the alternative manufacturing and product concepts. They are not generally successful. When one is concerned with using distributors as channel members, the marketing concept is the only viable option as customers are the base of the business and the company objectives can only be met through customer satisfaction. The whole organization supports the task of the marketing function. This is the first guideline of the marketing concept.

The concept of marketing includes the process of working with markets in order to make exchanges happen, for the purpose of satisfying human needs and wants. The core concept of marketing is illustrated by the seven conversion processes that take place (see Fig. 4.1).

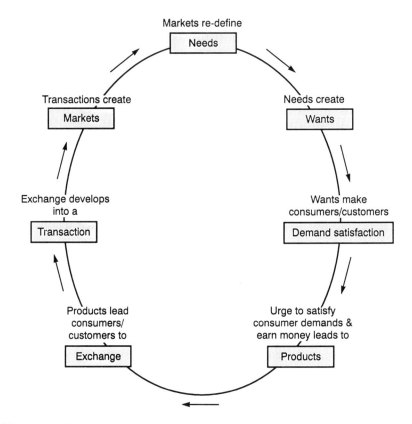

Figure 4.1   The core concept of marketing

Consequences of the marketing concept

A considerable effort is devoted to understanding the customers' demands, current and future, and the market structure (market and marketing research/identification of market segments). Market segment selection – selecting those market segments which can be best served while meeting the company's objectives – is the next step. Once this critical decision has been made, all the resources of the company are used to achieve the objective through strategic marketing planning. This planning and co-ordination responsibility is the core of the marketing function. This approach does increase the chance of success as the company's objectives/strategies are adjusted to the customers' expectations and not vice versa.

The marketing function, including channel management, is therefore the focal point in the company since it is the interface between the external world and the internal resources. This implies an adequate organization and company structure with all company employees dedicated to satisfaction of the customers and to the achievement of the marketing programme. The marketing function in a company has also to take account of the scenario as it develops. Any marketing decision taken at a point in time affects the immediate and near term future of the business, if not its long term future. Scenario building must be an integral part of marketing. The changing conditions in different fields – social, political, economic and technological – and in customer preference, when they happen simultaneously, are often in conflict. It is important to conduct a rational and systematic analysis of the future impact of each environmental factor on a specific business; and to avoid being trapped in a last minute crisis, under the pressure of events, when it may be too late to adjust to them. Marketing is all about taking account of all these factors and determining what courses of action are in the best interests of the company and of its chosen groups of customers. Often a balance has to be struck and the company's business profile redefined. In short, marketing involves market research, product planning, pricing and planning, advertising and sales promotion, selling, servicing, marketing administration and other general matters.

Competition, both local and international, is now intense in most businesses. On the production side, there is a trend to concentrate on large units as being more economical. Every company must be selective in many fields. Selectivity has the unique objective to be **competitive** in the market. The adoption of the marketing concept in every company is merely a consequence.

The marketing plan

Every company must be selective in many respects relative to the business portfolio the company wishes to keep, the market segments it wishes to operate in and the range of products/services offered. Product positioning with regard to the market and to the competing products is important for two reasons: to differentiate the product from the other products and to price it correctly.

The basic choice for a commercial organization is between market orientation or product orientation. The most frequent approach is a compromise. A key factor in building a marketing strategy is the concept of product differentiation. There exist several ways of differentiating one product (or service) from another. The difficulty lies in assessing the relative importance of each factor in the decision-making process of the customer and then exploiting only the 'key' differences. Product differentiation is directly associated with market segmentation; the desire to cover a number of market segments causes an increase in the number of different products and this adds to the costs. Finding the right balance and the correct compromise is part of strategic market planning.

Having decided on the kind of business the company wishes to operate in, the supplier's first task is to identify the market segments and rank them. The second is the selection of the segments that the supplier wishes to enter. The third is implementing a marketing plan. The marketing plan is part of the business plan; its five-stage process should be adjusted and included in the process of the latter. The five stages are:

1. Collect and analyse the information (basic data).
2. Set the objectives of the plan.
3. Select the strategies (the marketing mix).
4. Specify the action programme.
5. Forecast the financial impact of marketing initiatives.

George Day[1] has developed a framework for linking competitor analysis to marketing planning. His main thesis is that the various analyses should first lead to assumptions about the environment, competition, the company's resources and its competitiveness, followed by a SWOT analysis. The results should lead a company to formulate its strategic direction. A strong market attractiveness, combined with a strong competitive position would point to a high overall attractiveness.

Once a company has evolved its marketing plan, it must develop appropriate product promotion programmes and sales tasks with relevant profit and volume goals. In order to satisfy the customers, engineering has to design the product to meet customer needs; manufacturing has to produce the products on time and according to specification; and after-sales care and service has to be planned, geared and working. Therefore, it is vital that the marketing planning process integrates all other plans in the company in such a way that the annual planning and budgeting process becomes synchronized.

The marketing plan in its turn needs to take full account of the demands upon all the parts of an organization and to hold a balance between what is possible and achievable in the time frame and within the total budget, and what is desirable in an ideal situation. Only when top management have a satisfactory marketing plan can they turn it into a detailed expenditure plan and company-wide work plan. Integrating all the activities of a company and focusing them in the interests of the customer is vital if a company wishes to adopt the marketing concept.

The marketing manager plays a vital part in this total marketing process by representing the interests of the customer within the organization. The marketing manager has to take on the tasks of 'internal marketing', namely, educating the various divisions/functions within the company on various aspects of marketing, of articulating the impact of likely decisions of the company on the customer and of persuading other functions to follow the path dictated by the chosen marketing strategy even though it might appear to them to go against their individual points of view. The marketing function is at the interface between the market, the customers and the supply, that is, the product which the company wishes to and can offer. The adoption of the 'marketing concept' in the company means recognizing that the main base is the market and that the 'product' should be designed to meet customers' requirements to their satisfaction.

In practice, however, the company's products are 'already there' in most cases and the possibilities of finding and promoting new products are limited and costly. Therefore, there is and there must be a permanent dialogue between an external input, the market forces, and an internal input, the product. One of the major roles of the marketing function is to find the optimum fit between those two inputs, between the market–product pair.

A single market, or rather a single market segment, can be served by a large number of products, which differ in terms of performance, price, appearance, etc. Conversely, a single product, or rather a homogeneous group of products, can be sold in different market segments, which are different in terms of location, use, needs, motivation, etc.

Trade marketing

Trade in this context means the distributive trade which

> *brings together for the consumer as wide a range of items as possible from a great diversity of sources and makes them available from a single source.*

In the process of buying and selling, the trade makes its living from the difference in the prices. Its main reason for existence is that it knows what the consumer wants and how to make it available.

The distributor has to appeal to customers in their role as buyers, whereas the manufacturer approaches the distributors' customers in their role as consumers. In industrial selling, the consumer and the buyer may be quite different people, whereas in the selling of consumer goods they are likely to be the same person. It is better for the manufacturer and the distributor to work together on a joint appeal to both facets of the customer, rather than treat each other as antagonists.

Some of the large retailers sell the concept of their stores as their 'product' in its own right. They tend to usurp the function of deciding what the public wants and expect the producers to pay heed to what they, the retailers, want the manufacturers to produce. A manufacturer who markets through distributors has to develop a two-pronged marketing policy to attend to the needs of the distributors and the end customers. This will mean linking the planning processes of the functions of product and consumer marketing and sales to distributors.

The nature of marketing communications

There are two points of view regarding what constitutes communications with consumers: a limited point of view that identifies communications with advertising, point-of-sale material, personal selling and public relations; and an extended point of view which recognizes that all aspects of a firm's marketing activities represent an opportunity for communication. The first view is unrealistic. What marketers say in advertising and customer relations may be drowned out with what they do with the product, the package, the price or another aspect of visible marketing activities.

The nature of marketing communications can be explained through answers to the following questions which can be grouped under the three legs of a 'marketing' stool illustrated in Fig. 4.2.

1. Marketing research:
   - (a) Who are the intended customers?
   - (b) Who are the buyers and the decision-makers concerning the exchange of goods?
   - (c) Who signs the cheque?
   - (d) To whom do we tell our story?
   - (e) What do we tell?
   - (f) Who measures if the products and services bought result in the requisite satisfaction?

2. Marketing communications:
   - (a) When do we tell?
   - (b) How do we tell what we intend to tell?
   - (c) How do we get the customers to think of us and not of our competitors?
   - (d) How do we measure the effect of what we tell?

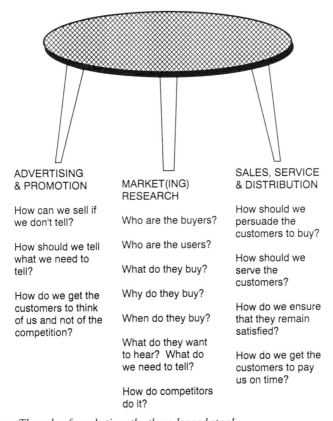

Gain customer satisfaction & satisfactory profits

ADVERTISING & PROMOTION

How can we sell if we don't tell?

How should we tell what we need to tell?

How do we get the customers to think of us and not of the competition?

MARKET(ING) RESEARCH

Who are the buyers?

Who are the users?

What do they buy?

Why do they buy?

When do they buy?

What do they want to hear? What do we need to tell?

How do competitors do it?

SALES, SERVICE & DISTRIBUTION

How should we persuade the customers to buy?

How should we serve the customers?

How do we ensure that they remain satisfied?

How do we get the customers to pay us on time?

Figure 4.2 The role of marketing: the three-legged stool

3. Sales and service:
   (a) How can we sell if we can't confirm what we told?
   (b) Did we tell what we set out to tell?
   (c) How can we persuade buyers to buy?
   (d) Did we sell what we set out to sell?
   (e) Did we satisfy the needs and wants of customers?

CONSUMER ATTITUDES AND DEMANDS

Marketers aim to modify consumer attitudes concerning their products. Favourable attitudes are held to increase the probability of purchase of those products. Advertising and promotion is used in a variety of ways to change consumer attitudes, by the provision of favourable product information, creation of favourable feelings towards the brands or through an effort to change consumer behaviour, or through a combination of all of them.

Marketing theory and practice place a lot of emphasis on attitudes and their measurements. There are a lot of problems associated with the prediction of behaviour through attitudes. Attitudes towards different attributes of the same object can cancel out each other. Thus, while consumers may think very highly of some object, say a Mercedes car, their attitude towards its cost in relation to its advantages to themselves may mean they are very unlikely to buy it. Marketing is particularly concerned about these different attitudes and their importance in affecting the purchasing decision.

Attitudes are formed through experience and learning, and the pattern of attitudes of any individual and the reasons for them can be unique to that individual. Therefore attitudes can only predict behaviour in very large populations and not on an individual basis. Marketing management is concerned with adjusting the amount, timing and type of demand so that the organization can achieve its objectives. According to Philip Kotler[2], demand can be measured for six different product levels, five geographic area levels and three time levels, making ninety types of demand measurement, and each of them can be used for different purposes to carry out the analysis of market opportunities, the planning of the marketing effort and the control of the marketing performance.

> *Market demand for a* **product** *is the* **total volume** *that would be* **bought** *by a defined* **customer group** *in a defined* **geographical area** *in a defined* **time period** *in a defined* **marketing environment** *under a defined* **marketing programme***.

These eight factors affect the measurement of demand. 'Company demand is the company's share of the market demand.' This is affected by the effort needed in marketing the company's products.

The measurement of potential demand is essential whether the seller wishes to introduce a new product, drop an existing product or expand into a new market. In fact, it is necessary before any strategic decision can be made. Various methods are available for estimating the market potential and for forecasting future demand. The choice should be made after taking into account the purpose of the forecast, the type of product and the availability and accuracy of the data.

Retailing influences

The majority of consumer goods are sold through retail outlets which determine the consumer shopping environment. Some of these retailers exercise great influence, for example when a small number of them control a large share of the market. Keeping the interest of these large distributors is then a problem for the manufacturer.

Most companies selling consumer products find that own stores is a costly and inefficient alternative. This means that the retailers retain ultimate control over which products reach the market at the end. Even after that, the display and other retailer-controlled factors can influence the sales of the product.

Factors which influence choice of shops

Generally, consumers choose shops on the basis of their past experience in familiar areas. Although research into elements influencing consumer choice has not been very successful, the following factors are thought to be important:

1. Shop location, including such elements as ease of parking, travel time, etc.
2. Shop characteristics, including design, range of goods, quality of service provided, personnel, price, advertising and promotion, atmosphere, the shoppers patronising the shop.
3. The consumer types, split into those who:
   (a) shop for enjoyment;
   (b) shop because they have to;
   (c) derive moderate pleasure from all aspects of shopping;
   (d) wish to obtain the best value for money;
   (e) shop to fulfil needs with the best available choice;
   (f) are motivated by a combination of the last two.
4. The image of the shop, with the consumers trying to match their requirements with their perception of the shop.

The image question has to be considered by the retail management with regard to the type of market targeted, the competitors, the objectives that need to be fulfilled and the ways to adjust the image to conform with all of these factors. The manufacturers have to reconcile the store image with the brand image which they are trying to establish, especially in the case of selective distribution. The way a product is treated inside the shop is considered to influence the sales of branded products to a great extent. The following elements influence the sales:

- stockouts
- price
- display and product grouping
- shelf location

Basically, the association between the manufacturer and retailer is one of necessity. Manufacturers are primarily interested in their own brand products, wide distribution, sales, low retail margins, consumer loyalty and display facilities, all pertaining to their products and the profits to be made from them. Retailers are interested in their store sales, profits, exclusive distribution, high retail margins, consumer loyalty to their stores and displaying the most profitable items.

Some retailers have introduced 'own labels' to reduce manufacturer dependence. This means the product is marketed under their own brand name and can be manufactured by anyone. Such products have high profit margins, are exclusive to the particular retail chain, can be priced below equivalent branded goods and allow retailers a greater degree of flexibility in pricing and promotion. Some generic products, which have no brand name and no promotion and can therefore be priced low, are also achieving success. Consumer attitudes are mixed on both these alternatives to manufacturer branded goods.

It must be expected that retail management will favour their own label products over other brands in such matters as store display and shelf positioning. Own brands and generic products tend to do better during times of economic stringency. Nation-wide own labels are bound to make inroads on manufacturers' brands. Consumer laws place restrictions on advertising claims, packaging and pricing practices and this adds to the problems of manufacturers.

Life-style influences

The family is unique among other groups in society, because of the emotional commitment involved and its institutionalized position in society. However, the family pattern regarding such things as leadership, norms and sanctions resembles other human groups.

The family life cycle
This concept has been in use in marketing for about forty years. An individual and a family pass through several stages in their lives which influence their shopping habits. It can be used for segmenting markets in an effective way and in identifying markets for particular products and services, e.g. launderettes are generally in demand in single person families.

The family life cycle stages are:

- young single
- young married without children
- young married with children

- older married with children
- middle-aged with dependent children
- middle-aged without dependent children
- older retired

However, these stages no longer include all common family patterns. Single parent households, dual career families, people living together without marriage, all make up a substantial part of society today in the developed world.

The family life cycle can be easily used in marketing since it combines such essential elements as income, social perceptions and family needs in one concept, and family statistics are easily available in most countries. The stages can be measured in terms of the number of families existing in each stage, these numbers are large enough to use for market segmentation and known types of media can be used for reaching the various stages.

On the other hand, there exists no standard way of categorizing the stages and comparisons are therefore difficult. Certain definitions may either narrow down the number of families in a category or broaden it to include different consumption patterns making them useless for marketing purposes; and some households do not easily fit into any life cycle stages.

Some theorists feel that the concept of the family life cycle should be augmented by the concept of life-style, to add the dimensions of attitudes and behavioural patterns. Consumer groupings based on attitudes, interests, opinions and activities have been tried, each group being a potential market for various products and services. One such grouping is on the basis of low income consumers driven by needs, another group driven by perceptions of others and the third category satisfying their own needs and wants without outside concerns.

Life-style categorizing is supposed to provide marketing insights into consumer behaviour. The types do overlap considerably but the marginal differences can sometimes be sufficient for marketing decisions.

Packaging

Packaging is basically needed for protecting the product during its transport and storage. It may also be required to protect the user against damage or harm. The protection needed depends upon the value, the composition and toughness or otherwise of the product concerned, as well as the length of the distribution channel, the handling the product is likely to receive and the possible effects of the climatic and other conditions it may encounter. However, the basic consideration of protection of the product has recently been superseded by the promotional and design aspects, although in most cases the requirements do not conflict with each other.

As transport and storage costs depend on the weight and/or volume of the goods concerned, the manufacturer's primary concern would be to make the best use of a given space. Retailers also often use sale per square foot as a measure of productivity and would therefore prefer less bulky packaging. Both manufacturer and retailer may, however, bow to the need for promotional appeal and accept extra packaging. Often, the only means of differentiation available to the manufacturer may lie in the packaging.

While manufacturers may prefer to sell their products in large amounts, small families may prefer to buy small quantities of products despite their comparatively higher prices. In a free market, the consumer generally wins, although sometimes at the cost of paying more for the inconvenience caused to the manufacturer.

Technology and competitive impact

The changing technology provides many long and short term business opportunities, although many businesses tend to see them as problems instead. Suppliers must be alert to customer perceptions and attitudes to technological advances and cater to new demands. The following information is vital in this process:

1. Which customers are keen to use new technology and what steps have they taken most recently to do so?
2. What advances can one expect from them in the future?
3. What can be done to encourage key customers to make use of such innovations?
4. What are the sources of innovation used in the past and whether there is any change in them?
5. What ways are available to persuade customers to use innovative methods with a view to a more beneficial collaboration with the supplier?

Most customers would like to see better new product management with fewer hold-ups in the process which can cause loss of competitiveness. New technological advances can change the structure of an industry almost overnight and a sharp look-out must be kept to keep the business competitive in such fast-changing circumstances.

The strategic use of relevant new technology has to be combined with customer orientation to profit the business in the best possible way. In particular, the strategic needs of one's key customers must be kept in mind at all times. It is necessary to establish strategic alliances with the main customers and make effective use of new technological advances. The following developments in the market-place point out the necessity for such close relationships:

1. Product life cycles are becoming shorter and shorter, with the product quality and design improving with every change. The markets for such products are now global and the best international suppliers are the most successful. A focus on total quality should be built into the market strategy as shown by the Japanese example. Customers are looking for suppliers who can match their strategic needs and develop with them.
2. The emergence of new trade blocks and new markets together with international industrial investment makes it even more crucial to maintain close contact with the key customers and to keep in step with them.

Case illustrations

The fact that Jaguar is flourishing can be attributed to Sir John Egan. When he arrived in 1980, the company was losing around £1 million a week and was perilously near closure. While efforts were continuing in the areas of quality, timing and productivity, Egan was looking at ways of improving the product, its marketing and distribution – in fact, the whole strategy, the objective being to pay more attention to detail without altering the basic design. Information was drawn from a feedback programme in which 300 customers were contacted every month and every aspect of design from fuel consumption to interior trim and detail styling was tackled. On this basis, map pockets and extensive tool kits were supplied with the car, and the leather and walnut trim retained. The management concentrated on communication and the creation of a 'family atmosphere'.

> We want to foster a sufficiently inspirational environment for workers to succeed, [said Egan.] You don't feel like giving your best if you don't think the company's worth it. We want our workers to feel affection for Jaguar and see it as more than a place where they spend their working hours.

Egan denied that he was trying to foster a Japanese-style approach. At the same time, he was acutely conscious of the effect of Japanese work ethic on the workers' productivity. In his belief that an educated work-force is a plank of success and that ignorance isolates people, he set up an open-learning centre at Jaguar where all employees could train in their own time. Subjects range from English for ethnic minorities and 'O' level mathematics to MBA degrees carried out in conjunction with Warwick University.

Staff recruitment also became more scientific. A battery of psychological tests tried to ensure that candidates were 'social and intelligent human beings and could cope with the job as we know it's going to be over the next five or ten years'.

ICI spent heavily in careful testing and brand promotion of Dulux as a decorator's friend, and positioned the product to achieve the required retail distribution. This helped Dulux to reign as the brand leader in the paint market and to retain this position; wholesalers and distributors world-wide have appreciated this fact.

In aggressive marketing, distribution channels should be given the necessary priority so that new approaches can be fully and adequately tested and methods of distribution can be improved before new or superior products are developed with heavy costs.

EVALUATION OF THE COMPETITION

In marketing in today's business environment, the knowledge and the evaluation of the competitors is a key input in strategic marketing planning. I have heard it said 'Too many companies look in the mirror and not enough through the window'; this is still true. For many reasons ranging from lack of information to overconfidence, many companies do not conduct a systematic and analytical survey of their current as well as potential competitors, despite the fact that they profit from the process. Examples show that in this way they can:

1. Learn from others' successes and failures as to how to conduct their own business.
2. Improve their knowledge of the market by considering the link between the suppliers' actions and the customers' reactions.
3. Identify the strengths and weaknesses of the competitors and use them to spot relative opportunities fitted to the company resources.
4. Select the business mission and objectives, in the light of the above, and design the best strategy to achieve them; this should include the attitude to be adopted towards the competitors.
5. Differentiate the company (image, products, etc.) positively from the competition.

The following case shows how the analysis of competition helps a company choose the correct alternative when entering a new market. Nabisco had a local subsidiary and a large share of the biscuit market in Denmark. United Biscuit (UB) tried at first to enter the market by means of a distributor, Copenhagen Bread Factories (CBF) which did not work very well as the small bakers who were CBF's main customers, did not have the demand for biscuits in large quantities and CBF did not have contacts among the high volume retailers. Later, UB set up their own sales subsidiary on the lines of Nabisco. After two years of various teething problems, they increased their market share substantially in Denmark.

Before going on to the techniques and format of the exercise, it is worth considering the major guidelines. The first list of competitors should include most, if not all, of the competitors operating in the whole field of the total business definition. When the company mission has been selected, then the direct competitors can be identified and a detailed evaluation conducted.

Though it is not often possible to gain precise knowledge about competition, this should not prevent the exercise from being carried out using the best possible estimates; they can be changed later on if the facts become available.

There are two distinct steps in the evaluation of a competitor in a specific business. The first is to make an 'absolute evaluation' whereby a competitor is checked against the industry and the market; i.e. to answer how well they fit in with the demand, in all respects. The second step can be called a 'relative evaluation' of the competitor's strengths and weaknesses *vis-à-vis* the company, the basis for comparison being the company resources. Confusion occurs when these two steps are combined and an objective analysis is superimposed on a subjective input.

Absolute evaluation

This should consist of a comprehensive assessment of the competitor company, beginning with its origin, historical growth, its aims, objectives, strategies, chosen markets, products and services offered, style of management, culture of the company, perceived image, financial performance and key motivational aspects of the managers among other things.

An in-depth analysis of the specific product lines should include historical performance of the product lines versus apparent market trends, total sales, market share and financial performance. In addition, an evaluation of existing business resources must be performed in a quantified manner as far as possible in common with the historical performance above, but should then be translated into a simplified 'rank' with selection amongst five grades: excellent, good, medium, below average, poor.

All company resources, which are ultimately used to achieve sales and profit, can be grouped in three basic categories as: money (financial), physical (products and capacities) and people (human resources). Depending upon the nature of the business and the stage of development of the company in the business, each of these resources influences the ultimate result in a greater or less degree. The overall assessment (rank) which will result from the detailed evaluation should take this into account. The analytical table Table 4.1 can be used.

Apparent mission, objectives and strategy

A detailed survey conducted as above, should allow an assessment of the competitor, including the business mission, long term objectives and the strategy they appear to follow. The product range offered and the degree of market coverage give a good indication of the business mission of the competitor and the selected markets/products segments. It is easier to

	Past Performance	Existing Resources
Market position		
Market coverage		
Sales (units)		
Sales (%)		
Market share		
Price position		
Overall appraisal in business		
Finance		
Return on investment (profitability)		
Capability of investment		
Physical resources		
Production capability		
Cost competitiveness		
Product range		
Research/innovation		
Physical distribution		
People		
Management quality		
Management dedication		
Organisation structures/ efficiency		
Marketing talents		
Margin management		
Sales force (direct/indirect)		
Technical service to customer		

Table 4.1 Competitor evaluation checklist

understand the competitor's objective and their strategy, after determining the broad profile of their mission, although there is a wide range of objectives and a wider one of strategies, even for similar companies.

Competitors have been broadly classified in four categories; a company is considered a leader if it holds a large share of the market; a challenger is a company which is hoping to grow into a leader; a follower holds a comparatively small share of the market and does not aspire further; a nicher focuses on a narrow segment of the market or on a speciality product.

Sometimes the 'me too' approach of copying a company's product or modifying it is not necessarily a bad thing. Brooke Bond introduced their Brazilian brand coffee and Bird's Eye their frozen pancakes in imitation of their competitors. It is possible to seize a new opportunity in this way if an analysis reveals that the competitor has omitted from their product line some specific features that could exploit a specific segment of the market. This is especially the case if the market is growing and can support a larger number of brands.

Following a study conducted on the subject, R. G. Cooper[3] suggested that a manufacturer who is 'first in' in any market can be matched by those coming in later.

Relative evaluation – major strengths and weaknesses

This is the second step of the exercise and probably the most important; the **par** for evaluation is now the own company resources, though the 'average competitor profile' can also be used for comparison. Only major points should be highlighted in the relative evaluation in order not to swamp the final profile with secondary details.

Sources of information

It is impossible to know everything about one's competition. It should be an ongoing and important task of the marketing management to watch it and be prepared to react to their actions when necessary. There are many useful and readily available sources of information about competitors, within the limits of business ethics; for example:

1. Their reports, brochures, speeches, interviews.
2. Their organizational and personnel announcements.
3. Customer views regarding them.
4. Publications by independent consulting firms concerning them, e.g.:
    (a)   industry studies
    (b)   security analysts' reports
    (c)   magazines, newspapers, etc.
    (d)   government attitude

Conclusion

Watching competitor moves pays. Differentiation also pays.

In a world where most whisky brand names are owned by large multinationals, Macallan Glenlivet is a small independent distiller of whisky situated in the Scottish Highlands. On the famous Black Monday of the stock-market crash, it managed to maintain a stable share price. The shares had a scarcity value because of the small shareholder base. Much of the rest of the industry is controlled by multinationals from abroad. Despite a small work-force, it manages to produce a world-class whisky.

Macallans frown on price-cutting because whisky is made by a slow and expensive process. Producing whisky is a long term business where the standard export product is twelve years old.

Whisky giants are sometimes ready to cut the prices to a ridiculous extent causing difficulties for such a small company. Macallan's steadiest and most important customers are in Europe.

Changes in the strategy of the United Distillers Group (UDG) had eased the strain on Macallan. Their decision to buy out their distributors had caused some independent distributors to look for small specialists to fill the gaps. Macallan wished to keep its premium image and did not countenance any strategy which would detract from it. The wholesale price of whisky rocketed up fourfold in 1988.

The descendants of the founder of the company still owned large chunks of the equity and this made it difficult for outside bidders to try for a take-over or merger. The management is concerned to keep up its reputation even if the company is taken over. They do not like the insistence of certain other competitors on high rates of return in the short term while ignoring the need for quality and long term potential.

In another instance, a watch manufacturer benefited from watching competition. In the past, most watches were sold through department stores and jewellers' shops. One manufacturer, looking for a new distribution strategy, did some market research and found that most watches were bought as gifts. The company then decided that such purchases would not merit the thought and time that is spent on personal purchases and went in for a more intensive distribution through other types of shops. This policy was also followed by Timex to make their products more easily available and because a lot of jewellers would not accept the lower mark-up on Timex watches as compared to the other makes of watches.

One of the problems in business today is the amount of information available which few have the time to collect, read and understand. It may be worthwhile giving the task to someone responsible, in order to keep up-to-date on all business matters. In most businesses today, a condition of success is to 'do something better than the others'; in other words, to beat the competitors. Words such as offensive, defensive, surrounding, direct attack, squeezing, are part of the strategic marketing literature. It could almost be described as 'marketing warfare'. It is no longer enough to swim the channel; one has to be among the first to reach the other side.

TARGET MARKETING AND BENEFIT SEGMENTATION

The manufacturer is the principal authority for describing the product, its features and benefits and holds the responsibility to ensure that the product is merchantable and 'fit for the purpose'. So the manufacturer has to set the purpose and the goals clearly so that there is very little chance for the channel members to change them, and, as the campaign leader, must define very clearly the specific groups of customers for whom the product is intended and spell out the target markets. Dependence on the channel sales force to get the required sales volumes may mean the manufacturer has to gain the commitment of the channels to the segmentation. In a value-added sense, the benefits must also be clearly understood by all the parties involved from the manufacturer to the end customer.

The success of a marketing campaign can only come from all the parties working together in a motivated and co-ordinated manner; effective segmentation of the market and the identification of specific benefits to the target market is the starting basis for such a campaign. Markets consist of groups of consumers which may have different needs and may expect different benefits from the product. Philip Kotler has described market segmentation as

> *the subdivision of a market into homogeneous subsets of customers, where any subset may conceivably be selected as a market target to be reached with a distinct marketing mix.*

A market should be segmented according to the needs and desires of the customers in that market. The segments should be capable of definition and measurement, so that their marketing potential can be measured. For example, segments based on demographic data are relatively easy to measure, whereas those based on abstract values such as appreciation of art are very difficult to measure. Segments must be large enough to make a separate marketing effort worthwhile and it must be possible to reach them through advertising and promotion.

Segmentation is sometimes global; it does not recognize national or cultural boundaries. For example, well-to-do youngsters living in cities own walkmans, drink Coke, wear Levi jeans, sport Nina Ricci fashion clothes and wear Swatch watches. Some of them also eat at McDonalds. This pattern seems to be repeated from the Far East to the west coast of the United States and beyond.

The main reason for market segmentation is to improve the market position of the company together with its profits. A market segmentation strategy can assist in the attainment of these objectives by:

- identifying new opportunities
- better promotion of existing products
- better response to marketing influences.

Market segmentation can reveal new opportunities by identifying unusually profitable segments of the market or discovering better channels of distribution for existing products. The market research that is necessary before market segmentation can be attempted, can itself lead to a better understanding of the marketing processes and thus improve the marketing decisions. One of the purposes of test marketing is also to understand the process of segmentation better than would otherwise be possible.

Distributors can play an important part in test marketing. Procter & Gamble, Unilever and General Foods, to name a few, rely on test marketing to prove product innovation, customer appeal and promotion testing before embarking upon national/international launches. Test marketing is an important way of reducing risk and distributors have a valuable contribution to make.

In Search Of Excellence[4] describes 3M and Hewlett Packard as companies which encourage innovation not only among their staff but also among their distributors. Heinz and Crosse & Blackwell both came out with spaghetti hoops at about the same time without being aware of each other's interest in this idea. Did the idea originate with their suppliers?

Market segmentation can lead to increase in costs of market research, research and development, production, administration, inventory, distribution and advertising and promotion. There is always a point beyond which further segmentation is inadvisable because it is unprofitable. Also, some markets are found not to yield to segmentation. In either case, product differentiation can be tried instead.

Market segmentation strategy consists of identifying particular segments of the customer base and developing a product or a variation of an existing product specifically for those segments. It can be considered an extreme form of product differentiation. Sometimes the product differences in the various segments are quite insignificant. However, so long as the segments are separately identifiable and merit different marketing programmes, these product differences matter. It can happen that product differentiation itself causes the segmentation of a market. Segmentation exploits known differences among the consumer population whereas product differentiation attempts to create differences among a population where they did not exist before.

The main population characteristics used for segmentation are geographic, demographic, psychological or behavioural. Markets are segmented according to whatever variable or combination of variables is suitable in any case. Different geographic regions may make good segments because of their history, climate or physical properties. Age, sex and social class are often used for segmenting markets. The psychological make-up of a population segment can make a difference, for example, where products are differentiated by their prestige factor or their appeal on health grounds. An example of behavioural segmentation occurs when the basis is the benefits expected by the buyer from the product.

Many different methods are used for market research designed to identify market segments. However, the experts differ about the efficiency of these methods.

EFFECTS OF VOLATILITY OF HIGH TECHNOLOGY PRODUCT LIFE CYCLES ON THE CONTROL OF THE CHANNEL

A high technology product comes under pressure from:

- new innovations
- new technological advances
- substitute products with cost advantages to the manufacturer
- shorter and shorter sales life cycles and sometimes installed life cycles
- competitive inroads into an established customer base
- customer demand for enhancements and improvements
- competitive launch of improved products for the same value margin when volumes drop.

The time available for developing and learning about the product and establishing oneself gets shorter and shorter every year as the years roll by. The squeeze on margins from established products generally means that the channel members are always seeking additional incentives and compensation to top up the profit contribution and to make up for reduced margins. If the channel members are not able to pay for good staff and to retain them, they continually feel the absence of skilled resources at the appropriate levels. The channel members tend to become restless, go in search of other avenues to achieve their goals and to complain about the lack of incentives in dealing with the products.

At the same time, most customers wish to buy proven products which fit their purse. The only pressure the channel members feel they can bring to bear is by complaining to the manufacturer that the product does not offer adequate profitability and that the manufacturer does not support the channel members in their areas of need.

PRICING AND DISCOUNT STRATEGY

The first rule is that the company's costs of production, marketing and distributing the products to the customers' satisfaction must be recovered. Here costs plus a minimum margin is a good starting point. The second rule is that one must have clear objectives for the market-place one is addressing. Is the objective to gain a share of the market? Or is it to cream the market? Or is it to penetrate the market? Or is it that the company just wants to be there – in other words, they just need a presence, but do not care about the market share? Or is it some other objective?

Manufacturers generally want the end consumers to be charged a price which will be attractive and which will make sufficient profits both for themselves and the distribution channels involved, and which is neither too high nor too low. However, they usually have little control over this end price. The best that can be done is to plan what the price should be and try to influence both the retailer and the distributive trade to keep to it.

The distributor's level of profit is affected by the net margin, the amount of goods sold, the stock turnover rate and the amount of credit allowed by the manufacturer, who can thus help the trader in many ways. During negotiation, all these aspects should be emphasized and used to influence the traders.

It is vital that the end prices should be known to the manufacturer to allow an estimate of the distributor's margins. This should be done through periodic surveys to help control the distributive process. The amount of margin to be allowed to every trade sector must be carefully calculated with allowance made for sales volumes, stock turnover and other factors, so as to keep the distributive trade interested in the transaction. Inflation can complicate these calculations and allowance has to be made for it. The manufacturer's accounts should make provision for the total costs of the sales including the distributive costs.

It is generally possible to control the prices charged to the consumer in a competitive market by setting realistic recommended prices using judicious judgement concerning the level of distributive trade rewards. A flexible and differentiated system of rewarding trade is necessary to stimulate trade sales, to motivate the different sectors to achieve the set objectives and to preserve equitable prices in the different sectors. Care must be exercised in setting a price guidance policy for the trade because within the European Community it is illegal to control sale prices by taking away the independence of the distributors.

Cost considerations

Cost control should be considered an important part of marketing. Proper information regarding costs could reveal ways of making better use of scarce resources; it is also necessary to make the correct decisions regarding prices. It is always more effective to combine suggestions for marketing expenditure with positive cost-cutting proposals. Costs can be assigned to different functions in order to determine the responsibility for them. For instance, it is salutary to ask and gain answers to some interesting questions. If an end customer/consumer pays $100 to buy a product or service, what proportion of this price is attributable to the various functions? How does this compare with the competitors? What business are we really in? Figure 4.3 illustrates this situation.

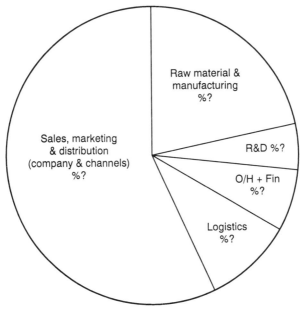

%? = What is the percentage of end customer sales revenue?

Figure 4.3 Sales, marketing and distribution business

Marketing costs are more difficult to measure and control than say, production costs. The latter can be attributed to products and processes, while marketing costs can be assigned to products, customers, territories, order sizes, channels of distribution and sales force. The marketing effort consists of intangibles and it is more difficult to assign the costs of obtaining a specific order than of creating a product or service. The effects of adding an extra machine or worker to the production process are easier to estimate than those of extra advertising or of dropping a sales executive from the force.

Pricing strategy

The pricing strategy, in terms of the price to the end-user, must therefore be based on 'marketing objective', i.e. 'creaming or skimming', 'being up-market', 'penetration', or 'neutral', or whatever. Managers ought to first consider what price the market will bear and the actions of their competitors. Afterwards they should set target costs for production so that they will leave sufficient profit margin. Most companies do it the other way round, calculating their production costs first and their price last.

The idea is to become a specialist; to discover something customers want before most other companies offer it, making it really well, pricing it at a premium and marketing it hard. Costs should only be used to set a bottom line. Sell to customers who have got the money to afford your products and target not the professional buyers but the people who will use your products.

Pricing policy requires special attention in a business since so many factors affect the decisions. In order to succeed at very low prices, companies have to be super-efficient. For them, the boundary between profit and loss is especially thin. It must be remembered that low margin lines need high margin lines to balance them. The product mix should be correctly balanced, with flexible prices and the best advantage being taken of price changes. The products should be sufficiently and advantageously differentiated from competing products and the difference should be promoted till the customers ask for it. The discount policy should be firmly controlled.

An examination of management ratios in seven different UK industries, covering a large number of firms in each, showed that 90 per cent of the variations in rates of return on assets, measured over three and a half years, were due to profit margin on sales. This shows how important the influence of pricing policy is on profitability, at least in the short term.

A long-standing marketing question is whether sales personnel should be given authority over pricing. Management should have access to information on costs, profit and the results of price changes on sales results and avoid unnecessary discounts. The strategy of allowing sales force personnel to make pricing decisions itself leads to aggressive bargaining by purchasing agents. Among a sample of 108 firms, those giving sales people the highest degree of pricing authority generated the lowest sales and profit performance. These research results imply that pricing should not be left in the hands of the sales force. Managers should make the final decision while taking sales force recommendations into account where pricing flexibility is needed. This is even more important when a low price strategy is adopted, because then gross margins are low and price discounts can result in disproportionate reductions in net profits.

In a cross-border situation, it is important to differentiate which channel will be marketing and delivering the product/service to the end customer. If it is a subsidiary, then a transfer price policy is appropriate. However, care must be taken to ensure that a justifiable element of profit is available for tax purposes both to the host and the subsidiary country so that the respective exchequers are not unhappy. Of course, in the 1990s, tax authorities do come to know of the transfer prices offered to different subsidiaries in different countries. It is important to ensure that a uniform policy is applied and discrimination is avoided.

Transfer Pricing

Sometimes a company can market its products through a subsidiary or a joint venture with a partner in one country and through a distributor in an adjacent country. The pricing strategy adopted for shipments of products to the two countries may come into conflict. It is important to understand the concept of transfer pricing which is adopted for transfer of products to a subsidiary.

Having set up a profit centre, a company wishes to evaluate its performance and to motivate the management to achieve objectives set for it. In order to do this, a rational system of transfer pricing is needed. Transfer prices are the prices paid by a division of a company (in this case, a profit centre) for the goods it receives from the parent company. These prices have to be set so that the management responsible for the profit centre has sufficient leeway for motivation and for achieving the set objectives, and the parent company can obtain sufficient profits.

When this concept is carried across to a foreign country, it can cause complications involving, among other factors:

- taxes on income, duties and tariffs
- conditions in the local market
- the creditworthiness of the potential customers
- government rules regarding imports
- the rules regarding profit transfers
- the possible conflict between the objectives of partners in joint ventures.

The transfer price can be set at:

1. The direct cost
2. Direct cost plus overheads and margin
3. A figure after consideration of the price paid by the end customers
4. Level which an unconnected buyer would pay for the same transaction.

All these possibilities have their own advantages and disadvantages. Price 1 is used by some companies on the basis that the foreign sales help them achieve scale economies in domestic manufacturing. Price 2 may be used by businesses operating on the basis that the foreign sales must earn a profit at every stage of their movement to the end customer; this may end up in non-competitive prices in a foreign market. On the other hand, Price 3 is expressly designed to be competitive in the designated market. Another possibility is to use such a pricing policy and also use foreign sourcing to gain a foothold in a new market considered too small to allow local manufacturing. After the products are established in the market and some experience is gained, the company can develop other effective strategies. The difficulty with Method 4 is to decide what a hypothetical buyer would pay for the product. It is easier to establish a range of prices within which the price should vary.

As the rates of taxation vary in various countries, international businesses are naturally trying to minimize the total taxes they pay while the national governments are trying to counter their moves and maximize their own tax revenue.

The US Treasury transfer price review programme is one of the most comprehensive in the world today and can be used to obtain guidelines for management of international companies. It covers the sale of tangible property from raw materials to half-finished and finished goods; the use of tangible property; the pricing of all services, financial, R&D, consulting, etc.; and transfer or use of intangible or intellectual property such as patents, copyrights, trade marks, procedures, forecasts, estimates, customer lists, etc.

When such transfers are made across national boundaries, the transfer prices have to be accepted by different national tax authorities who may have conflicting interests themselves. For example, the customs authority may wish to have high prices for the tangible property being transferred so that they can charge high duties; whereas the inland revenue may wish for low prices, so that the local business makes more profits which can then be taxed by them. International businesses have to examine tax laws carefully to make them work to their best advantage.

In the US Treasury regulations, the preferred rule applying to sales of tangible articles is Method 4 above with three possible methods. The idea of the first is to establish what price would be paid by a buyer in an ordinary market situation who is not connected to the selling company. This is usually difficult. Secondly if the buyer has not appreciably added value to the products before reselling them, then the resale price for an uncontrolled sale can be used after deducting an appropriate mark-up, which is defined in the regulations. The cost-plus method has the lowest priority and is specified in detail. However, this method is the easiest to apply in practice. These regulations do, however, allow a company to reduce prices to gain an advantage in foreign markets.

It is necessary that international marketing managers should study such regulations which may apply to their operations and make sure that their pricing procedures conform to their provisions so that they do not tangle with the tax authorities. It is possible to adjust pricing policies to local tax rates so as to minimize the company tax burden. Sometimes, the different tax rates may signal in different directions, as in the case of a country with high import duties and a low income rate. Many companies either ignore the tax situation or pay it minimum of attention for the following reasons:

1. The tax savings are small compared to the efforts needed to minimize them.
2. The effort is more profitably spent in effective strategies for motivation and resource allocation.
3. It is better to have a simple and straightforward pricing policy and avoid costly disputes with the local tax authorities.
4. The developed world is tending towards similar tax policies anyway and the efforts to avoid taxes are not going to be worth it.

Some countries require importers to keep funds proportional to the price of the imports in a non-interest-paying deposit for a fixed period. This provides an incentive to reduce the amount paid for the imports. On the other hand, if the amount of profits which can be transferred out of a country is restricted, this provides an incentive to increase the price paid for imports by a subsidiary. Other government regulations may control market pricing. It is necessary to study the local rules and regulations in order to manage the company operations in the best way possible.

In the case of joint ventures, a company has to share the profits of the venture. Therefore the incentive is to price the transfer goods at a higher price than if they were being transferred to a subsidiary. It is best to work out an acceptable pricing arrangement in advance and it should be one that the relevant tax authorities will also accept. At the same time, the relationship with distributors in neighbouring countries or territories within a trading region must be carefully weighed before deciding upon what pricing strategies to adopt.

In the EC, the Single European Market will take effect at the beginning of 1993. Price harmonisation will soon become the regulatory policy. Discrimination which may eventually affect the consumers must be avoided.

The third rule is that all the channel members must have an opportunity to earn a living. It is demotivating for a member to play an important part and find that they are losing money, while others earn a good living. The fourth rule governs competition and anti-trust laws. Any pricing practice which has as its object or effect, limiting, distorting or eliminating competition will be illegal in most countries. It is certainly so in the EC, USA and almost all developed nations.

Discount strategy

In a similar manner, care should be taken that discount policies, especially quantity order discounts and rebates, do not discriminate against channels or consumers. For instance, an offer of a discount to a large company buying a product in volume must not mean that the cost to a small customer is so high as to be put into an uncompetitive situation.

Although several types of discounts are possible, depending on the industry and nature of the products, generally speaking rebates and discounts must not be 'discriminatory'. In the United States, for example, the Robinson–Patman Act makes it illegal to grant an extra discount to a customer on account of their size and order potential. In a similar manner, the Treaty of Rome which governs the EC competition laws prohibits 'dissimilar conditions to equivalent transactions'. The different types of discount are:

- Quantity discount
- Discount as a percentage of the value of the goods supplied
- Discount as a value against the value of goods supplied
- Discount for growth
- Discount for delivery size
- Cash discount
- Discount with payment terms
- Terms of reward for incremental sales
- Co-operation discounts

These are discussed in further detail below.

Quantity discounts encourage the trade to buy more, but they also eliminate the smaller customers in the long term and this means more discounts to the others who tend to control the market in larger shares. Concentration of trade in fewer hands means lower prices for the consumer and lower profits for the manufacturer who loses control over the distribution system. Discriminatory pricing is not allowed in the Unisted States and similar implications exist under the Rome Treaty, although they are not as strictly enforced. The system of quantity discounts causes a number of problems, among which are retaliation by competitors, the need for confidentiality and consequent leakages, difficulties regarding the actual method of paying the discounts and the danger of the trade taking the discounts for granted. **Discounts for growth** are subject to similar disadvantages as quantity discounts.

Discounts for delivery size are more relevant as it actually does cost less to deliver in large quantities, in terms of administrative costs and transport, for example. It also motivates the trader to sell more. These discounts can be paid for out of savings on cost rather than out of profits and cannot be considered discriminatory. They need not be confidential and the administration process of payment is comparatively simple. Multiple stores can have deliveries made to their own warehouses which in turn can deliver assorted stock in large lots to their own branches. This system can still encourage large buyers, but the process stimulates an increase in efficiency in the whole chain if the discounts exceed the increase in costs in handling larger deliveries. The only drawback is in case of perishable goods. Delivery-related discounts are the best procedure for a manufacturer to stimulate sales, motivate distributors and improve the efficiency of the distributive chain while maintaining some control over the whole process of distribution.

Differentials between distributive functions can be used when a manufacturer sells to different levels in the distributive chain, e.g. to retailers as well as wholesalers. The difficulty arises in distinguishing between the different levels and deciding on the prices used for them and in avoiding discrimination when it is not legally permissible. Quantity discounts for total sale or for deliveries may solve this problem automatically. However, it is necessary to be vigilant in order that the various members of the distributive chain get their level of reward, which is not always achieved by this process. The best way to achieve such differentials is to allow co-operation discounts for performing services which the manufacturer does not have to perform, such as redistribution in smaller quantities. These discounts should be related to the savings made and either renegotiated periodically according to the expected level of sales or fixed provided certain conditions are met.

Cash discounts are made for prompt payments within the agreed credit or current account terms. The general system is that the customer checks the delivery against the invoice and pays within a stated time limit, which is usually but not necessarily one month. In practice, most suppliers close their ledgers periodically, usually once a month, and send in their bills, counting the time allowed from that date. With computers, it is feasible to send in the accounts and to settle them separately instead all together once a month. Direct debiting is a useful system of payment in this respect if it can be negotiated.

As the objective of a cash discount is to encourage early payment and facilitate cash inflow, the possibility of a cash discount offer must be taken into account in quoting the price to the customer. The discount must also be sufficiently attractive to entice the customer to pay rather than 'borrow' from the supplier on a credit basis. Some suppliers may have a policy of offering credit facilities to their customers as an incentive, either through a financial institution or with their own resources. Such loans should be separately covered by relevant paperwork and not mixed with the papers relating to the actual sale of goods. They should conform to any relevant legal rules. It is also essential to make any other discounts conditional on prompt payment; in that case, a cash discount may not even be needed.

After a decision is made on the form of the discounts to be paid, it is necessary to work out the rules and to consider the implications. It is best if the same scale can be applied to all company products and to quantities purchased instead of their money value, so that inflation does not erode the advantage. It may be necessary to adjust the scale in proportion to the value of or the margin on each product if the range varies widely in terms of value or margin. When discounts are being offered on the basis of savings made, a good model of all relevant costs should be constructed in order to help fix the scale, starting at the point where the savings first arise and stopping where no more savings are possible. Discounts on quantity sales should be applied to the incremental quantity only; this process makes the increase smooth and avoids anomalies. There is usually a high 'ceiling' set in this process.

The objectives to be achieved by a manufacturer through the terms to the distributive chain concern:

- end prices
- reward obtained by the various members of the trade
- incentives offered to the trade
- performance levels
- payment terms
- likely effects of discounts, etc.

The possible effect of any alteration in the terms should be carefully estimated as well as the amount of opposition the change will provoke. Incentives may be needed to help bring about the change.

Pricing approaches

In pursuing an international or global marketing strategy, a company may wish to adopt an ethnocentric or polycentric or geocentric approach to pricing. There are advantages and disadvantages in all these approaches.

An **ethnocentric approach** has the advantage of simplicity because it is based on keeping the price the same world-wide in a base currency, with the customer absorbing the exchange, freight and import duties. No information on market conditions or competitive situation is needed; but the company's profits in each national market are not maximized. This is a philanthropic approach.

The **polycentric approach** is based on transfer prices set by the headquarters and the local managers are allowed the freedom of action. This approach takes account of local conditions, but there is no co-ordination of pricing strategies applied in the national markets. There is the risk of local managers taking advantage of product arbitrage potential when the landed costs and local prices in markets allow for an entrepreneurial manager to buy in the low price market and sell the product in the more expensive market.

A **geocentric approach** recognizes that local conditions, which include costs, income levels and competition and marketing objectives, call for special attention. It therefore participates in setting a price level that is appropriate for each market. In this manner a company can adopt a global posture rather than maximizing the potential in each country.

Cost-plus pricing

At its simplest, this means calculating the cost of producing an item and adding on a profit margin. This makes no concession to the market or to the fact that price is an important determinant of demand. At the other extreme, the price is raised until the sales fall seriously and the cost of manufacture is largely ignored. In both these methods, no attempt is made to equate what the customers are prepared to pay with the price which gives the producer a reasonable return.

Absorption (full cost) pricing

Total costs are reduced to unit costs according to the accounting convention that costs can be split into direct costs and overheads. The former are relatively easy to allocate in this way, but the latter do not depend upon output directly, although they increase as the organization expands. Machinery incurs fixed costs and these have to be arbitrarily distributed over a range of products, based on a percentage of all sales or the factory area used for the manufacture of each product. The overheads are then allocated to each unit of an estimated sales volume. The direct costs per unit and a percentage margin for profit are added on and this gives the selling price. This implies that profit can be made from the very first unit sold which is obviously not true.

Marginal cost pricing

The marginal cost of production is the additional cost incurred on the production of one more unit of output. This method differentiates between those costs which vary with output and those which do not. A price is set on the product and the direct costs are subtracted from it, the balance representing a contribution to the overheads. This allows an examination of profitability as sales increase or decrease. This method has the advantage that it enables firms to set prices purely on direct costs when sales are sluggish as in seasonal businesses like hotels and airlines in the tourist trade. It is also frequently used by firms which are not operating at full capacity.

Many large retailers carry 'own brand' products made by established manufacturers which sell at lower prices than their own products, but relieve the manufacturer of selling and distribution costs. If the sale of 'own brand' lines does not affect the manufacturer's sales of established brands, the profits will rise. This method is also used by retailers when they select 'loss leaders' to attract customers to their shops hoping they will then buy enough of other stuff to make up for the losses.

Little attempt is made to determine the strength of demand apart from the estimate of total sales. It assumes a clear definition of costs which may not exist in many cases. It can be difficult to decide the extra cost of producing just one more item. One of the pitfalls can occur when a lower priced product, which makes little contribution to cover overheads, becomes so successful that expansion of capacity is called for, increasing the overheads; or the other products fail to perform so well and do not cover the overheads any longer. In this case, the price of the lower priced item may have to be increased, possibly causing a drop in its sales.

The 'mark-up' method

Many retailers apply a standard mark-up on wholesale prices to give them their profit. Manufacturers have no control over the final price since the abolition of the resale price maintenance in most countries. Mark-up pricing takes the state of demand into consideration, with slow-moving products having a lower mark-up than others, luxury goods having a higher mark-up, and so on.

Break-even analysis

The break-even price is arrived at by determining the unit price at which the net sale proceeds will cover all the variable costs attributable directly to the product and the share of the fixed costs allocated to it, when a given volume is sold. In a similar manner, the break-even volume is that volume of the product which must be sold at a given price in order that the sale proceeds can fully cover the variable costs and the fixed costs attributable to the product. This analysis is very important for establishing the survival levels. Of course, care must be taken to include costs of inflation and other costs likely to be incurred so that one is not suddenly caught out by selling at too low a price.

The break-even price or the break-even volume, does not by definition yield the profit requirement. For this, the selling price must be substantially higher than the break-even price or the volume must be adequately higher so that the profit objective of the organization can be achieved.

Psychological price

Price is a factor which is often researched when products are being tested in the market to determine their 'fit' with consumer needs. When similar products are already on sale, their prices obviously affect this perceived value, but consumers quickly put their own value on new products and it is important to price products to give 'value for money'. Frequently, panels are set up to evaluate the product and suggest a range of prices they would be prepared to pay for it. This gives the manufacturer some idea of acceptable prices, although, in practice, the consumers might act differently. If the price set is too low to give a reasonable profit, the firm may decide not to go ahead with the product. However, if the acceptable price is higher than the 'cost-plus' or marginal price, the manufacturer may wonder what to do. If it is set well below the perceived price in the hope for extra sales, this can make consumers suspicious. If it is well above the perceived price, then they may question its special benefits.

Distributors

The effect of pricing on distributors must be foreseen and guarded against. A distributor can be alienated by constant price changes, since it adds to the paperwork and upsets the routine. If a manufacturer's marketing strategy needs strong support from intermediaries, the price-setter must adapt to the policies adopted by the distributors, such as price-lining (where the retailer selects certain prices, quality levels or price zones, and carries merchandise only at those levels), or mark-up policy.

Prices and discounts to the distributors and dealers must reflect a level of reward sufficient to motivate them to perform the functions and tasks allocated to them without jeopardising the resale price levels planned.

A CHECKLIST FOR ENSURING EFFECTIVE MARKETING THROUGH THE DISTRIBUTOR

1. The role of the distributor is not just selling. Everybody sells, but the distributor's role as an important member of the marketing channel route, must be fully recognised by the manufacturer.
2. The function of marketing is all pervasive – the essence of marketing is identifying the needs and wants of the customers, and matching them with the company's products and services. The distributor is a marketing agent.
3. The appropriate skills of marketing must be present in the chosen distributors.
4. The will to engage in marketing must also be evident in the distributor

organization. The necessary investment in marketing is a prerequisite in today's world of industry and commerce.

5. The marketing activities of the manufacturer and the members of the channel must be complementary and not competitive.
6. The activities of the members of the channel must be co-ordinated and integrated.
7. The distributor relationship must not be perceived as a short term one.

References

[1] Day, George, *Strategic Market Planning*, West Publishing Company, St Paul, Minn, 1984.
[2] Kotler, Philip, *Marketing Management*, Chapter 6, Prentice Hall International Inc., London and Englewood Cliffs, p 118, 1976.
[3] Cooper, R. G., 'The dimensions of industrial new product success and failure', *Journal of Marketing*, Vol. 43, Summer 1979.
[4] Peters, T. J. and Waterman, R. H., *In Search Of Excellence*, Harper & Row, New York, NY, 1982.

5 THE IMPORTANCE OF A GOOD LOGISTICS CHAIN

In this chapter, a broad outline is given of the principles of a good logistics chain and the role of a distributor in this regard. Many of the readers will be familiar with the story told in a Rank Video film titled *Who killed the sale?* A lot of things can go wrong in the process of satisfying a customer's need right from the beginning of the selling process and right up to the point where the customer accepts the product as being satisfactory. This is where logistics also plays an important part, besides its effect on company profits and well-being.

THE LOGISTICS CHAIN

The logistics concept

The term **logistics** has been interpreted in a number of ways. Sometimes it is used synonymously with distribution, but as a concept of management it covers a broader area, being concerned with all the tasks involving the movement of materials into and through the business on to the customer. Sometimes the sales function is also included in it. In common with marketing, the concept emphasizes the optimization of costs and customer service as well as the improvement of services to the customer. It tries to hold a balance between the opposing objectives of marketing and distribution; e.g. marketing may want to hold high inventory levels while distribution may want to cut costs by reducing them.

By looking at the functioning of the logistics process it is possible to examine ways of improving efficiency. Many managers are unaware that the storage of finished goods and their distribution are merely the last links in the supply chain and focusing on them can mean missing other major opportunities for improvement in logistics. The best possible distribution system cannot guarantee customer satisfaction if the customer is dissatisfied with the product itself. All elements of physical distribution influence each other. Efforts made to improve one element on its own will cause changes in the other processes and the objective may be thwarted by the deterioration caused in another process. It is best to address the process as a whole, which converts the supplier's raw materials into finished goods for the end-user as quickly as possible, to the right quality, at the right time and at the lowest possible total cost.

The flow of information is just as important to the efficient functioning of the logistics chain as the flow of materials. Information flows from the component suppliers into the company in one direction and from the company to the customers in another direction. On the other hand, information from the market-place flows into the company and from the company to the suppliers. Materials, however, flow from the suppliers through the company to the customers, value having been added in the process (Fig. 5.1). The most common barriers to the flow of information are the functional boundaries that the logistics process has to cross and clashing objectives and geographical separation of key functions.

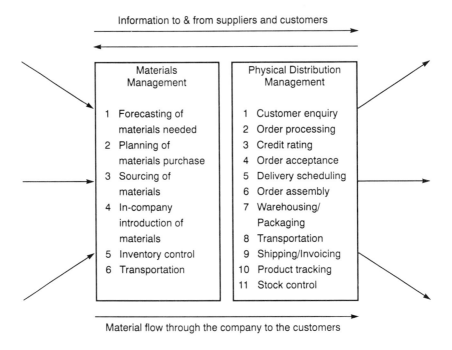

Figure 5.1 The logistics concept

The logistics function is usually charged with responsibilities covering:

- inventory: quantities, order frequency, location, handling methods, warehouse management

- transport: purchasing, route and mode decisions, own account or bought-in
- information
- packaging
- service: stock availability, order processing and delivery times, transit times

Every firm has to decide whether a separate logistics function should exist or this task should be part of a cross-line functional role. Many businesses do not realise that a more efficient logistics management can make a great difference both to the achievement of their strategic goals and their financial returns. Logistics management helps determine a company's market share; it can also materially improve operations management through a more efficient use of resources. The following are ways in which logistics can affect costs and revenue:

1. The efficiency of a company's customer service can affect its market share.
2. Considerable economies may be made in purchasing and production by better integration/co-ordination of the two functions.
3. Selling and administrative expenses can be controlled through improved logistics management.

In all businesses the product has to be moved at the right time in the right amounts to the correct destination in order that the product be delivered efficiently to the end-user. In most firms, however, the organization of the physical flow of goods or services and the management of the relevant information are managed in separate but connected phases.

Materials management

The materials management cycle consists of the inflow of goods through materials acquisition whether it is by outright purchase or partially or fully on credit basis, plus internal transport and inventory management. The relevant strategies regarding purchasing, transport and warehousing must include cost-effective methods in these functions. The materials flow involves vendors and suppliers, and is integral to the operation of the business. Purchasing forecasts are directly based on production schedules or other internal usage plans. Highly integrated materials management is possible given a disciplined internal planning process.

The logistics activity in a company acts to co-ordinate the flow of material and the related information through the system. It has to co-ordinate production planning; delivery frequencies are required to match sales demands and customer order frequencies. All this has to be achieved through shared information. This requires an integrated information system in which:

1. Data entering one subsystem is also available to any other subsystem requiring it; for example, data concerning customer orders should be available to inventory control, production scheduling, sales forecasting, etc.
2. All inter-related subsystems should have access to data in a common data base.
3. Closely connected activities are integrated into the same procedure, order processing, credit checking and stock allocation.

A high degree of sharing of expensive capital equipment should be allowed for; for example, the central computer installation, the data base and the application packages, among others, can be shared among the various functions.

The logistics information system consists of two subsystems dealing with supplies and customers. The supply subsystem input consists of the materials requirements plan, indicating how many of what types of items are needed and when they are needed for production; this has to be checked against the standing inventory and any orders outstanding. If necessary, sources of supply for any extra materials needed will have to be decided upon and purchase orders generated. This process appears simple but a company may have a register of hundreds of suppliers and maintain an inventory with many thousands of stock-keeping units. Also a sharp look-out must be kept for possible shortages and the suppliers checked for their reliability, prices and service. At the same time, the inventory must be minimized while making sure that production is not held up due to a stockout. It is obvious that a sophisticated information system is necessary to balance all these factors simultaneously.

In many ways, the customer subsystem is the mirror image of the supply system. An order from a customer is the start of the process. Hundreds of such orders per day have to be monitored against customer records for creditworthiness and special terms or needs, among other things. After which stock has to be assigned to the order, replenishment of inventory catered for if necessary, delivery and invoices as well as other complementary activities arranged for. A host of other information regarding achievements of service levels, re-order levels, etc., has to be gathered at this point to assist in making demand forecasts.

These two subsystems come together in the manufacturing function and have to be integrated through production control so that the supply subsystem generates what the customer subsystem demands. Many companies have installed materials requirements planning (MRP) systems. Basically these forecast the components and materials needed from the company's master production schedule (MPS) and the bill of material (BOM) for each end product. The requirements are calculated by taking existing stock levels and orders already placed into account, as well as the times when the items will be needed and the supply lead times. A successfully implemented MRP system can reduce inventory levels, speed up changes in the production process to meet changes in demand and increase the level of service in meeting demand. The basic idea is simple but the control of such multiple activities has only become possible through the use of advanced computer technology.

Other methods such as the just-in-time (JIT) system can reduce inventory levels while maintaining service levels. The idea is that the materials needed should arrive just in time for their use in manufacture. Reliable lead times are necessary for these systems to work properly. A similar development in the distribution field is the distribution requirements planning (DRP) system. This starts from the demand for the finished product and produces requirements schedules at each level of the distribution chain. This is a 'pull' system in that the end demand 'pulls' the required products down the chain rather than a centrally decided production plan 'pushing' the products down the line. Since the emphasis is now on customer needs, the former makes more sense than the latter, though both have their advantages.

The latest innovation is a combination of the MRP and DRP systems into logistics requirements planning (LRP) systems, which will link the end demand through the whole chain back to the suppliers. This has a number of complex requirements which must be satisfied before such a system can be contemplated, including a high degree of dedication on the parts of the management and the whole organization.

Physical distribution

This term is usually applied to the outward flow of goods from the firm to its customers through the distribution network. The customers may be wholesalers or retailers or manufacturers who use the product in their production process. Thus the physical distribution cycle of one firm may be the materials management cycle of another business. In that case, the decisions concerning the former can often be tied in with the buyer's materials management process. When distribution is fully dependent on customer demand in the market-place, finished goods inventories are often managed separately under traditional re-order point systems. The management of inventory of raw material and work-in-progress (WIP) is undertaken within production.

The term logistics management includes the total flow of materials from raw material acquisition to the delivery of the finished products to the end customer, and the counterflow of information controlling this movement. The terms logistics and physical distribution are often used interchangeably.

The importance of physical distribution

In recent years, firms have realized that physical distribution costs can amount to as much as a quarter of the gross national product (GNP). This has increased its economic significance. Its importance to management has also increased significantly because:

1. Logistics is now an important competitive tool in the struggle to control distribution. It is also considered an important strategic factor.
2. It is now realized that logistics cannot be dealt with piecemeal; improving efficiency in one area, say warehousing, is no good if this throws other operations into confusion.
3. Systemized technological developments in recent years have forced management to consider logistics as a whole.

The physical distribution concept

This emphasizes the connection between costs and service levels and aims to minimize the total distribution costs at a given service level, when backed by an integrated logistics network. Its four main components are:

1. The total cost approach: this considers all the costs of the physical distribution network, visible and invisible, while trying to achieve a given service level. It is necessary to remember the interdependence of all these elements and to try to minimize the total costs instead of attempting to reduce them piecemeal.
2. Trade-offs in costs: certain costs may increase while others are being reduced, but the objective should be to reduce the **total** distribution costs.
3. Minimum suboptimization: owing to the interdependence of all the distribution functions, any change in one will affect the others. When these functions are integrated, the goal should be to minimize sub-optimization through systems management.
4. The total system perspective: this takes the concept a stage further by considering the costs in the entire marketing process from the beginning up to the sale to the end-user. For example, instead of the retailer pricing the goods received, which is a time-consuming and therefore expensive process, the retailer can provide the manufacturer with up-to-date price lists, the manufacturer can price the products and charge the retailer for the service; the result being lower costs in **total.**

Physical distribution management

Since the costs of physical distribution can amount to more than a quarter of sales price at manufacturing level and the necessary assets can amount to as much as a third of the corporate assets, it is important for management to keep these costs down. It is possible to keep visible costs, such as warehousing, inventory and transport, down when the logistics functions are integrated. The invisible costs are due to customer dissatisfaction caused by late deliveries, lost sales/orders, etc. Control of these costs, both visible and hidden, is very difficult owing to the effect of any changes on customer service levels. Improvement of the latter can increase costs and a decrease in costs may mean a drop in the quality of the service. Physical distribution management provides guidelines for keeping a balance between cost and service levels.

TRANSPORT

Transport is an important part of logistics since inadequate transport provision can increase inventory costs prohibitively, as well as the investment in inventory; it can also cause customer dissatisfaction and increase the invisible costs dramatically. Therefore the selection of the right mode of transport, which is efficient and dependable, is essential for the achievement of distribution objectives. The five modes are: rail, road, sea/waterways, air and pipeline, plus combinations of some or all of these. The possibilities must be considered for cost, reliability and possibility of risk/damage.

WAREHOUSING

This can be either company-owned or leased/rented from others. The advantages of company-owned warehousing are: greater flexibility and control, better information feedback and potentially lower unit costs. Regional distribution centres serving regional markets are a new development in the Europe of today; if they are highly automated and can cater for packaging of orders, maintenance of full inventory and combining products from different production centres, they can go a long way towards achieving improved efficiency and increased customer satisfaction. For example, some companies are considering locating regional distributor centres in Maastricht in the Netherlands, Colmar in Alsace and in Bavaria. These regions are also developing the type of infrastructure needed for the functioning of such centres.

The advantages of leasing are: location and space flexibility, and possibly lower costs for seasonal businesses. There is also wider choice available for the type of warehousing needed, e.g. special commodity warehouses for storing agricultural products or refrigerated warehouses. Warehousing firms may also offer a variety of extra services to compete with each other.

It is possible to reduce the need for warehousing by choosing a slower form of transport, e.g. storage in transit. The number and location of warehouses is decided by their purpose and the level of customer service to be provided. They should be so positioned that they will yield the desired service level after all the variables are considered. This solution is unique to each business. The transportation costs decrease as the number of warehouses increases; while the inventory and warehousing costs increase at a diminishing rate. The objective is the lowest total cost of the whole system at the point where the curves meet (see also Fig. 5.2).

The locations of the warehouses affect the customer service level and the total costs; they also have a significant effect on the competitive powers of the business. A number of models have been developed to help management make better decisions. The significant factors are the estimates of lost sales due to the distance of the warehouses from the customers, and the costs of operation and of transport.

INVENTORY MANAGEMENT

Inventories may be held in the material management cycle to supply the production function or in the distribution function to meet customer demand. Inventory control in the latter is crucial to efficient physical distribution. Inventory represents the largest single investment for manufacturers of packaged consumer goods, amounting up to a third of their asset investment. High inventory levels are necessary in competitive conditions where the market segments are diverse in nature and customers are used to obtaining goods quickly.

The objective of inventory control is to minimize total inventory costs subject to demand and service level constraints. The main costs are due to holding inventory, ordering and the risks of stockouts. The system has to figure out how much to re-order, when to re-order and how to control stockouts at the minimum cost.

There are a number of inventory control systems available, depending on the type of business. Distribution requirements planning (DRP) systems deal with connecting the production process with the other inventory levels further down the channel. They operate on the assumption that they are managing inventories intended to resupply other inventories.

An accurate forecast of future demand is obviously essential for any inventory control system. Lack of such a forecast or inaccuracies can wreck havoc throughout the physical distribution channels. Unpredicted increases also cause stockouts and loss of orders in the future. Every firm and every channel member has to balance the costs of holding higher inventory levels against the costs of stockouts.

PRODUCTION CONTROL AND MATERIALS REQUIREMENT PLANNING

These, together with purchasing and raw materials handling, are generally grouped under the materials management function. Sometimes the objectives set by the management for these functions clash and cause a drop in the level of the customer service and/or a rise in physical distribution costs as a whole. Production is the focal point of all this activity, because production levels determine the needs for raw materials, parts, etc., and also the amount and types of finished products, which in turn influence the delivery times and modes for the distribution function.

Materials management is the 'single manager' organization concept embracing the planning, organizing, motivating and controlling of all activities and personnel principally concerned with the flow of materials in an organization. If the physical distribution concept is adopted by a business, it is usual to combine all activities concerned with raw materials under a single manager, who is sometimes also responsible for production scheduling. These activities are similar to those concerned in physical distribution of finished products, the difference being in the materials handled and their recipients.

Just-in-time (JIT) logistics systems

This is a logistics system by which materials arrive at the point of use just in time, thus saving on inventories and warehousing. Their implementation affects the purchasing, transport, warehousing, production, quality control and data processing functions, and requires an amount of discipline which many businesses find difficult to create and sustain.

In order to be successful, it has to be operated by all channel members in a given channel. It calls for all materials to be part of the work-in-progress, without pausing to collect storing expenses. Each part of the manufacturing process has to get the right elements in the correct amounts just in time. JIT is found to work best in repetitive manufacturing situations where the suppliers are close by, the forecasts are accurate and there exist significant levels of inventory to start with. Significant cost reductions can be made if JIT is successfully applied.

Order processing

The distribution process is activated by a customer order. The order cycle includes the time spent in processing the order as well as the time taken by the physical motion and therefore depends on the speed and efficiency of these operations. Electronic systems are now available to reduce the time needed for the flow of information and communications.

Planning a logistics strategy

Strategy for the logistics process requires the evaluation of possible physical distribution systems which meet the customer service standards required at the lowest possible cost. A system thus properly planned will increase the response of the various elements in the process, the sensitivity to the distribution environment, knowledge of the possibilities of cost reduction and service optimization in the function, and the awareness of the effect of corporate strategy on the process.

The planning begins with deciding on the customer service strategies and goals, and goes on to the functions and investment involved in physical distribution, to decide on systems and procedures for the functions and then developing these strategies in human resource terms and implementing them. After this process is complete, the criteria for the selection of channel members have to be established. The performance of the strategy has to be monitored periodically and action for improvement taken if needed.

The logistics strategy needs to be updated whenever there is an appreciable change in one or more of the following:

- demand
- customer service levels
- products
- distribution costs
- pricing policy

INTERNATIONAL LOGISTICS

In both national and international business the tasks of moving goods through the firm to the customer are similar. However, some differences do exist. Order processing and transportation are especially important in exporting and the manufacturer's responsibility often ends with maintaining stocks with wholesaler agents/subsidiaries. Export order processing is complex and so is the transport documentation. International transport costs are often large, transit times long and deals less reliable. It is often necessary to deal with numerous transport firms. In most cases it is more important to process orders and obtain transportation rather than the physical moving of the goods themselves, though this may vary with the type of business. In fact, international logistics is best considered in terms of moving **the order** through the business and out to the customer.

The manager in charge of exports may well be in charge of all but the production process. Each order goes through a number of stages, such as the inquiry from the customer and the arrangements for credit. The export manager's area of influence could also include product design, warehousing, packaging and production planning, among others. Product design can influence transport costs and damage in transit. The terms of sale should take into consideration such factors as the best unit of sale for advantageous transport terms. Producing the right goods at the right time is essential for export orders. Warehousing and packaging have to liaise with the export management to make sure that the packaging confirms with the order and the case markings coincide with the letter of credit and are in the right language. Lastly, the international distribution function is the best source of sales information and should be used as such.

For importing goods, the management role is similar to materials management. It should be integrated into the function responsible for the smooth flow of materials into the business or else be managed by someone who can impose the necessary system on the organization. The function is closely associated with production planning and purchasing. The import and export tasks are dissimilar in their nature and it is not advisable to combine them into one function.

It is possible to organize the export division either vertically, with each task in charge of a specialist or else horizontally, with each specialist in charge of a product and/or an area. Export logistics concerns bringing together diverse elements and their co-ordination. Many shipping managers have a wide range of disciplines within their sphere, but few have the authority to optimize the logistics task.

IMPLEMENTING A CUSTOMER SERVICE FUNCTION

Logistics and customer service

These are linked in the sense that logistics affect customer satisfaction and good customer service calls for a complementary logistic function. Service provided to successive buyers in a distribution channel has an impact on distribution effectiveness and growth, especially in the dealings between producers, wholesalers and distributors.

The market institution that controls the channel of distribution is referred to as the channel commander. The channel commanders are beginning to realize that marketing strength and stability are more likely to result when all critical firms in the channel make a fair profit; the concept that support and expertise should be geared to the solution of all problems is spreading.

Though all concerned firms recognize that the customer services, whether service analysis or technical aid, are the responsibility of the firm involved, these areas have special cost reduction opportunities where special skills are required. A majority of customer complaints involve distribution problems which do not concern sales personnel. A customer service programme including both service analysis and technical aid should be administered as a function separate from sales.

It is well-known that many Japanese companies have committed themselves to total quality management. Some have extended this to marketing functions and distribution as well. Toyota showed a classic example of this total quality strategy, when entering and establishing their position in the US car market.

Customer service and care

Customer service has many dimensions and has to be adapted for every market segment in which the company competes. A genuine policy of customer service can pay high dividends in cost efficiency. Logistics is all about making the product or service available to the end-user. Availability is affected by many factors which all come together in the concept of customer service. The following are the main elements in this concept:

- order cycle time
- consistency/reliability of delivery
- inventory availability
- order size constraints
- ordering convenience
- delivery times and flexibility
- invoicing procedures and accuracy
- claims procedure
- condition of goods on arrival
- sales executives' visits
- order status information

This list is not exclusive and different market segments will need emphasis on different factors and some may be influenced by other factors outside this list. In fact, it is best to treat each market segment on its own in this respect. Customer service can be the most important element in the company's marketing mix. Market research has shown that if a product is not available when wanted by a customer, the likelihood of the sale being lost to a rival brand is very high.

The following are considered as the three basic factors in customer service requirements:

1. Definition of the company's customer service policy as a whole, laying down the attitudes, organization and responsibilities.
2. The laying down of internal customer standards after a cost–benefit study in each segment of the market.

3. Information in general terms for the customers concerning what they can expect in customer service from the company.

The following six steps have been proposed in establishing a cost-effective customer service policy:

1. Identify the key elements of customer service according to the opinions of the customers – these may differ significantly from the company's perceptions.
2. Rank these elements according to the importance attached by the customers to them.
3. Decide on the company position on these factors after consideration of the competition.
4. Segment the market according to the service needs.
5. Work out the customer service packages for these segments.
6. Establish the management and control procedures for customer service.

Market research is a vital ingredient for all these decisions and this needs to be carefully considered and conducted over all the important market segments.

Customer service standards

The elements of customer service are split between pre-transaction, transaction and post-transaction elements. It is necessary, first of all, to establish through market research which of these elements are the most important to the consumers. The answers will be different for different businesses and different markets, and definitely so for different industries. The amount of control exercised by the distribution manager over these elements will also vary widely.

Once the most important aspects are established, then:

1. Set quantitative standards of performance for each service element, according to customer needs.
2. Measure actual performance for each of them.
3. Analyze variations between standards and actual performance and report them regularly to the appropriate management level.
4. Take measures to diminish these variations; these should be part of an overall strategy confirming to the objectives of the firm.

Logistics decisions involve trade-offs. Such trade-off decisions need to be taken with the full knowledge of what effect a decision is likely to have on the customer, the distributor and the company's total costs, which reflect the costs of inbound and outbound logistics and inventory costs (Fig. 5.2).

It is better to have distribution controlled by a single authority if stock levels are to respond to changes in demand, deliveries are to be prompt and the finished products in the inventory are to be the right ones at the right time. Unfortunately, finance directors, who are best placed for the role, rarely bother with distribution except to question the contract after it has been signed, generally after complaints have been received from another department.

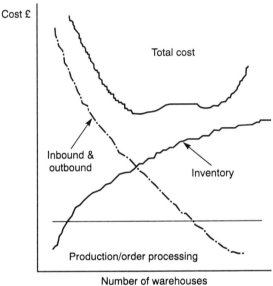

Figure 5.2   Logistics costs

Closely relating distribution activities to costs of inventory, production and sales and marketing can pay handsome dividends. Logistics management is closely connected with financial management. It is possible to conduct the distributor relationship on the basis of 'open book accounting' by buying distributor services in which all contractors' costs are identified and profit margin are agreed beforehand with built-in bonuses for achievement of performance targets set and penalties for underperforming. This benefits both parties who tend to co-operate to find the best methods of distribution to suit them both and are willing to consider changes in established methods to improve things.

Before considering contracting out distribution activities, companies should consider the following:

1. Do they know their business well enough to convey the knowledge to a contractor successfully and achieve desirable results?
2. What exactly do they wish to obtain from their distribution contractor? Are they prepared to pay for the best possible service and does their

profit margin support that level of service cost? Would they reduce their margins to pay for it with a view to using it as a promotional tool to increase sales?

3. What method are they planning to use to pay the contractor, cost per item of delivery, open book basis or another method? In any case, it will be necessary to monitor the contractor's performance to make sure the specified service standards are being adhered to.

4. Is a contract necessary? If so, they must make sure it is tailored to suit their needs.

Tony Sellick, logistics manager responsible for purchasing, production planning, warehousing, transport and the sales forecasting system at Wavin Building Products, a company with a turnover of £50 million plus, is reported, according to Semple[1], to have said:

I personally think the logistics manager should also control sales administration. His transport operation – comprising a central stock point and a mixture of own-account, contracted haulage and a parcels service – responds to customers' demands, which vary widely according to urgency and order volumes. The work patterns may soon have to be changed extensively.

CHECKLIST FOR A GOOD LOGISTICS CHAIN

1. Cost-effective sourcing for flexible demand situations
2. Choice of suppliers to match customers' strategic response
3. Standards of quality and inventory performance to match changing demands
4. Packaging regulations for a cleaner and greener environment
5. Good inventory management to achieve a balance between quantities, order frequency, location, handling methods, warehouse management
6. Efficient and cost-effective transport management across inbound logistics, i.e. purchasing, route and mode decisions
7. Balancing the flow of goods along the logistics pipeline
8. Good information dissemination
9. Pricing for value addition in a competitive environment
10. Quality of service starting from stock availability through order processing, delivery times and transit times, to pre-, during and after-sales service.

References

[1] Semple, Jack. 'A stock response is not enough', *Financial Director*, pp. 63–71, September, 1991.

6 ROLES OF THE MANUFACTURER/ SUPPLIER AND DISTRIBUTOR

In this chapter, we consider the comprehensive roles of the manufacturer/ supplier and distributor, and also how the roles complement each other. We have already established that in marketing a product and getting it to the final consumer/customer, a number of organizations may be involved besides the producer/manufacturer. When the channel includes more than one party, for example, a manufacturer and a distributor, it is important to recognize the mutual obligations and the way in which the roles can be distinguished. Without a clear understanding, the functioning of the relationship may become suspect at best and ruptured at worst. There are also questions about who exercises the leadership and how it is exercised.

CHANNEL LEADERSHIP

A number of factors influence the extent to which a channel leader can manipulate other channel members and lay down their marketing policies. The ability to control a channel is dependent on power-generating characteristics such as experience or past history of the firm, or it may be dependent upon environmental factors such as demand, technological levels, competition, legal constraints, etc., and the channel member's expertise in manipulating these factors.

A manufacturer gains a channel leadership position by having:

- a strong market share (twice the share of the nearest competitor/brand leader often gives this position, e.g. IBM, Procter & Gamble)
- good customer knowledge and understanding of their needs (e.g. Seiko)
- strong brand identity (e.g. Heinz, Cadbury)
- good product innovation capability (e.g. BMW)
- good customer service
- good quality of service
- financial strength.

In this type of situation, all other channel members tend to listen to the channel leader, follow their lead and play their tune. In other words, they are truly the leader of the pack. The control of a channel leader is greater when:

- the demand is declining
- the demand is unstable
- personal selling and post-sales service are important factors
- competition is strong among the channels.

This seems to indicate that a threatening state of the market makes it easier for a channel leader to emerge. Retailers obtain more control over marketing decisions in heterogeneous marketing environments.

Control and leadership depends very much on the degree of originality and ownership of the concept, product ideas, brand image, the number of channel steps and the consumer appeal of the products. BMW, VW, Audi cars, Coca-Cola, Pepsi, Nestlé and Gillette are all examples of well-known brands with the necessary pull and in-built characteristics for channel leadership. These companies also possess a degree of originality and ownership besides the brand image and consumer appeal.

In contrast, magazines and newspapers lack some of these attributes and in that market, the fight for circulation is very fierce. Moreover, the main distribution channels such as the confectioners, tobacconists and newsagents (CTNs) find the demand unpredictable, the products bulky in relation to the retail value and needing awkward display space. While magazines and newspapers attract customers and are not subject to price competition in the same way as some other products and the margins are tolerable, the channel arrangements are not ideal.

A channel leader can be a manufacturer/producer or a wholesaler or a retailer. General Electric, General Foods, Siemens and IBM are examples of the manufacturer as channel leader. Major furniture wholesalers and their outlets such as Wickes, and Marks & Spencer and Sears as major retail chains are examples of other types.

COMPLIANCE TO STRATEGIC POLICIES

Strategic policies can be defined and communicated but the test of the policies lies in their execution and the results. It is important to ensure that the implementation of the policies is monitored and the results measured. Only from the monitored results does one come to know about the divergences; they in turn lead to the kind of profitable improvements which generate the much needed ROI.

It used to be said of sailors that they only did what was inspected and not what was expected. Marketing channel members, for instance, in the high technology business, are no different. Motivation plays an important part – not only 'the carrot and stick' type of motivation but also 'relationship' motivation built on an understanding of the needs and wants of distributors, their strengths and weaknesses, their problems and the opportunities available to them. However, all these factors cannot help if the roles are not clear in the first place.

THE DISTRIBUTOR FUNCTIONS

These functions are as follows:

1. Movement of ownership
   (a) buying and selling, including advertising, product service, consultation and training;
   (b) risk taking with respect to the ability to sell the goods to the next level of ownership.
2. Movement of goods
   (a) transportation
   (b) storage, including material handling
   (c) division or assembly
   (d) packing
   (e) grading
3. Marketing management
   (a) credit financing and collections
   (b) market-decision information gathering
   (c) decision-making

THE DISTRIBUTOR'S ROLE

Within marketing

The distributor's role consists of:

1. Buying the products from the manufacturer
2. Selling the products to customers which fit the manufacturer company strategy
3. Maintaining the manufacturer company image
4. Provision of after-sales support and service
5. Local promotion
6. Maintenance of required 'price' image

 7. Paying the manufacturer on time
 8. Achievement of minimum target levels
 9. Collection of monies due from customers on time
10. Maintaining terms of trading as agreed
11. Obtaining information regarding the market, the competition and the product on a continuous basis
12. Feeding back this information to the manufacturer
13. Maintenance of agreed inventory levels
14. Maintenance of agreed channel and sales coverage
15. Compliance with 'statutory' requirements.

In shaping distribution policy

The distributor has to:

1. Articulate the changes in demand
2. Identify the required level of service
3. Comprehend the product characteristics
4. Estimate the distribution costs
5. Contribute to the establishment of an appropriate pricing policy
6. Provide feedback from the market-place – a vital input to determining any revisions to policy
7. Participate in a review of the existing distribution policies.

The distributors have an important role to play in providing such feedback. Efficient physical distribution is a necessity for effective marketing. Physical distribution absorbs a surprising amount of resources and it is necessary to keep a strict watch on possible ways of cutting costs especially when demand is sluggish. Control of physical distribution costs can only be exercised if both the manufacturer and the distributors have a good understanding of their roles in this context.

As a result of detailed product analysis and marketing feedback received from their subsidiaries and distributors, W & T Avery, a weighing machine company, concluded they were not developing new products fast enough to meet the market demand for electronic scales. This resulted in the production of scales which could calculate the calories, fat, carbohydrate and fibre content of many hundreds of foods. These scales varied from kitchen scales to industrial scales for a variety of different purposes. In 1985, the company won an Engineering Industry award for this innovation.

Importers and distributors can reinforce the market position of a manufacturer's products. For example, Astra have contributed to the reinforcement of Boots & Co's drug, Brufen for arthritis sufferers by distributing it in Denmark and Norway.

In the early 1960s, BMW were in serious trouble. In order to effect a turn-around, they searched for and identified Opel's top wholesale distributor and appointed him as the chief executive. He was able to discover an unexploited market because of his viewpoint as a distributor. This was for a sporty saloon car; Mercedes were not exploiting this market segment. By catering for this market, BMW launched their well-known success story.

In controlling inventory

The distributor has to minimize the inventory held, subject to demand and service constraints. Inventory management is very important in controlling costs and in avoiding shortages. The manufacturer and distributor both have a part to play in controlling inventory, though such control has to be exercised through co-operation between these two independent parties.

In demand management

The distributor has to:

1. Provide an accurate sales forecast to support the ordering operation
2. Constantly update the parameters on which an informed demand assessment can be made
3. Take preventive measures so that stockouts do not occur because they can have a detrimental effect on the demand.

The forecasting model depends upon the nature of the demand, whether it is predictable or unpredictable, seasonal or otherwise, and so on. The model also depends on who needs the forecast. The nearer the channel member is to the end customer, the more volatile their demand pattern.

THE MANUFACTURER'S ROLE

The manufacturer's role is comprised of the following:

1. Supplying goods of merchantable quality, suitable for the market for which they are destined, reflecting the 'image' conceived in the campaign which has been agreed upon.
2. Creating sufficient margin in the product so that the channel member, i.e. the distributor, receives adequate returns from the sale.
3. Providing the following:
   (a) product training
   (b) benefits training
   (c) sales training

    (d) sales guides
    (e) price guidance
    (f) handling of objections
    (g) advertising and promotion material
    (h) contacts and service points
    (i) incentives and motivation

4. Keeping the channel 'informed' of business developments, new product lines and competition.
5. Providing 'campaign' leadership and 'business' leadership.
6. Motivating the channel principal and their sales force.

THE IDEAL HIGH TECHNOLOGY CHANNEL MEMBER

In the case of high technology industry, the channel member must, in the first place, possess an inherent interest in marketing and selling technical products which involves:

- an understanding and comprehension of the technology
- the will power to sustain the lead time involved in technical selling
- an appreciation of the nature of the support requirements that follow in such technical sales situations.

High technology products tend to be facility rich and therefore call for applications selling – this in turn requires an in-depth understanding of the customer requirements and needs which must be matched in order to gain a commitment from the customer to purchase. It may be necessary to suppress the urge on the part of the sales force to give an elaborate description of some of the features and benefits which may not be relevant to the customer; they should only concentrate on those that will interest the customer and yield value for money.

The channel needs to be equipped for stocking the products as necessary and provide demonstration facilities – this requires a professional business approach to channel management. Unlike the consumer durable type of channel, the high technology channel member needs to be fully conversant with approaches to industrial product marketing and service product marketing.

In most high technology product areas, there exists a varying combination of factors for sales situations. For instance, in selling sophisticated hardware like computers or control systems, the emphasis must be on applications marketing, i.e. how far are the features of the product relevant in the customer situation and what is involved in using the product.

7 LEGAL ASPECTS

INTRODUCTION

In today's rapidly changing world environment, governments are keener than ever to deregulate the businesses operating within their countries but within a framework which allows for fair competition, consumer choice, consumer protection and protection for the interests of society.

LEGISLATION AFFECTING BUSINESS TRADING IN GENERAL

Legislation affecting business has increased considerably over the recent years and the enactment has happened for a number of reasons. The protection of businesses from each other and a sense of fairness feature prominently among the reasons.

The United Kingdom

As an example, in Britain alone, the laws affecting marketing are many in number. An abbreviated list would include:

Advertisements Act	Insolvency Act
Bills of Sale Acts	Mercantile Acts
Carriage of Goods by Air,	Merchant Shipping Acts
Railway, Road, Sea Acts	Misrepresentations Acts
Carriers Act	Resale Prices Acts
Consumer Credit Act	Restrictive Trade Practices Acts
Consumer Protection Act	Sale of Goods Acts
Copyright Act	Supply of Goods Act
Exchange Control Acts	Trade Descriptions Acts
Fair Trading Act	Unfair Contract Terms Act

Understanding competition plays an important part in this game; technology and innovation affect this market both in terms of the rate at which new products emerge and old products become obsolete. Due to pressure to achieve economies of scale, components manufacturers tend to merge and become larger units. Thereby many high technology product components achieve a commodity status. Differentiating a product from its competitors is therefore vital.

Other important characteristics are:

1. Financial soundness (a) ability to finance operations
                                    (b) skill in managing financial aspects of what is essentially a marketing, sales and distribution business.
2. Territory coverage: organization and people to cover the territory adequately so as to achieve the agreed objectives.
3. Technical support and service.
4. Keenness to maintain trained and knowledgeable personnel as the business involves 'value-addition'.
5. Commercial acumen.

Reference

[1] Thomas, Doina, 'Second Bite at BMW', *Management Today*, January 1971, and Business Week, 20 May 1970.

Food & Drug Act   Unsolicited Goods and Services
Hire Purchase Act   Acts.

There are other laws which could have marginal effect on any trading or marketing activity.

The United States

Similarly, a short-list of the federal laws would include:

Anti-merger act	Fair Packaging and Labelling Act
Automobile Information	Federal Cigarette Labelling and
Disclosure Act	Advertising Act
Child Protection Act	Federal Food and Drug Act
Clayton Act	Federal Trade Commission Act
Consumer Goods Pricing Act	Meat Inspection Act
Consumer Product Safety Act	Miller–Tydings Act
Federal Trade Commission	Robinson–Patman Act
Improvement Act	Sherman Anti-trust Act
Fair Credit Reporting Act	Wheeler–Lea Act
Fair Debt Collection Practice Act	

Other countries

Other countries have similar acts governing business activity, some of which are complex. The statute books of many countries get filled with new legislation and amendments to existing laws, and it is no wonder that some business executives feel that there is a need for every firm to have ready access to at least one legal advisor on a regular basis.

However, these laws differ from country to country and when an international dispute arises, it becomes necessary to find out first which law is applicable. Attempts are being made to ratify an international business law code because of the difficulties of adjudicating between parties who have differing legal systems. This is being attempted at least on the basis of economic groupings such as the European Community.

Managers and other company employees can be considered parties to a legally binding contract simply on the basis of their actions, e.g. acceptance of an order. 'In law, all contracts stem from an offer which is made by one party and accepted by the other.'

Jurisdiction

Sometimes the court that sits in judgment on the case may have to apply a foreign legal system. It is therefore important for the parties to any contract to know beforehand which law will apply to any disputes. In order to make sure of this, a clause should be included in any contract specifying that the contract will be ruled by the law of the seller's country or the law of a country chosen by the seller. Let us explore in some detail the laws applicable within the European Community.

EC COMPETITION LAWS

Competition rules and regulations

The aim of free competition is to guarantee a wide choice for consumers and help keep prices down and standards high, while providing a powerful stimulus to economic and technological progress. This is compatible with a degree of public control. The objectives of European Community competition policy are to prevent:

1. Excessive concentrations of economic power from damaging the interests of consumers, competitors or subsidiaries.
2. Companies from re-establishing trade barriers by means of agreements and export bans.
3. National assistance/aid from distorting competition so that the existence of the Common Market is threatened.

Equality of opportunity is guaranteed to all companies in the common market by the European Commission which monitors the activities in the market and occasionally punishes offenders. Businesses who believe themselves to be victims of infringements of Community competition rules may bring direct action before national or European Community courts.

A blanket ban applies to all agreements and concerted practices which have as their object or effect the prevention, restriction or distortion of competition within the common market by enterprises operating within the Community (or outside it), whether European or not, whether public or private. This is in the main enshrined in Article 85 of the Treaty of Rome. Article 86 prohibits abuse of a dominant position.

For thirty years, the European Commission has been dealing with various forms of agreements and practices:

- market sharing agreements, creating protected markets
- price-fixing agreements
- exclusive purchase agreements, sharing the market and distorting free trade
- agreements on industrial and commercial property rights
- exclusive or selective distribution agreements

The Commission is not opposed to encouraging co-operation between small and medium-sized companies to boost economic progress. Agreements between small firms, which have a combined annual turnover of less than 200 million ECU – about £ 140 million – **and** where the products covered by the agreement account for less than 5 per cent of the relevant market, are not caught by the EC competition rules. This is a matter of commission policy only – not binding on the Courts. Mergers posing a threat to effective competition in the Community are also subject to EC control under a regulation introduced in 1989.

A major development is the exemption of certain categories of agreement meeting the criteria of distortion laid down in the EEC Treaty. Agreements prohibited by Article 85 of the Treaty of Rome can be exempted either by an individual Commission decision in a particular case or by virtue of a block exemption applying to a particular category of agreement, if their pro-competitive effects outweigh any anti-competitive effects. These 'block exemptions' are laid down in Commission regulations (enacted by virtue of authority delegated by the Council) which define the scope of the exemption and the associated conditions and safeguards. Agreements within their scope are automatically exempt without the need for notifying the Commission. They include certain agreements in the fields of exclusive purchasing and distribution, patent licensing, co-operative research and development, selective distribution systems, motor vehicles and others.

Article 86 of the Treaty prohibits the abuse by one or more undertakings of a dominant position within the common market or in a substantial part of it where it may affect trade between Member States. There is no exemption available for such abuses.

The Commission has the power to investigate complaints and to penalise infringements in virtually every area of economic activity within the Community. At the same time, in consultation with the Member States, the Commission is continuing its efforts to clarify the application of the above articles to particular kinds of agreement and practice so as to give greater legal certainty to Community businesses.

The Single European Act established a European Court of First Instance to reduce the burden of work on the European Court of Justice. Competition cases are included in the jurisdiction of this court, offering speedier justice on appeal and a fuller investigation of the facts and economic arguments. The right of appeal on points of law to the European Court itself is maintained.

The development of a clear, viable and strong merger law is considered by the Commission to be one of the main essentials to be put in place before 1992. The basic principles agreed on were:

1. Assessment of mergers within the Community in the context of a single market must be on the basis of European dimension.
2. Undertakings covered must have legal security and there must be rapid, fair and clear procedures laid down.
3. Clear criteria must be laid down for prohibition and authorization and for the demarcation line between Community and national laws with the essential consideration that dual control of mergers under the new regulation and under Articles 85 and 86 must be avoided.

National controls on company restructuring are incompatible with the existence of a really integrated market and with the increasing geographical extension of a large number of markets. It is imperative to have a fully formulated and clearly expressed competition policy which is coherent and predictable in the areas of merger control, joint venture control and the licensing of inventions. Community level control over European scale company mergers and concentrations is essential provided it is in a form acceptable to governments and industry, and exercised on the basis of pre-defined economic and legal criteria.

The Merger Control Regulation came into force on 21 September 1990. It applies only to mergers with a 'Community dimension', a test based on both geographic and financial criteria. The Regulation will apply to any transaction which has the direct or indirect effect of bringing about a concentration between undertakings or groups of undertakings:

- where the aggregate world-wide turnover of the undertakings concerned is more than 5000 million ECU and
- where the aggregate Community-wide turnover of each of at least two of the undertakings concerned is more than 250 million ECU,

unless all of the undertakings concerned derive more than two-thirds of their aggregate Community-wide turnover from the same Member State. The turnover thresholds will be reviewed in 1993.

Mergers outside the scope of the regulation will continue to be governed by natural law. However, in view of the relatively high thresholds for the application of the Regulation, the Commission has reserved to itself the power to intervene in the case of certain mergers even if they fall outside the scope of the Regulation.

Joint ventures are generally not covered by the Regulation unless the joint venture performs on a lasting basis all of the functions of an independent undertaking and does not give rise to co-ordination between the parties. The Commission will examine proposed joint ventures with a view to any anti-competitive effects. In order to clarify its position, the Commission is currently taking steps to set out the framework of a competition law and policy in the shape of guidelines, within which joint ventures can be established.

Comparison with US laws regarding competition

Sherman Anti-trust, Clayton, Robinson–Patman, Miller–Tydings and Consumer Goods Pricing Acts all have the collective effect of prohibiting:

- monopolistic policies
- practice of restraint of trade
- practice of price discrimination, unfair trading terms, tying clauses and exclusive dealing
- deceptive acts and practices regardless of whether the competition is affected
- intercorporate acquisitions with substantial effect on competition
- the use of price maintenance agreements in interstate commerce.

DISTRIBUTION AGREEMENTS

A distribution agreement may be defined as an agreement whereby a supplier of goods appoints a distributor to resell the goods. In EC competition law terms, the distributor takes title to the goods supplied and resells them to a retailer, another wholesaler or the end-user. There are three types of distribution agreements: non-exclusive, exclusive and selective.

Non-exclusive distribution agreements

Non-exclusive distribution agreements are likely to come up against Article 85(1) if they restrict the parties' freedom to take independent commercial decisions; usually this concerns decisions regarding the products. Some typical restrictions are:

- fixing or recommendation of retail prices
- limits on quantities of goods to be manufactured or distributed or services to be offered
- obligation not to sell competing goods
- restrictions on purchases from or sales to third parties
- export bans or restrictions on active or passive selling
- restrictions on dealer's choice of markets
- tie-ins and full range restrictions.

If such clauses have to be inserted in a non-exclusive agreement, the parties should notify the agreement to the Commission and request exemption on Form A/B; otherwise those clauses and perhaps the whole agreement could be void and unenforceable and the parties liable to fines. Any clause enforcing export bans, customer restrictions or resale price maintenance is unlikely to be exempted and is very likely to attract fines.

Exclusive distribution agreements

These come up against Article 85(1) but they can usually qualify for exemption under the block exemption Regulation 1983/83 applying Article 85(3) if they lead to an improvement in distribution. This provides that the prohibition in Article 85(1) does not apply where the supplier agrees only to supply the distributor with certain goods for resale within the whole or a defined part of the Common Market and the agreement contains no other prohibited restrictions. This clause for exclusivity must be inserted in the contract in order to qualify under the regulation. The definition of resale allows hiring out and leasing but forbids additional operations which add more than a small permitted value to the goods, e.g. through packaging. No restriction can be imposed on a supplier apart from an obligation not to supply the named goods to users in the contract territory.

Only the following restrictions are allowed on the exclusive distributor:

1. No manufacture or distribution of competing goods.
2. Exclusive purchase from supplier.
3. Ban on active sales outside the contract territory.

The following restrictions are also allowed as they do not restrict competition:

1. Purchase of complete range of goods.
2. Selling under specified trade mark/packaging/presentation.
3. Promotion and sales obligations
   (a) advertising
   (b) maintenance of sales network/stocks
   (c) provision of customer and guarantee services
   (d) employment of specialized or technical staff.

No restrictions apart from those specified in the regulation are allowed. The block exemption does not apply or may be withdrawn in certain circumstances such as:

- Reciprocal exclusive distribution agreements by competing manufacturers, both with turnovers of over 100 million ECU
- Measures to prevent parallel imports
- If the contract goods are not subject to effective competition

- Refusal to serve certain customers without objective reasons or excessive prices charged by exclusive distributor
- Agreements concerning resale of petroleum products in service stations or drinks in premises used for sale/consumption of beer.

Selective distribution agreements

A manufacturer, usually of technical consumer equipment, may implement a selective distribution system under which dealers are selected according to some criteria. For example, a computer manufacturer may wish the distributor to employ specially trained staff to sell their products. Such systems have to examined under Article 85(1) and have to satisfy the following:

1. All dealers who meet the qualitative criteria concerning their technical qualifications and those of their staff and suitability of their premises should be allowed into the selective distributor network.
2. The products must justify such criteria. Technically advanced products as well as some products like perfumes and newspapers merit them.
3. The imposition of the following obligations is likely to be allowed:
    (a) to have a specialized and specifically equipped department
    (b) to provide after-sales service
    (c) to display the products attractively
    (d) for wholesalers only to supply appointed wholesalers/retailers
    (e) for wholesalers not to supply private customers.

Quantitative limits have to be exempted by the Commission as they infringe Article 85(1). The following clauses must be notified to the Commission and are unlikely to be exempted:

1. The dealer to meet a sales target set by the supplier.
2. Restrictions on where the goods can be sold.
3. Prohibition on supplying certain types of customers.
4. Prohibition from cross-sales to other appointed dealers.
5. Resale price restrictions.

Selective distribution agreements regarding the sale of motor vehicles can benefit from automatic exemption under Regulation 123/85 if they meet the conditions laid down in it in detail.

AGENCY AGREEMENTS

The European Commission considers that an agency agreement between a principal and its agent is not normally caught by Article 85(1)). However, if an agreement is not a genuine commercial agency agreement and is in reality a distribution agreement, then the Commission will be able to spot it and in such a case, it will fall within the scope of the EC rules. Businesses with such agency agreements should consider whether they are likely to infringe the rules and if so, what the consequences will be. The Commission has produced new draft proposals to clarify the relation of agency agreements with Article 85(1).

An agent is regarded as an auxiliary organ forming an integral part of the principal's business. Agency agreements did not generally fall within Article 85(1) as agents working for a principal and carrying out their instructions could be considered as part of the principal. Therefore the principal could exercise far greater control over the agents. The new proposals introduce the concept of integrated and non-integrated agents to determine how far it is permissible under EC competition law for a principal to place anti-competitive restrictions on its agents.

A principal may impose the following restrictions on an integrated agent:

- an obligation not to handle competing products for the duration of the agreement;
- the grant of an exclusive or sole territory;
- an obligation not to sell outside their territory;
- a non-competitive clause for up to two years following the expiry of the agreement in respect of the products and territory covered by the agreement.

The above restrictions may not be lawfully imposed on a non-integrated agent. The Commission will continue to treat a non-integrated agent as an independent trader with the effect that any restrictions on competition will be governed by Article 85. The concept of integrated and non-integrated agents is derived from the case law of the European Court of Justice, though it may prove difficult to apply in practice.

The important criteria for an integrated agent are:

1. The agent does not assume the primary responsibility for the performance of a transaction.
2. The agent does not assume any financial risk in relation to such transactions;
3. Remuneration comes from the commission paid by the principal on each transaction.
4. At least one third of the turnover must be with a single principal;
5. The agent must not have significant outside obligations which could conflict with any obligations under the agency agreement, e.g. where the agent deals in competing product ranges.

Non-integrated agents may be assessed on the basis of whether they act for a number of principals and/or carry competing product ranges on behalf of other suppliers.

The Commission's new proposals are likely to be adopted by 1993. There will clearly be agency agreements which will be considered in breach of Article 85, and they will run the risk of having to pay heavy fines which the Commission has the power to impose. The offending restrictions in the agreement will automatically become null and void, and unenforceable. In addition, if a third party has been excluded from operating in a particular territory because the principal granted an exclusive agency to another company, such a third party may sue either of the contracting parties for damages of loss suffered as a result of such restriction.

EXCLUSIVE PURCHASING AGREEMENTS

Such agreements bind one party to purchase all its supplies exclusively from another without being assigned an exclusive territory. These contracts may infringe Article 85(1) if they distort competition or affect trade. Such agreements may qualify for exemption especially in cases affecting small/ medium businesses. They may benefit under the block exemptions if the terms of the regulation are strictly adhered to. Apart from the exclusive purchase, the only other obligation that can be imposed on the purchaser concerns the manufacture or distribution of competing products. In most cases the following restrictions may be imposed:

1. Purchase of a complete range or a minimum quantity of goods.
2. Sale under trade marks or with specific packaging/presentation.
3. Measures for promotion of sales including:
   (a) advertising
   (b) maintenance of sales network/stocks
   (c) provision of customer and guarantee services
   (d) employment of specialized staff.

The only restriction which may be imposed on the supplier is the obligation not to distribute the contract goods or any other goods which compete with them in the reseller's 'principal sales area' and at his level of distribution. If any other restrictions are imposed, the agreement should be notified to the Commission in order to claim exemption. The block exemption will not apply if:

- the exclusive purchaser consumes the goods bought;
- the period of agreement is either longer than five years or indefinite;
- the agreement covers two or more unconnected products;

- manufacturers of identical/competing goods enter into reciprocal purchasing agreements except when one has an annual turnover less than 100 million ECU.

DISTRIBUTION CONTRACT

Why a written agreement is necessary

A contractual relationship exists in law whether there is a written or a verbal agreement to trade with a distributor. A signed, witnessed and sealed legal document is not necessary for the legal existence of a contract. However, a written agreement is advisable and it is the common practice adopted by enlightened companies; the basic reason is to provide certain safeguards:

- confirmation of the verbal relationship
- the need for security of tenure
- the minimization of risk to either party arising from the actions of the other.

It also insures against the following possibilities:

1. The representatives of either or both parties may change over time and in the absence of any written accord, successors may develop different perspectives which may hinder the relationship between a manufacturer and a distributor.
2. The understanding reached between two parties at one time may be inadvertently forgotten by one party and this may lead to arguments later on and contribute to a deteriorating relationship.
3. The objectives and/or strategies of either party may change; this may lead to a change in the policy of one party towards the other and the scope for adequate consultation may not exist as a result of the day-to-day pressures; the consequences to the relationship may be ignored.

Typically an agreement should cover at least the following areas (Fig. 7.1):

- business definition
- territory to be covered by the distributor concerned
- products/services that the distributor will be selling
- duration
- manufacturer's obligations to the distributor
- distributor's obligations to the manufacturer
- targets/goals that the parties agree as relevant for a satisfactory relationship
- supply/payment terms

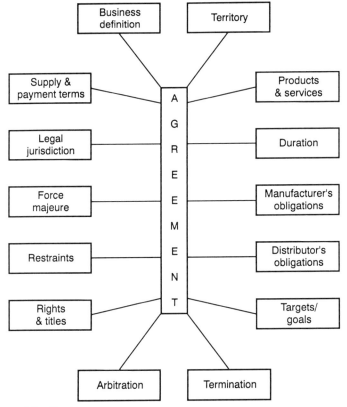

Figure 7.1 Distribution agreements

- restraints/reservations on the business, if any
- rights/titles
- termination terms
- *force majeure* clauses as needed
- arbitration procedures in the event of disputes arising
- legal jurisdiction.

Do not fail to consider the following before entering into an agreement:

1. The national law will apply to the agreement unless legally specified otherwise.
2. The distributor must be given adequate notice before the contract is terminated.
3. The distributor's staff may have to be compensated for loss of employment and this may become your liability.
4. The amount of compensation increases with the length of time the contract has been in operation and indefinite terms carry stiffer penalties.

5. Such compensation may not be dispensed with by the terms of the agreement.
6. The distributor is generally compensated for the increased market share created by them.
7. 'Just cause' can be defined either by the agreement or the existing law. It is best to quantify the terms of the agreement precisely so that the breach of contract can be clear. Otherwise it may be difficult to prove it in court. The distributor may ask for arbitration to decide whether 'just cause' exists and unless it can be proved, the principal may be forced to renew the contract. Even if 'just cause' is shown, the distributor may still be compensated for any continuing benefits to the principal after the agreement expires.

A written and signed contract gives the principal an advantage in court. The most important sections are those dealing with termination. A breach of contract should be defined precisely as well as the provisions for dealing with such a breach; there should be no possibility of expensive misunderstandings later. The transfer of all physical and intellectual property should be laid down in detail as should that of the list of customers and contacts. The following points are important and should be firmly laid down in the agreement:

- period of notice
- which law should prevail
- what should be the place for arbitration
- language for communication.

STATEMENT OF SALES POLICY

As the business situation changes during the course of a relationship, it may become cumbersome and costly to review the contract or to insist upon a new legally drawn up contract every time such changes warrant it. This is the reason for a living marketing instrument which sets forth the changes in the policies of the business and which is issued to the channel members, stating the company's trading methods and the specific commercial aspects concerning the sales of the company's products.

This marketing instrument is enshrined in a Statement of Sales Policy. If the contract does not clearly spell out some aspects, such as the definition of a distributor, including the basic qualifications that must be possessed, such as reputation, facility to carry inventory, delivery requirements and the method(s) of distribution, then the Statement of Sales Policy should include clear definitions of those aspects. The products to be so distributed should also be clearly defined as well as the prices to be charged, discounts offered, terms of payment, performance criteria and warranty terms.

The amount of assistance to be expected by a distributor and the training help offered by the company should be stated, as well as the marketing and A&P facilities on offer. It is advisable to have some representative body set up to resolve problems and offer advice. The conditions of sale should be set down in full and a price list included if possible, with the clear proviso that the latter will be updated from time to time with an explanation of the way price increases should be implemented. The sales policy document must also include a statement of the period of notice to be given prior to changes in price, trading and commercial terms.

The sales policy document issued to a distributor tends to spell out relevant changes to:

- prices, discounts and terms of payment
- inventory to be held
- variations in targets as agreed
- performance criteria
- training requirements and training offered
- liability
- warranty
- campaign stock
- sales promotion aids
- marketing assistance
- campaign planning
- reviews and co-operation.

TERMS FOR AGENT/DISTRIBUTOR AGREEMENTS

In the context of an international agreement, the following are relevant for contract provisions associated with particular problems. It is important to identify exactly what your relationship with your distributor is going to be. There are significant distinctions between a distributorship and a sales representative or an agent that will directly impact the form of your contract.

Corporations versus individuals

It is better to appoint corporations or other legal entities as distributors rather than individuals for whom the local labour laws may apply. One of the major reasons for doing business through a distributor or an agent is to limit foreign taxes. Review the appropriate tax treaties before finalising your relationship with the distributor. In general, the more independent the distributor, the less likelihood of your being subject to the local taxes.

Duration

Provision for the duration of the agreement is important; if the term appears to be indefinite, the chance of a demand for compensation upon termination increases. A short, specific term of one or two years is best for agency or distributorship agreements; a new agreement should be signed at the expiration, instead of providing for an extension, as some jurisdictions treat extensions as an indefinite term. It may be better to change some clauses in each new contract to make it clear that the agreement was renegotiated.

Termination

Terminal clauses that focus on the commercial viability will probably be enforceable, but it is best to check what constitutes 'just cause' in the relevant jurisdiction and delineate reasonable causes for termination. It is important to give adequate notice of termination; this may pre-empt an inquiry into the justness of the cause. List the causes, separating those for which termination is automatic from those for which a period of grace is provided.

Before entering into an agreement, an analysis should be made of:

1. What rights and obligations the parties will have after termination.
2. Which contract provisions survive termination.
3. Who will keep the customer lists and similar information.
4. Who will handle outstanding orders and inventory.
5. Whether the terminated distributor will be subject to a non-compete clause.

Product sale or service agreement

A sale contract should offer the goods for sale, indicate the purchaser's acceptance of your offer and acknowledge the obligation to pay. In a distributor contract you should appoint the distributor and have them accept the appointment. The functions and responsibilities will vary depending upon the nature of the product or services to be offered, the services requiring a great deal more in the way of follow-up. With respect to product sales, it should be identified whether the distributor is to sell only one line of products, or whether the products are to be offered as a range.

Territorial and customer restrictions are generally acceptable, but each set of facts must be reviewed for legal implications in both countries. The area in which the distributor is to operate must be specified, otherwise the goods may be sold world-wide. When considering exclusivity, keep the legal implications for both countries in mind, especially if the arrangement is reciprocal. While a resale price for your product may be suggested to the distributor, it should not be enforced.

Arbitration and governing law

One way to limit termination disputes is to provide for arbitration and choice of law outside the distributor's jurisdiction, thus avoiding the necessity of litigation in the local courts. In providing for arbitration, pay attention to the procedure for selecting arbitrators and to the site of arbitration, with consideration for the laws to govern the dispute and the language used. Often, each of the parties select one arbitrator and the two so chosen choose a third, the three functioning as a panel to resolve the dispute.

Payment and compensation

In sales contracts, payment will generally be of one of the following forms:

1. Cash in advance: payment is usually received before shipment and the importer has total risk while the exporter has none.
2. Letter of credit: payment is due when shipment has been made and documents have been presented to the correspondent banks. The exporter's risk depends primarily on the terms of the letter and the goods become available after payment is made.
3. Documentary collection: involves a sight draft or a time draft. In the first case, payment is made on presentation of the draft to the buyer and the goods become available to the buyer after payment to the buyer's bank. If the draft is not honoured, the exporter will have the goods returned at extra cost. In the second case, payment is made on maturity of the time draft and the goods become available to the buyer before payment, the exporter facing the risk of relying upon the buyer to honour the draft later.
4. Open account: if payment is made by open account, the goods become available to the buyer before payment which is expected at some agreed date.

Terms and conditions of sale

Always specify price and credit terms, shipment terms and passage of title terms in a foreign distributor's agreement.

1. Price: distributors should be given enough notice to adjust their prices in case your prices change. An agent should also be informed, though you generally control the final price there. An attempt to control the distributor's prices can raise anti-trust/competition concerns.
2. Credit: you have to determine whether to give credit to the distributor and to allow them to give credit to their customers in your name, as well as who will be paying for and arranging for credit insurance.
3. Shipment terms: these require special attention as someone has to arrange for overseas transportation and to decide whether special packaging is needed. Responsibility for clearing customs, passing inspection and for arranging inland transportation and warehousing should be stipulated.
4. Passage of title: is directly related to the question of risk. Before the transfer of title, the supplier bears the risk; after it, the distributor or customer does so. It should therefore be clearly stipulated at what point the title passes from one party to the other and who provides for insurance at what points before, during and after the transfer. The location of the passage of title will determine whether the supplier receives income from a local bank or from a foreign correspondent bank or a foreign bank financing the buyer. The method of payment could affect the tax position, as in some countries there could be withholding taxes.

Facilities and personnel

If you are providing for facilities and personnel in the distributor's country, there is a greater chance that the distributor becomes integrated with your business and can be treated as your employee, which will mean that you may be subject to local labour laws.

Inventory

Inventory considerations call for a close analysis of risk of loss, passage of title, insurance and warehousing cost issues. The parties should agree whether the seller will buy back inventory on termination of contract.

Confidentiality

Foreign distributors that are exposed to a company's confidential information, especially proprietary information, should be required not to disclose it to third parties, the provision being drafted to survive termination.

Requirement to maintain records

You may want to include a clause requiring the distributor to keep usable and clear accounting records. Such records may need to be audited from time to time for purposes of ensuring quality of service, status of inventory, etc. In addition, you may need other information to be provided and records maintained in cases where an export licence is needed.

Reporting requirements

You may need feedback on marketing and sales performance in the distributor territory, information on the general competitor situation, market statistics, etc., for the purpose of improving your and your distributor's position in the market-place. Other information gathering requirements may be specified in the agreement.

Proprietary information, trademarks/tradename and copyright

The distributor should be required to acknowledge the supplier's right, title and interest to any proprietary information or material that comes into the possession of the distributor from the supplier. The distributor's use of trade marks and trade name should be restricted and there should be an agreement to report any infringement and to assist in obtaining protection against such infringement. The distributor, in general, only gets user rights in this case.

Copyrights, trade marks, trade name and patents should all be registered in the supplier's name in the territory. Make sure that upon termination, no right will be held by any foreign party with respect to any such property.

Advertising and promotion

Closely aligned with the above is the responsibility given to the distributor with respect to promotional materials. A decision should be made whether you retain a right of approval with regard to promotional materials produced by your distributor and to control the use of trade marks, etc.

Force majeure

These are included in agreements protecting both parties from a claim of failure to perform as a result of some uncontrollable event. The most controversial section is usually the acceptance of labour trouble as one of the causes.

Compensation arrangements for agent or distributor

It is important to draw a distinction between payment, which is made to the supplier for their goods, possibly including an element of compensation to the distributor; and compensation, where the payment is made to the agent or distributor as a commission for performing their job. For an independent trader, this is derived from the mark-up; for an agent, you specify whether they receive a commission or a salary.

1. Commissions: some attention should be paid to how they are calculated; this should be on a net, not a gross figure, and should be paid on money actually received from the customers and not on orders booked. Check whether the country of jurisdiction stipulates a maximum rate allowed on sales.
2. Currency: care should be taken in negotiating the currency in which payments to the supplier and the distributor are to be made; losses in currency exchange can wipe out profits.
3. Third-country payments: the jurisdiction in which the payments are made to the distributor should also be carefully considered.

Depending on the laws of the country of origin, it might be necessary to obtain representations from the distributor that bribes or gifts will not be offered.

Other provisions

Standard contract provisions such as severability, assignment, waiver and notice should also be part of the contract. In addition, you may want the foreign distributor to agree to assume responsibility for compliance with all other local laws, rules and regulations.

A formal contract with overseas distributors or agents is necessary because it sets out points of prior agreements and ways of resolving possible points of conflict. Whereas such a document may not cover all possible eventualities, it usually follows a standard form suited to the export market concerned. A comprehensive agreement document leads to a tendency of referring to it for each and every dispute, however small. A short but basic document may be preferred in cases where the parties wish to conduct their relationship with mutual understanding and trust.

CASE ILLUSTRATIONS

The following is a summary of brief notes on some cases illustrating the legal conclusions drawn by the relevant courts and showing the way in which some disputes were settled. Some of the cases arose out of competition considerations and Articles 85–86, but other cases concern non-competition issues.

Appointment of authorized retailers

1 Re *Omega Watches* (No. 70/448/EEC) [1970] CMLR (RP Supp) D49

Omega of Switzerland made the following arrangements for distribution in EC countries. There were five exclusive distributors each with a defined territory to which their sales were confined. Their supplies had to be obtained from Omega only and they could sell only to certain retailers in their area which had been recommended by Omega. Each retailer had to sign an agreement to buy only from their relevant distributor and to sell only in their own territory. Although the whole arrangement contravened Article 85(1), an exemption was granted for the control of the number of retailers per distributor as being necessary to ensure sufficient level of business to each retailer in order to provide the right quality of customer service.

2 Re *Bayerische Moterenwerke* [1975] 1 CMLR D44

In West Germany, BMW appointed exclusive distributors for defined territories which were also exclusive to the relevant dealers. Each distributor could appoint exclusive sub-distributors on the same principle in their area, subject to approval from BMW. BMW undertook not to supply directly to third parties, and the various distributors and sub-distributors agreed to obtain supplies only from authorized dealers in the EC. The selection of these distributors and sub-distributors was subject to both quantitative and qualitative criteria, the latter relating to adequacy of business facilities and the willingness to abide by the rules imposed by BMW. BMW only appointed enough dealers to ensure that each had a sales level high enough to support their business. The Commission, although holding that the arrangements contravened Article 85, granted an exemption because they held that for expensive and high quality products like BMW cars, it is necessary to ensure that a high level of technical expertise, after-sales service and maintenance is available, and the number of dealers could therefore be restricted.

3 Re *SABA* [1978] 1 CMLR D61

SABA was a German subsidiary of a US company manufacturing consumer electronic goods such as radios, televisions and hi-fi. It employed both wholesaler/

distributors and retailers to sell its products. There were conditions for a dealer to be approved as a SABA dealer and regarding the distribution channels to be employed. There were qualitative criteria and necessary agreement for various promotion activities, sales targets, etc. The Commission held that the arrangements contravened Article 85(1) because some dealers who could satisfy the qualitative criteria might not agree to comply with the other criteria. However, an exemption was granted under Article 85(3), because they held that the efficiency of the operation meant better service for less price for the consumer.

4 Re *Kodak and Omega* [1970] CMLR D19

In one of earliest of selective distribution decisions, the Commission permitted Kodak to restrict its film retail outlets to photographic film retailers who possessed suitable premises and storage and display facilities. It similarly allowed Omega to impose qualitative restrictions on its retailers by only approving jewellers or watchmakers. Neither was considered to need an exemption under Article 85(3).

5 Re *IBM Personal Computer* [1984] 2 CMLR 342

IBM were having trouble with outlets selling their larger and more expensive micro-computers to inexperienced users who were not being given the proper advice about the right equipment to suit their needs. This led to customer disappointment and loss of reputation. IBM wished to establish a network of dealers with sufficient expertise to give the proper advice as well as follow-up service and after-care. IBM declared it intended to appoint as many qualified dealers as possible who satisfied its objective criteria. There was to be no attempt to maintain resale prices for the products. The Commission granted IBM an exemption under Article 85(3), making it clear that it was based on the prevailing conditions in that market and on the consumer need for proper guidance and after-care.

6 Re *SABA (No. 2)* [1984] 1 CMLR 677

Originally, SABA had the sole right to decide which outlets met its criteria and take as much time as they wished for the decision. This was considered to 'open the door to discriminatory application of the admission criteria', especially at the retail level. SABA then restricted its time for replying to an application for admission to four weeks, after which it must sign an agreement with the applicant if no reply has been sent by it. All wholesalers were allowed to sign agreements with retailers admitting them to the system but they had to notify SABA, which could check the application for confirmation to its criteria and expel any applicants who did not comply with them.

Copyright

7 Re *Deutsche Grammophon GmbH* v. *Metro SB Grossmarkte GmbH & CO KG* [1971] CMLR 631

A Metro subsidiary in France bought DG records cheaply and Metro re-imported them into Germany and sold them at a low price through its outlets. DG invoked German copyright law for preventing this happening. They were prevented from exercising their rights under German law by the court on the grounds of contravention of Article 30–36.

8 Re *Industrie Diensten Groep BV* v. *JA Beele Handelmaatschappij BV* [1982] 3 CMLR 102

An injunction was granted under the Dutch law which forbade the marketing of copies of another's products which were 'slavish imitations' to a Dutch company against a German company. The latter was importing into Holland German goods which were 'slavish imitations' of Swedish goods which the Dutch company had marketed for many years. There were no existing industrial property rights in the goods, so that both could market their goods in EC countries and the abovesaid Dutch law was the only legal objection that the Dutch company could bring into court. The European Court was asked whether the Dutch law could be considered to be against Articles 30 and 36. The Court found that the slavish imitations were neither necessary or justified on any technical, economic or commercial grounds. Thus the Dutch law was protecting consumers against confusion.

9 Re *Danske Supermarket A/S* v. *Smerco A/S* [1981] 3 CMLR 590

In this case the copied products were marketed in the United Kingdom with the consent of a Danish firm which then tried to stop them being imported into Denmark under a national fair trading law. The Court found against the Danish firm.

10 Re *Keurkoop BV* v. *Nancy Kean Gifts BV* [1983] 2 CMLR 47

Nancy Kean obtained the exclusive right to a ladies' handbag designed in Taiwan via a Swiss firm and registered it under the Benelux Uniform Law on Designs. Keurkoop started selling identical Taiwanese bags by mail order in Holland. Nancy Kean obtained an injunction against Keurkoop in the Dutch courts. The Dutch Court of Appeal turned to the European Court for an opinion whether the Benelux Uniform Law on Designs was within the Articles 36 or 85. The Court found the law was within the said articles and that

> the protection . . . established by Article 36 would be rendered meaningless if a person other than the owner of the right to a design in a member state could be allowed to market in that state a product which is virtually identical in appearance to the protected design.

11 Re *Criminal Proceedings Against Karl Prantl* [1985] 2 CMLR 238

A German law made it an offence for any wine to be sold in Germany in a particular shape of bottle called Bocksbeutel unless it was made in certain parts of Germany which traditionally used that bottle. Prantl imported wines into Germany from parts of Italy which also traditionally used that shape of bottle. Prantl was judged to have broken the German law but the law itself was referred to the European Court to find out if it contravened the rules for free movement of goods. The Court held that the

German law ignored the traditions of the Italian Bocksbeutel users and could not be used in this case to bar the imports from another EC state. The EC Commission had already provided comprehensive requirements on wine bottle labelling to prevent consumer confusion.

12 Re *British Leyland Motor Corporation Ltd* v. *TI Silencers Ltd* [1979] FSR 591 (Ch. Div.)

British Leyland (BL) tried to stop parallel imports by means of its ownership of design copyright and copyright in spare parts for its motor vehicles. The defendant argued that they were in contravention of Article 36 and were impeding the free flow of goods in and out of the United Kingdom. The English Court applied the EC laws directly and gave judgment in favour of BL, since BL had a policy of granting licences freely on a non-discriminatory basis and offering all infringers a licence; the case was taken to court only if the offer was refused.

Excessive prices

13 Re *General Motors Continental* [1975] [1]

The Court confirmed that it is an abuse to charge prices which exceed the 'economic value' of the supplied product or service.

Exchange of information

14 Re *Fatty Acids* [1986] [1]

An agreement was made between four major producers of the product in question operating in the EC to exchange information concerning the total sales of their products per quarter in the EC, thus effectively removing one element of uncertainty in their competitive monitoring of each other's activities. The Commission imposed a fine on the participants.

Franchising agreements

15 Re *Pronuptia de Paris* [1986] [1]

Although franchising agreements contain restrictions regarding exclusivity, know-how and dealing in competing goods, the court held in the above case that franchising agreements can be compatible with EC competition rules. These agreements lead to efficiency in distribution of goods and services as well as other benefits for consumers, therefore a block exemption regulation has now been adopted with respect to them. Individual notification will still be needed if the terms of the agreement are outside the terms of the block exemption.

Good business practice

16 Re *Industries & General Mortgage Co. Ltd* v. *Lewis* [1949] 2All ER 573; 93 SJ 577

An employee who receives a bribe in relation to their employer's business has a civil liability to account for the bribe to the employer. In some cases the employer can also proceed against the person who gave the bribe. In a contract of sale obtained by bribery, the price is presumed to have been increased by the amount of the bribe and therefore the buyer can claim as damages the amount of the 'excess' price from the seller as well as the actual bribe from the employee, thus recovering double the amount.

17 Re *Foster* v. *Driscoll* [1929] 1 KB 470

A contract which is opposed to British interests and may endanger relations between the British Government and any other friendly government is considered void. A contract to import whisky into the United States during Prohibition was not held to be enforceable.

18 Re *Peter Buchanan Ltd* v. *McVey* [1955] AC 516

UK courts, while not enforcing foreign laws, will take notice of them where 'one of the terms of a legal contract are rendered invalid by the foreign law'. In this case, arrangements made to avoid paying tax in Scotland, which were illegal under Scottish law but not under Irish law, were declared invalid by an Irish court.

Horizontal groupings

19 Re *Peroxygen Cartel* [1985] 1 CMLR 481

A series of companies called Interox were jointly owned by certain manufacturers of chemical products. The overall policy for Interox was decided by a committee made up of senior directors from the manufacturers but it had no management or control powers. The Interox workings were managed by the employees of the manufacturers for which they were paid. The Commission decided that Interox was not sufficiently separate from the manufacturers for them to deny responsibility for its actions under Article 85. The question whether Interox was itself responsible to Article 85 for its actions or whether it was a joint venture between the manufacturers, was left open.

Joint ventures

20 Re *Agreement between Volvo Flygmotor AB and Sauer Getriebe AG* [1985] 1 CMLR 663

This case illustrates the position of the Commission regarding joint ventures involving small- and medium-sized businesses. Sauer was a very specialized medium-sized company and Volvo Flygmotor was part of the large Volvo group of companies. So their agreement required a specific exemption as the market share provisions infringed the regulations. The product range in question was available in the EC from a number of suppliers, some of whom belonged to powerful multinational companies. The Commission agreed to a specialization agreement because it enabled Sauer to enlarge its range of products and thus made it able to compete with its larger and stronger rivals and because it also allowed Volvo to enter a new market where it lacked sales organization and experience.

21 Re *Mitchell Cotts* [1986] [1]

A joint venture between competing companies infringes Article 85(1) and even when the companies are potential competitors, the article may apply to the venture. Although in the past the Commission has applied the article very broadly to joint ventures, there is now a sign of tightening up as in the case above.

22 Re *Optical Fibres* [1986] [1]

When one company participates in many joint ventures, the resulting interaction of the agreements may itself restrict competition. In the case above, the companies in the joint ventures found themselves prevented from competing freely with each other.

Loyalty and target rebates

23 Re *Suiker Unie* [1975] [1]

A group of sugar producers granted a rebate to buyers who bought exclusively from the group members. The Court held that this was an abuse according to Article 86, since the reward was not for the amount bought but for loyalty to the group.

Manufacturing agreements

24 Re *The Agreements Between Schlegel Corporation and Compagnie Des Produits Industriels De l'Ouest SA* [1984] 2 CMLR 179

A know-how agreement which granted the right to use the know-how for manufacturing the product anywhere in the EC and marketing it world-wide was not considered to be in breach of Article 85(1). In this case the agreement also contained provisions to limit the licensee to use a named component and to exclusive purchase of that component from the licenser for a period of five years. This part was considered to contravene Article 85(1) as the period was too long for a normal sale agreement.

Market sharing agreements

25 Re *Consten and Grundig* [1966] CMLR 418

Market sharing agreements are considered serious infringements of Article 85(1). Usually the market is partitioned geographically, thereby adversely affecting the establishment of a single, integrated market. The same result can be achieved by a division of customers as through an export ban.

Mergers and acquisitions

26 Re *Continental Can* [1973] [1]

If a business acquires a competitor and thereby increases its dominance of its market substantially so as to restrict competition, this is considered an abuse of its dominant position.

27 Re *Philip Morris* [1987] [1]

The Court held in this case that Article 85 is contravened when a company either arranges to co-operate with its competitor or gains control over it by buying shares. It depends on whether the company gains any kind of control over the other's business.

Patents

28 Re *Parke Davis & Co.* v. *Probel* [1968] CMLR 47

Parke Davis of Detroit held patents in Holland for an antibiotic. In Italy no patents were granted for antibiotics and an Italian firm produced the drug in Italy without any connection with or permission from Parke Davis. Probel imported it from Italy into Holland. Parke Davis applied for an injunction to stop the imports on the grounds that they infringed its Dutch patent. The Dutch court referred the case to the European Court for advice. The Court held that Parke Davis was not contravening Articles 36, 85 and 86.

29 Re *Centrafarm BV* v. *Stirling Drug Co. Inc.* [1974] (No. 15/74)

As in the following case concerning trade marks, Centrafarm attempted to import drugs from Stirling's UK subsidiary into Holland. Stirling tried to prevent it by exercising its Dutch patent rights; it also held patent rights in the United Kingdom. The Court refused this, defining the right of a patentee within EC as

the exclusive right to use an invention to manufacture industrial products and put them into circulation for the first time. Where the product has been put on the market in a legal manner, in the member state from which it has been imported, by the patentee or with his consent, then a derogation from the principle of free movement of goods is not justified.

30 Re *Merck & Co. Inc.* v. *Stephar BV* [1981] 3 CMLR 463

A patentee gave consent for his product to be marketed in Italy without patent protection. The Court held that he could not then exercise his patent rights in another member state to prevent imports of the goods from Italy.

31 Re *EMI Records Ltd* v. *CBS UK Ltd* [1976] 2 CMLR 235

The mark Colombia was owned world-wide by CBS from the United States, who assigned it to EMI in all of Western Europe. EMI now wished to prevent imports from the US of records bearing the trade mark. CBS put up a defence of common origin but were turned down by the court who ruled that the doctrine did not apply when the trade between EC member states was not affected.

Price-fixing agreements

32 Re *Polypropylene* [1986] [1]

Price-fixing agreement always contravene Article 85(1) and cannot be exempted under Article 85(3). A price-fixing agreement together with a market sharing agreement between the members of a cartel in the case above resulted in a large fine being imposed on them.

33 Re *European Glass Manufacturers* [1974] [1]

Agreements fixing a maximum price which must not be exceeded are unlawful even though they appear to benefit the consumer. If only domestic or local outlets can afford to sell below that maximum price, this isolates the market and distorts the competition.

34 Re *Roofing Felt* [1986] [1]

Agreements to stick to a minimum price or to keep to a given price list are also illegal.

Product market

35 Re *Continental Can* [1973] [1]

The question of whether two products have the same market is decided by the degree of interchangeability of the products. In the above case, the court decided that limited interchangeability means the products belong to different markets and reasonable interchangeability means they do belong to the same market. In this context, it is necessary to examine their nature, price, use and the conditions of supply and demand in their markets.

36 Re *United Brands* [1978] 1 CMLR 429; [1978] 3 CMLR 83

It was found that the banana market differed sufficiently from the other fresh fruit markets to be considered on its own. This was because consumers needing bananas were not generally satisfied by purchase of other fresh fruits. Therefore the competition between the two markets was very limited.

Refusal to supply

37 Re *Commercial Solvents* [1974] 1 CMLR 309

A refusal to supply on the grounds of nationality is considered an abuse since the EC treaty generally forbids discrimination on grounds of nationality. In the above case, CSC, which dominated the raw materials market for the production of ethambutol, took the decision to stop supplying them within the EC and its subsidiary started to manufacture ethambutol itself. The case arose when it stopped supplying Zoja in Italy with raw materials for its production. This was held to be an abuse of its dominant position as it would force the Italian firm to withdraw from the market.

Retailer requirements

38 Re *The Guarantee by Industrie A Zanussi SpA* [1979] 1 CMLR 81

The Commission declared that the Zanussi guarantee had to be honoured by any Zanussi dealer irrespective of where the product was purchased. Zanussi agreed that in future after-sales and warranty service would be available through the Zanussi dealer in the country of use, thus removing an indirect ban on parallel imports.

Sales and marketing policies

39 *Hoffman La Roche & Co. AG.* v. *Centrafarm VPE GmbH* [1978] and *Centrafarm BV* v. *American Home Products Corporation* [1978] ECR 1823

In both these cases Centrafarm purchased goods in one country with a legal trade mark upon them. In one case it repackaged them into a larger pack and put the original trade mark upon them. In the other case, it exported them to another country, repackaged them and added another trade mark to them. In neither case was it authorized to use the trade mark affixed to the goods and the owners took them to court to stop them. The court decided against Centrafarm as an unauthorized infringer. A caution was added that if the motive behind the actions had been to stop parallel imports, this would have changed the decision.

40 Re *Pfizer* v. *Evrim* [1982] 1 CMLR 406

The repackager enclosed the original package into a larger one with the Pfizer trade mark clearly visible. The Court held that protection of the trade mark did not prevent this activity.

41 Re *BAT Cigaretten-Fabriken GmbH* v. *EC Commission* [1985] 2 CMLR 470

BAT in Germany and a smaller firm called Segers in Holland both dealt in tobacco products. BAT had registered a mark called Dorcet in Germany which was dormant and could have been struck off for non-use after a certain period. Segers also registered a mark called Toltecs Special in Germany and this was contested by BAT who said it resembled their Dorcet mark. Segers did not wish to fight it out with a larger company and agreed to certain restrictions regarding their mark and to further registration of the Dorcet or similar marks by BAT. The Commission fined BAT for operating an agreement which in effect partitioned the market between the two companies.

Selective distribution

42 Re *AEG-Telefunken AG* [1982] OJ L117/82

The Commission imposed fines on AEG because after notifying the Commission regarding their selective distribution arrangements and obtaining an exemption, they had applied the arrangements in such a way that dealers who reduced prices could not become members of their network. This was the first time that a fine had been imposed for the manner in which selective distribution terms were applied rather than the terms themselves.

43 Re *BMW (Belgium)* [1980] 1 CMLR 370

The Commission gave BMW Germany an exemption for its selective distribution network because of the efficiency and after-sales service generated by the arrangement for the consumer. The original arrangements required the trade to be confined to consumers and members of the network throughout the EC and this was followed by BMW Belgium. In 1975, the BMW prices were lower in Belgium than elsewhere in the EC and this caused cross-border trade in those cars to become advantageous. Against the wishes of its parent company, BMW Belgium warned its dealers not to sell outside the network; the dealers themselves told all members not to sell outside Belgium. The Commission moved against BMW Belgium and the dealers, and found that they had contravened Article 85(1) by making an arrangement to prohibit exports. An appeal to the European Court was rejected.

44 Re *Gas Water-Heaters* [1973] CMLR D241

Three Belgian manufacturers and two importers of these products made a collective agreement on conditions of sale, terms of payment and conditions, and after-sales service, agreeing to supply only particular types of dealers and to give them discounts, including an aggregated rebate discount in certain cases. The Commission refused to sanction this agreement because it precluded other dealers who would also find it hard to compete against such heavy discounts. The aggregated rebate discount was disallowed since the dealers enjoying it were thereby discouraged from buying elsewhere.

45 Re *The Perfume Cases* [1979–1981]

The perfume manufacturers included Guerlain, Rochas, Lanvin and Nina Ricci. The commission had given them informal clearance by letters for selective distribution arrangements under Article 85. Retail outlets complained to their national courts in France, Belgium and Holland that these manufacturers of luxury perfumes and other beauty products refused to include them in their selective distribution systems, claiming a contravention of national laws against unjustified refusal to supply. The manufacturers relied on the Commission letters for their defence against contravention of Article 85. The Court gave a series of similar decisions holding that the letters could not prevent national courts from applying Article 85 to each case as known to them and deciding that it had been breached.

Supply of the products

46 Re *United Brands & Co.* v. *EC Commission* [1979] 1 CMLR 429

United Brands sold to almost all its distributors FOB Rotterdam and left them to sell in their territories at their own prices. FOB Rotterdam prices were set for the territories according to what the market there would bear without harming the market share of the distributors. The distributors bore the risks and United Brands simply took a profit. The Court held that United Brands could not charge differential prices for different territories because they 'took no risk of the market'.

47 Re *Nederlandsche Banden-Industrie Michelin NV* v. *EC Commission* [1985] 1 CMLR 282

This concerned discounts allowed by Michelin to its dealers in Holland. It was decided that a quantity discount on the basis of volume purchased is not an abuse. However, Michelin also had a sales target discount system which progressively rewarded the dealers for exceeding sales targets. There was no punishment for buying elsewhere. In spite of this lack of exclusivity, the system was considered an abuse of Michelin's dominant position in the market because it encouraged the dealers to buy from Michelin, especially at the year end and if the sales were not brisk enough. This prevented the customers from buying from other manufacturers, whatever their needs might be.

48 Re *The Distillers Company Ltd* v. *EC Commission* [1980] 3 CMLR 121

Distillers' wholesalers paid considerably higher prices for the products they bought for export because certain allowances and rebates were not allowed on exports to other EC countries. This practice was started after Distillers withdrew an export ban under its conditions of sale when asked by the Commission to do so. The Commission held that each such distribution agreement was contravening Article 85 and the Court confirmed this. In another Commission Notice to the Distillers Company plc in 1983, the Commission permitted the imposition of differential pricing for a transitional period after which it had to be slowly eliminated. Distillers were imposing differential pricing to their distributors of Red Label whisky which was re-introduced into the United Kingdom. It was being sold in Europe after being discontinued in the UK. Thus export sales were being priced at a higher level.

Termination

49 Re *SABA (No. 2)* [1984] 1 CMLR 677

The provisions for termination and expulsion from a network were permissible if not open to abuse. The only unconditional termination possible for the principal was if all dealership agreements were terminated. Termination for breach of selective criteria was possible but if the dealer questioned this, a court decision was necessary to make it effective unless it could be proved that the breach placed the distribution system at risk.

Third party rights

50 Re *Garden Cottage Foods* [1984] [1]

The House of Lords indicated in this case that damages or an injunction should, in principle, be obtainable by a third party if Articles 85 or 86 are breached.

Trade associations

51 Re *FEDETAB* [1981] [1]

Trade associations may not impose rules to make market entry more difficult or expensive. They can, however, impose qualifications on the type of company operating in the market which can be exempted by the Commission. In the above case, it was held that individual members of an association may be liable in respect of concerted practices with the other members when the rules of the association are binding on the members.

Trade between Member States

52 Re *Wood Pulp Decision* [1985] [1]

There is an effect on trade whenever the general pattern of trade changes; this effect must be 'between Member States'. But Article 85 applies even when the firms pursuing restrictive practices are outside EC and the practices concerned affect other markets besides the EC.

Trade marks

53 Re *Sirena srl* v. *Eda srl* [1971] 2 CMLR 260

Sirena from Italy took on a trade mark for a face cream from an American firm, who also similarly licensed a German firm. Eda bought the German product to market it in Italy and were sued by Sirena for infringement of an Italian trade mark. The Court held that the original assignment made in 1937 was restraining the free flow of goods and was therefore not enforceable. Trade marks are not considered as worthy of protection as patents and have to give way to the need for free flow of goods and services across the EC.

54 Re *Centrafarm BV* v. *Winthrop BV* [1974] 2 CMLR 480

Winthrop wished to prevent drugs from its UK subsidiary being imported into Holland on the basis of its trade mark rights. This was refused under Article 36.

55 Re *Terrapin (Overseas) Ltd* v. *Terranova Industrie CA Kapferer & Co.* [1976] 2 CMLR 482

This concerned two firms which were, respectively, British and German, both in the building trade. The first sold portable buildings and the second building materials. There was no link between the firms. When Terrapin tried to register its trade mark in Germany, Terranova opposed them on the grounds of similarity of the two names. The Court decided that the opposition was allowed under the rules of free movement of goods.

Unfair terms and conditions

56 Re *BRT* v. *SABAM* [1974] 2 CMLR 238

There is no hard and fast rule regarding what are unfair terms and conditions in any given case. This judgment involves consideration of the interests of the dominant party and the affected parties. A Belgian copyright collection society asked its members to assign to it all present and future copyrights and allow the Society their right for up to five years after the members had left the Society, thus acquiring a virtual monopoly of the copyrights. The Court considered that the compulsory assignments of copyrights, especially after the member's departure from the Society was an unfair condition.

57 *The Commission intervenes to improve competition in the market for sports goods* [European Commission press release IP/92/198]

Dunlop Slazenger International (DSI) is a subsidiary of the UK conglomerate BTR, one of the main European and world producers of sports goods and the leader within the EC for tennis and squash balls. Newitt, a UK distribution company, accused DSI of using various means to block its exports mainly of tennis and squash balls to other states in the EC. It alleged that DSI had first suspended deliveries and then applied discriminatory new tariffs in order to prevent it from remaining competitive in export markets.

The investigation following the complaint showed that DSI did indeed pursue a policy of restricting exports from the United Kingdom with the aim of protecting its sole distributors in other Community countries, amounting to a general ban on exporting addressed to all its UK traders. This ban was implemented by a series of concrete measures intended to prevent any exports to countries where DSI had sole distributors. In addition, the investigations showed that at least as regards the Netherlands, the implementation of these measures was undertaken in concert with DSI's distributors in that country and sometimes at their own instigation. The measures identified by the Commission during its investigations were as follows:

1. Specific refusal to supply products intended for export.
2. Prices imposed on UK traders with a view to preventing them from remaining competitive in export markets.
3. Buying in parallel exports at low prices to prevent them from exerting pressure on the prices charged by DSI's exclusive distribution network.
4. Marking products to establish their origin and final destination.
5. Exclusivity for the Dutch distributors in the use of the Dutch Tennis Federation's quality mark.

These measures clearly aimed to prevent any export bound for a country where DSI had a sole distributor, in support of its policy. At the end of the Commission's investigations, DSI recognized that it had infringed the Community's rules in a number of ways, and to a great extent (but not thoroughly) altered its practices.

Barriers to exports resulting from agreements or from concerted practices between companies have consistently been considered as serious infringements of Article 85(1) of the EEC Treaty, in the case law of the Commission and the European Court of Justice, as they challenge the free movement of goods which is a fundamental objective of the Treaty. The Commission therefore imposed a fine of 5 million ECU on DSI and 150,000 ECU on its sole distributor in the Benelux countries for the Dunlop brand.

Reference

[1] *The Competition Rules of the European Economic Community*, published by Simmons & Simmons, London, 1991.

8 SELECTING A SUITABLE DISTRIBUTOR

In this chapter, an analysis is made of the particular aspects that should be borne in mind in selecting a distributor as a channel member.

SELECTION OF A CHANNEL MEMBER

It is worth distinguishing between a foreign distributor, a domestic distributor, a dealer in a territory and a commercial agent. A foreign distributor is generally a wholesaler operating in the whole or a discernible part of a country – an agricultural machinery distributor based in Nairobi for the whole of Kenya would be an example. A software distributor based in Antwerp for the Flemish speaking part of Belgium is an example of a dealer. A domestic distributor for packaging materials based in Birmingham, England, to cover the Midlands region of England would be an example of a domestic distributor of a manufacturing company in the United Kingdom. A dealer for garden machinery could operate in a specific location from a shop and serve the needs of local customers. In most instances, the dealer would probably not carry more than a minimum stock, usually for demonstration or show purposes only.

The foreign distributor

Selecting an agent or distributor requires careful gathering and review of information. A study of several variables, here presented as the 'seven Cs', can help a firm analyze its needs before choosing a distribution channel.

1. Control: Tight control may be required over all distribution activities if the product is highly technical, sophisticated or difficult to sell; this may also require a reduction in the number of intermediaries in the chain.
2. Company objectives: These can be for market share, penetration or profitability, or a combination of these elements and the international marketer may have to work towards them.
3. Coverage: This refers to an appropriate sales representation and an

adequate sales force, necessary to cover the geographic width and the type of customers targeted.

4. Cost to the customer: This differs with different types of distribution channels.
5. Customer needs: These relate to the customers' specific requirements.
6. Competition: The international marketer must be aware of competitors' actions and structure the distribution channels to their firm's advantage. It is also necessary to gain an understanding of the strategies of current and possible future competitors. Competition in this context also includes competitors of potential distributors/agents.
7. Communication: The nature and extent of communication (media, promotional campaigns) that may be required to create/increase the awareness of the company and its products.

It is important to develop a profile of the potential distributor when a decision has been taken about the role of the distributor/agent and what kind of distributor is needed. One method is to rank and weight the factors attached to each characteristic of possible distributors. This should preferably involve prospecting by personal visits to the country concerned in order to interview potential candidates.

It is also important to recognize that the manufacturer choosing the agent or distributor will have different expectations from the latter. These expectations should be clearly spelled out as objectives and roles, so that each can understand what the other hopes to gain from the arrangement. Any differences should be ironed out, otherwise they can cause the agreement to fall apart later, at considerable cost to both parties.

One successful method of continuously updating this concord is a jointly drafted marketing plan. Most distributors will not be interested in a long and detailed plan, but a short, well-articulated document can often highlight trouble spots. A full plan can be written after a shorter one is drafted with the distributor. The following topics can be covered in such a document:

- description of the market and the environment
- market size and growth
- competition
- major opportunities
- marketing objectives
- marketing strategy
- target accounts and time-scales
- budgets
- assignments

This joint effort, expended in understanding what the marketing objectives and tasks are, is essential to establishing a good rapport and achieving success with an agent or distributor.

An agent/distributor development programme, usually a prepackaged presentation for gaining the interest and understanding of potential overseas partners, is a very useful tool, showing what the manufacturer will be offering the agent/distributor and conversely, what is expected from them.

Translating marketing plans into action is an important task of the link person. This requires dedicated effort in communicating the essentials of the marketing plan and the rationale behind it, to the relevant functions within the company, including the specialist marketing and logistics functions. Systems and the operational procedures within the company must be supportive of the marketing plan. A distributor or agent is performing an important sales and marketing role for the company and it must not be forgotten that the company's revenue and profit depends on their performance. Nothing happens until someone sells something – either the distributor or the agent or the sales force. If a company does not show enough concern for its customers, why should the customers bother to buy its products? In this context, distributors must also be seen as customers. Even a marketing plan has to identify benefits to the distributors.

It may become necessary to bypass the company's formal structures and procedures in specific instances.

Domestic distributor

Much of what has been said above is applicable in selecting domestic distributors, except that if the manufacturer is already well established in the domestic market then many of the top customers are aware of their presence, image and what the company stands for. The distributor essentially adds value through the distribution service. Coverage, communication and customer persuasion are the main ingredients supplied by the domestic distributor.

Dealer

The role of a dealer and the requirements placed upon them by a manufacturer may not be as tight or stringent as those of a distributor, and the selection criteria will therefore be different.

UNDERSTANDING THE FINANCIAL SITUATION

It is important to know whether the distributor's financial situation is sound. A number of questions need to be asked:

1. How is the distributor's business managed from a financial point of view?
2. Is there a suitably qualified financial person to manage it?
3. Who finances the business? What is the financier's relationship to the rest of the management?
4. What does the balance sheet look like? What does the trading account look like? How often are budgets set? How often is the performance reviewed and monitored? How are these activities undertaken?
5. What is the profitability of the distributor? How does it compare with others in the market-place? How does it compare with that of other good distributors already associated with the company?
6. What is the liquidity of the distributor? How does it compare with others in the market-place? How does it compare with the other good distributors?
7. How prudently is the business managed?
8. Has the distributor access to financial resources? What is the attitude of the financial resources to the distributor? What is the reputation of the distributor with them?

It is best and easiest for multinational companies to minimize financial costs and risks by improving their distributors' cash payments from other countries on a cross-border basis. If necessary, managers should be trained in cash management and adapt appropriate national techniques to their own territories.

A British company could have gained an order from a French buyer if the company had been clear at the outset as to how to cover the forward risk. The exporter provisionally obtained the order for the product at an invoiced sterling value for payment six months after the date of the order. The French buyer could not buy the sterling forward six months as the bank could only sell him forward up to two months – this naturally left the buyer exposed to currency risk for the remaining four months. The only option left to the buyer was to delay the order in order to find alternative suppliers who would be willing to offer better terms. If the British exporter had invoiced in French francs and sold those francs forward for sterling on the London Forex market for up to twelve months, the risk could have been covered. The French buyer would have been happy with this arrangement and would have confirmed the order straight away.

In another case, a British firm was asked to quote in sterling for a German contract and decided to quote in both sterling and D-marks. As the three-year forward premium on D-mark was then 15 per cent, the firm was able to reduce its D-mark quotation by 5 per cent as compared to its sterling one and to surprise the Germans who were comparing the various quotations.

The first step is to make sure that potential customers are creditworthy, but this is not easy to do in some countries. The rules for publication of financial statements differ from country to country. It may be necessary to find other sources. The next step is to establish credit terms which should conform to local standards to make their acceptance easy. The corporate culture in each country also influences the observance of these terms. It may be necessary to shorten the terms or offer cash discounts for early payments or charge penalties for late payments in order to speed up the process. The speed of these transactions is also influenced by the efficiency of national clearing systems, which varies widely.

Marketing/distribution managers need to work in conjunction with their financial managers. The efficiency and quality of national banking systems varies widely across the world. In order to make the best possible use of the banks in their country of operation, cash managers must consider the following:

1. The number of banks used: Reducing the number of banks in use is one of the best available ways to improve cash flows and reduce costs, through simplified administration and avoidance of excess cash build-up.
2. Idle balances: Preventing funds from lying idle is high on the list of cash management objectives; it reduces borrowing needs and costs. Bank balances should be kept to the minimum, especially those which earn little or no interest.
3. Obtaining good information on bank balances: Making sure that accurate, timely and detailed bank information is available.
4. Keeping track of costs and reducing them: Account analyses should be requested from all the banks in use. Persistence will be required in some countries for success. Companies should also develop good internal systems to check the accuracy of their banks' charges and compare rates.

Good treasury managers will already be aware of a number of cross-border techniques which can be adapted for use:

1. Transference of surplus funds from subsidiaries to a central corporate account where they can fetch higher interest.
2. Setting up of hold accounts to accumulate foreign currency receipts from exports, if the exchange controls allow it; these funds can then be used to pay expenses in the same currencies.
3. Delaying or hastening payments, subject to the national laws, to change the timing of intracompany trade flows, thereby shifting corporate

liquidity, reducing borrowing costs and protecting against currency risks.

4. 'Netting' intracompany payments among subsidiaries to reduce the total number of transactions within a corporate group.
5. Using re-invoicing centres to take title from the manufacturers and sell to other subsidiaries or to customers, thereby controlling the currency of billing and centralizing exposure marketing or enhancing marketing.
6. Developing finance companies or in-house facilities for re-invoicing, factoring and other aspects of international cash management.

PROFITABILITY OF A DISTRIBUTOR

The profitability of a distributor has to be measured in terms of:

- the return on sales as a percentage;
- the return on capital employed as a percentage per annum.

If one takes the first ratio, the return or profit is the result of the distributor's sales in a period less all the costs of operation, namely:

- the cost of goods sold (this is the landed cost of the goods purchased from the manufacturer) plus any costs incurred in the process of value-addition;
- advertising and promotion costs;
- sales costs including any commissions paid to the sales staff and commission agents;
- storage, transportation and handling charges;
- training and administration costs; and
- costs of capital employed (warehouse, transports, office, working capital, etc.).

The second ratio is the real return on investment and this is often expressed as:
(a) return on sales % multiplied by
(b) turnover of assets.

The first part has been described earlier; the second part reflects the efficiency with which the inventory and other assets are turned over. The first part indicates the margin on sales achieved and the second part indicates the administrative and managerial aspects of the distributor's business management skills.

OTHER FINANCIAL CONSIDERATIONS

Level of investment

The level of investment needed in the marketing channel depends very much on the type of channel and the goals set for it. A channel which merely acts as the sales agent, may only need investment in the form of skilled sales resources, sales material, sales training and perhaps demonstration equipment. On the other hand, an independent channel which acts as an importer/distributor covering a large territory may need to invest in inventory, warehousing, transportation, outbound logistics, and marketing/ sales and supporting resources. What level of resources is needed and whether some of these call for capital investment on a longer term basis, depend on the nature of the product, the agreed goals and the task in hand.

In general, fixed capital investment and working capital requirements are treated differently. Financial soundness of the channel is important for the manufacturer as well as the channel. A good financial strategy is a must. A professional financial approach to evaluating investment requirements and their sourcing is very important in setting up any channel operation.

Inventory management

The level of inventory appropriate for the type of product can be established by examining the industry statistics. In the case of a new innovative product, an initial estimate has to be based on the experience of a 'close-benefit' product and a view of the market characteristics, the launch programme and the product availability to meet customer demand. However, high inventory carrying costs must be avoided. A reasonably high inventory turnover rate is a prerequisite to getting a good rate of return on investment. As a high turnover rate has the effect of decreasing the operating costs (e.g. carrying costs, cost of capital, insurance, warehouse space, property costs, etc.) and reducing the need for a large amount of invested capital, it also leads to improved profitability and a better ROI. Yet inventory control and financial management have proved to be a problem for many channels. These are areas to which high technology channel management need to pay particular attention.

The cost of obsolescence can be very high if unsold items continue to remain in inventory. High inventory may lead to two side effects. If a product remains for a long time in inventory, it may be ageing and therefore, some provision may need to be made to cater for obsolescence, to the detriment of profits. If the product remains in inventory because it is unsaleable, then a write-off provision may be required – this may be due to a competitor launching a new product which gives more advantages and better benefits to the customer. Channel management must include monitoring and controlling inventory and maintaining it at the appropriate level. In addition, high inventory in an obsolete product ties up capital and therefore prevents a channel from investing in the currently demanded product.

Debtor management

The level of debtors outstanding at any given point indicates the degree to which customers are being financed by the channel. It is important to note whether the customers are being given credit in excess of the industry average, or if the customers are not being chased for payment, or if the problem is one of competing with others by giving extended credit. The more the number of days the debtors (receivables) are outstanding, the more is it likely that the channel is running out of cash. In any case, the terms of payment must include a clear assessment of the number of days of credit being given.

The age profile of the debtors, therefore, is an important factor to monitor. If customers are paying promptly, it is a good thing on the one hand, as it could mean that the customers are efficient and profitable, or it could point to inefficient financial management on their part. If the latter, problems may be accumulating only to surface later on. It is vital to recognize what is happening before it is too late. There is a danger that the long overdue debtor can become a bad debt. The nature of this adversity could also mean that the channel member is unable to make payments to the manufacturer.

ANALYSIS OF COST STRUCTURE – THE VALUE CHAIN

An important concept that highlights competition is the 'value chain'. This divides a company's activities into the technologically and economically distinct activities, 'value activities', which it performs to do business. The value a company creates is measured by the amount the buyers are willing to pay for its product or service. A business is profitable if the value it creates is greater than the cost of performing the value activities. To gain competitive advantage over its competitors, a company must either perform these activities more cheaply or in a way that leads to differentiation and earns the ability to change a premium price (i.e. the company's products or services command more value).

A company's value chain is a system of interdependent activities. Linkages exist between these activities when the manner of performing one activity affects the cost/effectiveness of others and creates trade-offs that should be used for optimization. For example, more costly product design and/or raw materials may reduce after-sales service costs. Careful management of trade-offs can be a powerful source of competitive advantage as it is difficult for competitors to copy.

The 'value system' of a company includes the value chains of suppliers and of distributor channels. The product passes through the latter on its way to the ultimate buyer and itself becomes a purchased input to the value chains of its buyers, who use it to perform one or more buyer activities. Linkages occur between the value chains of such a system and can be used to create competitive advantage and savings which can benefit all value chains in the system.

Competitive scope is a powerful tool for creating competitive advantage. It can be broad-based with a co-ordinated national or international strategy or narrow-based to serve particular or unusual needs.

Every value activity has both a physical and an information-processing component, which can be either simple or complex, a different mix being required for each activity. Metal stamping uses mostly physical processing whereas dealing with insurance claims needs just the opposite. Information technology is progressing faster than technologies for physical processing, so that the opportunities widen faster than management can explore them. The number of variables a company can analyze or control has grown dramatically. Information technology is creating new linkages between activities and enhancing a company's ability to exploit such linkages; e.g. by co-ordinating activities more closely with suppliers and buyers or in far-flung locations. The problem of dealing with too much information also means information technology is needed to store and analyse this information for the management. Most products have always had both a physical and an information component.

There is an unmistakable trend towards expanding the information content in products as well as processes. Together with the changes in companies' value chains, this emphasizes the strategic role of information technology; the role and intensity of information will continue to differ in different industries.

The structure of an industry is embodied in competitive forces that collectively determine its profitability:

- the power of buyers/intermediaries
- the power of suppliers/feeders
- the threat of new entrants
- the threat of substitute products
- the rivalry among existing competitors
- the pressure from the investors

- governmental/external influences

Information technology can alter each of these seven components and affect industry attractiveness. It has had an especially strong impact upon the first two. The cost of tailoring products to market segments is falling, affecting the pattern of industry rivalry. Reduction of the personal element has made many service industries less attractive. Management must look carefully at the implications of new technology to realize its advantages and be prepared for its consequences.

In any company, information technology has a powerful effect on competitive advantage in either cost or differentiation. It affects value activities or allows companies to gain competitive advantage by exploiting changes in competitive scope through:

- lower cost
- enhanced differentiation
- change in competitive scope
- spawning new industries

The information revolution is creating inter-relationships between industries that were previously separate. The merging of computer and telecommunications technologies is an important example. This convergence is having a profound effect on the structure of both industries. AT&T used its position in telecommunications as a staging point for entry into the computer industry. IBM, having acquired Rolm, the telecommunications equipment manufacturer, joined the competition from the other direction. Broad-line companies are increasingly able to segment their offerings in ways which were not feasible for them before. Telecommunications can profoundly affect each one of the value activities of a company, sometimes simply by improving effectiveness and sometimes by fundamentally changing the activity. In this process, the value chains of key customers and of competitors may change as well. In this context, the distributor's contribution to the process of value-addition must also be explored.

A CHECKLIST ON COMMERCIAL RISK

When a decision is being taken on selecting a trading partner and getting involved in commercial risk together, it is important to undertake appropriate research into commercial risks and to assess them before the relationship is finalized. Constant monitoring is equally important when the partnership is in existence. The following checklist is taken from a seminar conducted in 1991, by Phillip Day, Director of Finance, Booth & Co and a Director of EMSA.

Research implies making full use of all available sources (including a vital personal visit to discuss business with the prospective distributor), such as:

- credit reference agencies
- statutory returns
- banks
- trade missions
- commercial attachés
- trade associations and Chambers of Commerce
- other suppliers
- insurance brokers/associations
- police
- customer references

Commercial risk assessment is best done by:

- comparison with others in the same industry
- comparison with others among your distributors
- identifying any differences
- explaining the differences
- discussions with the distributor if appropriate
- discussions with your credit manager
- assessment in relation to the business contemplated

It should be recognized that the financial strengths and weaknesses of a distributor will be different from those of a manufacturer.

A decision on taking commercial risks in a specific situation can be 'yes' or 'no' or 'perhaps'.

1. If the decision is 'yes', agree with the distributor on:
   (a) frequency of delivery;
   (b) credit terms – currency value;
   (c) insurance;
   (d) forfaiting.
2. If the decision is 'no', tell the distributor to explore cash alternatives.
3. If the decision is 'perhaps', discuss the matter further with the distributor.
4. Regarding monitoring, agree the following with interested parties:
   (a) the criteria for monitoring;
   (b) frequency of monitoring;
   (c) the internal systems requirements;
   (d) responsibility for monitoring;
   (e) escalation procedures when things go wrong;

(f)   diary of visits and review dates.
5. In avoiding exchange risk:
(a)   determine what risk you are prepared to take;
(b)   define when you are on 'risk';
(c)   quantify the risk elements;
(d)   take action to:
- sell local currency forward;
- 'hedge' receivables in your own country;
- forfait (sell receivables).

A CHECKLIST TO GUARD AGAINST OVERTRADING

Overtrading occurs when a business expands quicker than it can make money. An increase in sales and profits may have happened, but there may also be a disproportionate rise in inventory, receivables and capital expenses, all of which contribute to a drain on the cash resources. The overtrading so caused is also referred to by some bank managers as the dark shadow of the expanding business. In the short term, the working capital cycle may not have been properly managed by the company management. The danger of overtrading in times of high inflation must be guarded against.

Do:

- Set conservative credit limits
- Monitor the settlement profiles
- Guard against sudden order increases
- Talk to the distributor
- Talk to the credit controller
- Recognise the problems that you can cause

Don't:

- Fool yourself – it can happen to you!
- Accept orders without thinking
- Sell without caring if the distributor can pay
- Accept silence as a sign that all is fine
- Ignore the problem after you have recognised it

SELECTION CRITERIA CHECKLIST

- Local presence
- Financial soundness
- Knowledge of the market-place
- Contacts with target customers
- Appropriate reputation in the market
- Shared values and aspirations
- Sales area coverage
- Competitive service skills
- Complementary lines
- Required skills and competence
- Appropriate facilities for inventory, warehousing and transportation
- Motivation to succeed
- Capable of marketing support to the manufacturer
- Capable of discharging the responsibilities
- Appropriate ethical practice
- Necessary leadership qualities.

ICI Fertilizers

(A case study was prepared by John K. Reynolds, Fertilizers Business Manager, and C. J. Murray, 'Bulwark' Project Manager, ICI Fertilizers (1992).)

By the late 1980s, it was evident from the political climate in Europe that pressure was mounting to reform the high cost Common Agricultural Policy, with its resultant overproduction which was also perceived as detrimental to the environment. The prognosis for the British farmer was not good, what with the advent of milk quotas, nitrate-sensitive areas and land-set-aside schemes; they feared it would lead to at best static and at worst declining incomes. All this was a far cry from the post-war agricultural policies of all British governments to produce more food at home for the balance of payment and national security reasons.

Throughout this period ICI Fertilizer (ICIF) business had made enormous contributions to technological advancement in agriculture, with consequent leaps in agricultural productivity, particularly in grass and cereal production. The contribution was based on pure research at Jealotts Hill research station in Berkshire and ICI-owned farms located strategically throughout the United Kingdom. Extension work with commercial farmers from this basic research was undertaken by a large techno/commercial sales team of agricultural graduates. Actual orders for fertilizers were taken by appointed agents, usually agricultural merchants or co-operatives, by means of sales representatives who called at farms, supported by the ICI Fertilizers field force. At the peak of the business, some 450 agents were active in Britain, with a probable combined sales force of 10,000. However, by the late 1980s, the agents usually sold many rival brands and traded in imports and increasingly ICIF's extension and market development work was not sufficiently rewarded. Farmers had less brand loyalty and were often sold inferior cheaper products by agents, who were keener to buy on behalf of farmers than to sell for ICIF.

Agricultural merchants prospered during the 1970s and 1980s; as agriculture expanded its production, it required more inputs and the increased output meant more produce for the merchants to buy from farmers and to trade on to consumers. Many local and regional companies merged or were purchased by international groups, often resulting in merchant sales forces being augmented by feed and chemical specialists, creating a duplication of effort with the ICI Fertilizers sales team on the farms.

However, with the realization of impending changes in the fortunes of farming and intensive intermerchant and intermanufacturer competition, margins were progressively eroded. Inevitably, this led to a review of corporate strategies, resulting in some companies deciding to exit from the agricultural supply sector. The fertilizer industry in Europe was now dominated by Hydro and Kemira, with ICIF being only strong in its home market, but being increasingly challenged there by the other two. ICIF's strategy review at this time concluded that the sales and marketing policy needed careful appraisal with particular emphasis on its channels to the market. The executives formed a project team of ICIF personnel from marketing, sales, logistics and legal departments, code named 'Bulwark'. Its remit was to produce and evaluate options for distribution from the factory to the farm, not only meeting commercial but also product stewardship objectives for the business. Options considered included a larger sales force employed by ICIF selling direct to farmers, modification of the existing agency system or creating a distribution system. Distributors were the preferred option to meet ICIF objectives, providing an extension of the ICIF marketing effort, charged with providing ICIF products and services to their farmer customers, and encompassing the ICIF values of quality, service and product stewardship. Distributors would also be responsible for handling any complaints that might arise from time to time on behalf of ICIF.

Having decided the way ahead it was evident to the project team that it lacked the necessary expertise and experience to formulate a distribution policy, which would meet all reasonable requirements of potential distributors within ICIF's commercial objectives. The author, Vinoo Iyer, as a result of lectures given on a Management Centre Europe course, was recommended by a colleague as a consultant with wide experience of marketing through distributors and expertise gained from working with companies in many industries and markets. It was quickly apparent from the initial briefing, that he had understood the requirements, by his preceptive comments on the agricultural supply industry and its problems.

An outline plan for the project had been developed based on a Gantt chart. This covered every aspect, from preparation of documents, evaluation of potential distributors through to internal communication and final launch. It was immediately recognized that the overall time-scale of July to end of October was only just feasible, since it was now the end of June. It would require highly focused effort and meticulous planning to seize the available window of opportunity. The author recommended that ICIF should produce a 'New Relationship Bible' as the key internal communication medium, with the following format:

1. Introduction
2. Objectives
3. Strategy
4. Benefits of the new relationship
5. The business and sales plans

6. Operation of the relationship
   and how it will work
7. Distributor selection
8. Sales support material/aids
9. Training programme
10. Schedule of activity

The document was produced rapidly by the project manager, after brief discussions with the business manager and the two regional sales managers. It pulled together all the activities to date, together with further proposals, proving to be an invaluable reference for all involved. The author led a series of meetings with the ICI staff who were to be engaged in the negotiations with prospective distributors. The aim was for a clear understanding of all the issues and the real consensus. It is often very helpful to have someone who can stand back and challenge the thinking processes, without getting bogged down in the detail that springs from familiarity. Around twenty people were to be involved directly in the negotiations and it was essential to have a high level of ownership and understanding of the task ahead. The future roles of the ICIF distributors and the ICIF sales force were the central theme.

Essentially ICIF was trying to establish non-exclusive distributorships throughout Great Britain, each with a principal area of operation, but with overlapping territories so that two or three distributors would cover the same area, affording the farmer some choice. The requirement was for the selected distributors to operate a professional sales approach, to promote the ICIF brand and embrace good agricultural practice and product stewardship, with due regard for the environment, health and safety issues. They would be required to provide a suitable level of technical service to farming customers, which would as far as possible replace the service provided previously by the company's own agriculturalists.

A 'war room' was set up with two telephone lines, one being for incoming calls. This was continually manned during the critical period after the launch and an answering machine was provided after the working hours. A simple data base was established in the 'war room' to monitor progress in each area of the country as negotiation started. National information was summarized at the end of each day and sent to key managers. Information was displayed visually so that internal staff who were not immersed in the project could readily see what was happening. Establishing this 'war room' was a key ingredient in the company's success. Staff were only a telephone call away from an immediate update as needed or advice on interpretation of legal issues, parameters for negotiation, etc.

Prior to the launch, 'cornerstones' in each area were identified. These were potential distributors who were regarded as essential to the success of the overall strategy. They were the target for ICIF's initial approaches and soon they provided a critical mass which significantly strengthened the negotiating position. All of the potential distributors had previously been merchants for ICI Fertilizers and it was simply not known how they would react to the proposals. If ICIF had been rejected by the 'cornerstone' distributors, they would have had to consider postponing the project until a later date and to spend some time working with these key distributors. The need for confidentiality had prevented ICIF from testing the ideas with all but a couple of very loyal agricultural merchants.

Regular review meetings were held after the launch to assess the progress of negotiations. Due to delaying tactics by some major merchants who saw such an agreement with ICIF removing some of their power and influence in the fertilizer market, it took some time to get all the agreements settled with a satisfactory mix of merchants in each area. However, the ICIF sales team did succeed after adopting a firm negotiating position. Rather like a general election result, the outcome became predictable with the first round of negotiations. These negotiations were carried out in a structured way, fully supported by briefing materials. The objective of the first visit was to develop an understanding of the implications of the new relationship for both parties. The ICIF negotiating team was certainly not trying to get the new agreement signed at this first meeting.

Any variation in terms between distributors that was not available to all or which could not be justified in terms of logistics savings, etc., was not only illegal but also extremely divisive and the ICIF team refused steadfastly to vary the terms of the proposed distributor agreement despite considerable pressure.

After the agreement was signed, the next step was to engage the ICIF sales force in developing individual distributor marketing plans for the coming year. They were developed using a 'skeleton plan' as the basis; this plan had been prepared prior to the launch.

Apart from the value of the 'New Relationship Bible' and the 'war room', the ICIF team identified a number of key factors which helped in the success of this project:

1. The commercial implications of change had to be fully understood so that judgements could be made.
2. It was necessary to assemble a data base of information on each prospective or potential distributor, including sales volumes, payment record, number of sales staff, etc.
3. Legal people were required to be involved at an early stage to help prepare distributor agreements and vet proposals, including outline (skeleton) distributor sales and marketing plans.
4. An agency (Plimsoll Publishing) was used to look at the financial viability/ structure and likely developments for each company that was to be considered.
5. ICIF seized the opportunity to change the basis of trading in favour of payment by direct debit or credit transfer. This was very successful and helped the company to eliminate overdue accounts. The incentive provided in the distributor plan for change to this method of payment was well worth the outlay.
6. It was easy to underestimate the strength of the company's negotiating base. The team was rewarded for being firm without being unreasonable.
7. Effective selection criteria which were as objective as possible were developed. Financial viability was most important. Effectiveness in the market and willingness to develop a strategic customer/supplier relationship in which both worked for the benefit of the other, were 'second equal'. Other criteria for selection were made more objective by constructing an assessment questionnaire which was answered by the company's own staff and also by end-users, relating to each potential distributor. By providing 'yes/no' answers to a large number of indivi-

dual questions, a comprehensive picture of each company could be built up.

8. All staff, particularly the senior managers, needed to understand the implications of the EC legislation. Advice from counsel had to be sought on the essence of the proposals **before** starting to prepare documentation. Any necessary modifications were resubmitted. Such modifications could take several months to complete, given the speed of the legal profession!

9. A document such as the 'New Relationship Bible' could not be written by a committee. It was best done by someone who had a deep understanding of the business and its markets, in consultation with key managers.

9 ESTABLISHING A GOOD RELATIONSHIP

A good relationship between a producer/manufacturer/supplier and the distributor organization cannot be established unless the two organizations and their key people share common values and goals. The two organizations must also appreciate the requirements of the legal systems under which they operate, what can and cannot be done legally, morally and ethically, and have a full understanding of the cultures of the countries and peoples concerned. This chapter deals with these important aspects and lists some significant points to be taken into account.

NEED FOR SHARED VALUES AND GOALS

A distribution system consists of inter-related and interdependent members working together to achieve satisfaction of a customer need on the one hand and satisfactory rewards for all the participants including the producer of the product designed to meet that need on the other. Each channel has limits, geographic, economic and human, as well as constraints imposed externally because of other channel members, the market or the larger environment. The channel evolves through adapting to these multiple factors. A systems theory framework has been proposed by Morris and Sirgy[1] for understanding the life cycle of channel members and systems, and can be summarized as follows:

1. A channel member is more likely to adapt and grow if:
   (a) it understands its role and objectives in terms of the channel network and especially in the context of the influence of the dominant channel member;
   (b) it keeps a close watch on environmental changes which may affect its role and is capable of changing when there are significant gaps between expectations and results;
   (c) it adjusts its expectations realistically when these gaps persist despite repeated action in an effort to bridge them.

2. A channel system is more likely to adapt and grow if:
    (a) its members behave in co-ordination with each other in a controlled way;
    (b) it can hold a balance between the internal and external expectations concerning its channel members;
    (c) its market performance is good and hence its channel members are satisfied.

Channel systems that are vertically integrated can influence their environment more but are less responsive to outside changes; conversely, non-integrated systems have less external influence but can respond more positively to environmental demands.

Good and understanding distributors and agents can contribute to the success of a product through their commitment. The Harris Corporation succeeded in short-wave radio products mainly because of the quality of the channel members and their commitment to the Harris product. Of course, the product was designed and priced to be competitive in the target market and the compensation available to the channel member was 15 per cent higher than that of the competition.

ESTABLISHING THE RELATIONSHIP

Effective trade marketing

Vertical marketing system
An ordinary distribution channel comprises one or more manufacturers of products, wholesalers and retailers, each being a separate business operating to maximize its profits even if this means reduction of profits for the channel as a whole. A vertical marketing system, on the other hand, consists of manufacturer, wholesalers and retailers all operating as a unified system, because one member owns or controls the others. They are becoming more common in the consumer goods sector in the interest of better control and greater efficiency.

When it is an administered system, there is a dominant entity or entities in the system which 'administer' it either completely or partially to their own advantage and that of the other members of the system. The idea is to minimize the costs through interchannel organization and joint strategies. While the members of the channel are independent, they agree to the system for the benefits which it brings them. American Airlines offers their agents a comprehensive system which automates their book-keeping, displays information regarding flights, makes reservations and prints tickets and itineraries. This has gained them a substantial market share. Kraft, who are a large market force in the dairies field, developed facilities management programmes which help to allocate space in supermarkets for dairy products.

In order to initiate such a system, it is necessary to convince the channel members that the aspiring 'administrator' can be trusted and is more knowledgeable than themselves. A new approach has been programmed merchandising plans for each different type of sales outlet. For this, co-operation in developing merchandising plans is needed. Some companies have successfully transferred this concept to the logistics field.

In a corporate system, one entity owns and operates all distribution levels in the channel system. If the dominant entity either franchises or licenses other channel members to use its products, trade marks, etc., then it is a contractual system. Different variations of this type are voluntary chains, where independent retailers can join the system originating with the wholesaler; co-operative chains are wholesaling companies owned by the retailers they serve; while manufacturer-sponsored franchises generally operate on the basis of exclusive territories for the franchisee dealers, in the field of soft drinks, for example.

A corporate system can come into being when a manufacturer decides to establish its own sales centres or wholesale outlets, or when retailers/ wholesalers integrate backwards. Such systems are organized for efficient division of labour within the structure, with commitment to the same objectives. It is possible for such a system to gain the power to manipulate the market. Achievement of scale economies is the most common reason for the existence of corporate marketing systems. Since their distribution is concerned with a broad range of products, the corporation is required to deal in them and control them. This, in itself, leads in time to diversity of objectives and interests among the members. The system can become unwieldy and suffer from the common defects of such organizations.

Multichannel marketing systems
These occur when a company uses two or more distribution channels to reach its customers, in one or more market segments. For example, a company may sell through wholesalers and through its own outlets at the same time, thus creating competition between retailers served by the wholesalers and its own outlets. If there is a clash, the channels may need to be placated by offering them rewards.

There may also be cases where the multimarketer's channels are all self-owned and controlled. Here the conflict will be mainly internal.

The change process
Effective trade marketing becomes even more necessary when circum-

stances are changing. The internal forces that cause changes to take place are:

- total quality/supply chain management
- pressure for cost-cutting and lessening of friction
- the increasing importance of account management
- the focus on increasing profits instead of on increasing sales
- lack of balance in information
- requirement of long term promotional cycle

The external forces causing change are:

- the increasing concentration of power in distributive trade
- the need for ever more complex segmenting and positioning
- retail selling on broader fronts
- advances in technology
- increased demand for professionalism
- the wish for long term, stable and profitable partnerships

Bond-building

The wish for long term, stable and mutually profitable relationships with distributors leads to examination of ways of cementing the ties, such as:

- creation of trust
- erection of exit barriers
- erection of entry barriers
- helping to fulfil consumer objectives

The effectiveness of these methods will vary according to the industry, markets, cultures, companies, etc. They have to be considered in relation to the prevailing circumstances.

Creation of trust can be effected through:

- distributor visits to factory head-office
- entertainment
- regular contact, eg newsletters, visits
- events promoted for trade
- fulfilment of promises
- open communication
- joint problem consideration and solution
- involvement of top management
- flexibility on rules and regulations

The following can act as exit barriers:

- custom/habit
- over-riders
- technical support
- procedures for resolution of problems
- a club for customers
- loan arrangements
- past investments
- distributor staff training
- formal contractual agreement
- spread of 'family' culture
- financial assistance

Custom or habit is a weak barrier; the next three are somewhat better; the last three are strong and the others are moderately influential.

Possible entry barriers are:

- low price
- superior product quality
- electronic linkage between channel partners
- regular scenario building
- building a strong network of channel relationships
- performance-based reward structure
- co-operation in long term planning
- co-operation in innovation

These vary from the first two which are fairly weak barriers to the three middle ones which are moderately effective, and the last three which are the most effective.

Contribution to fulfilling customer objectives can be made through:

- the sales force working for the customers
- market communications jointly planned and executed
- support in business management
- project teams drawn from both manufacturer and customer teams

The last two methods are more effective than the other two; all these methods are better as a whole at bond building than those in the other three categories.

The reason for building bonds is to ensure strong, trusting and long-lasting relationships between the channel partners.

Problems in establishing and managing international marketing channels

It is necessary for a marketing manager to be aware of the problems that are likely to be faced in the initiation of international trade in order to plan accordingly. The first difficulty is in finding the 'intermediaries', although several directories now exist to help in this task. After finding them, rigorous criteria have to be applied to:

- their financial strength
- their connections
- the businesses represented
- the quality of their facilities, personnel, etc.
- the match between skills needed for the product coverage and the skills available within the candidate.

It is all the more necessary to choose very carefully, as many countries have protective legislation to make it difficult to terminate the relationship easily in case of difficulties. The trading practices, the economic structure and cultural conditions of the host country can impose constraints on available channels. The resources necessary for advertising and promotion have to be larger in proportion, as the number of intermediaries to be reached may be large. Those in less developed countries, small intermediaries in particular, are not keen on innovation or on holding large inventories, owing to the risk involved and the capital investment or the effort needed. Motivating foreign distributors can be difficult. Financial motivation may not work in certain cultural conditions. It is essential that the international marketer exercise some form of control over the foreign channel members. Existing arrangements between industry and intermediaries can restrict or block access to certain markets.

All these difficulties and many more account for the increase in integration into manufacturing by intermediaries and into wholesaling and retailing by manufacturers. This in turn forms new financial barriers for new entrants into international trade.

Difficulties can be encountered in foreign markets, if the market background is not sufficiently researched. The French consumers rely heavily on their 'parfumiers' for opinions on cosmetics. These people are small retailers who specialize in cosmetics and French manufacturers traditionally grant exclusive distribution to a few of them. When a foreign manufacturer of cosmetics tried to distribute only through chain stores, so that the various costs could thereby be minimized, the parfumiers discredited its products and damaged its reputation and sales all over France.

CONFORMITY WITH SALES POLICY

As described in Chapter 7, the Statement of Sales Policy sets forth the policies of the business and is issued to the other channel members stating the company's trading methods and the specific commercial aspects concerning the sales of the company's products. It should clearly define a distributor, including the basic qualifications they must possess, such as skills reputation, inventory to be carried, delivery requirements and so on, and the methods of distribution. The products to be so distributed should be clearly defined together with the prices to be charged, discounts offered, terms of payment, performance criteria and warranty terms. A distributor must be able to conform to the sales policy.

CONFORMITY WITH COMPETITION AND RESALE LAWS

In some countries there are few or no laws to govern commercial transactions while in many others complex laws exist to do so. It is necessary to familiarize oneself with such laws of any country where the company is hoping to trade. The best way is to employ a very good law firm specializing in commercial and anti-trust laws of that country. There are no straight answers to any questions in this field. In the EC and USA, strict competition laws exist and these have to be observed. Firms with a strong market share must take particular care not to abuse their strong position by imposing conditions on the distributors or by entering into arrangements which infringe competition laws.

Effective organization of marketing channels requires power and this power is restricted by government legislation in many countries. Some of these laws restrain the use of the 'carrot-and-stick' method or coercive powers. Other laws may restrict vertical integration or other devices which reduce competition.

Resale price maintenance by a supplier specifies the limits, upper and lower, beyond which resellers, usually wholesalers and retailers, may not sell its products. It is 'analogous in motivation and effect to vertical territorial restrictions'. On the other hand, Posner[2] says

resale price maintenance is more flexible than exclusive territories as a method of limiting price competition among dealers and may be the only feasible method where effective retail distribution requires that dealers be located close to one another; any arguments that are available to justify exclusive territories are equally available to justify resale price maintenance.

Despite this opinion, price-fixing, whether maximum or minimum prices are set, is still illegal in the EC, USA and in many other countries.

STRATEGIC FOCUS

The following steps help to implement the chosen strategic focus.

1. A joint campaign should be planned by the manufacturer and the channel operator.
2. It is important to establish the channel operator's perception of the target market and its potential.
3. This potential must be corroborated through independent research by the manufacturer. An easy way is to engage business school students who are working on in-between semester projects for nominal payments.
4. The target volume from the top 20 per cent clients who yield 80 per cent of the business must be sought from the channel operator as also for each of the clients the target volume sales which can be reasonably expected in the planning year. The remaining 20 per cent must be estimated.
5. Establish whether this business level is viable and economic from the manufacturer's point of view; if not, renegotiate the volumes.
6. Establish the price at which the manufacturer supplies to the channel operator, making sure that the latter can make adequate profit.
7. This needs to be followed up by establishing what type and level of sales force would have to be engaged by the channel operator, the type and amount of training needed, e.g. product, sales, the support that would be required from the manufacturer and what promotional tasks would be undertaken by both parties.
8. The carrying out of the foregoing must result in a beneficial financial situation for both partners. Motivation must start from this point.

MANAGEMENT STRUCTURE

Relationship: close or detached

If the channel is an associated company or subsidiary, a close relationship can be developed with the chain of management in the hands of personnel belonging to the company. However, the staff at headquarters may be remote and answerable to a level of management which is not directly in control of the subsidiaries or associated companies. It is very important to have staff who have successful experience of the management of subsidiary or associated company operations and who therefore possess credibility when offering guidance or advice on channel matters. A suitable supporting marketing organization should be in place to lend credibility and weight to the link person. As regards international or export sales, there are often differences of opinion as to how the organization should be developed. The marketing and distribution views within an organization can be different. Some alternative views exist in companies as per Figs. 9.1 to 9.4. In the author's opinion, an effective organization would be a combination based on Figs. 9.2 and 9.4.

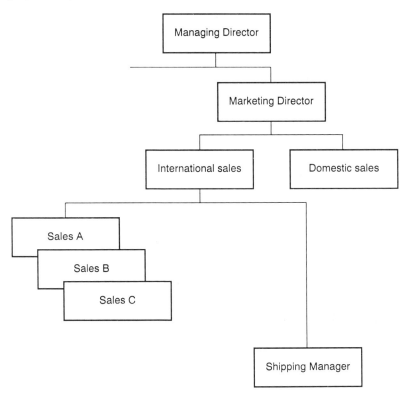

Figure 9.1 Marketing view 1

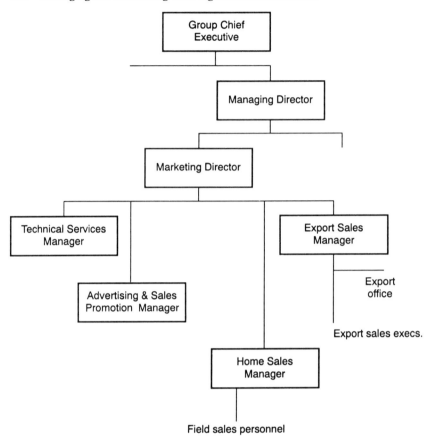

Figure 9.2 Marketing view 2

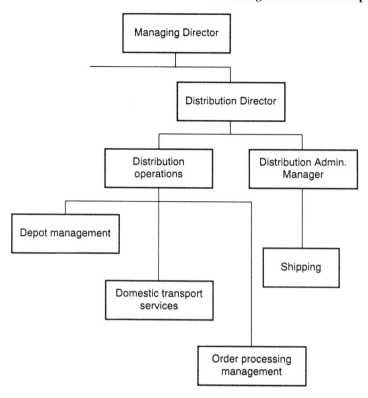

Figure 9.3   Distribution view

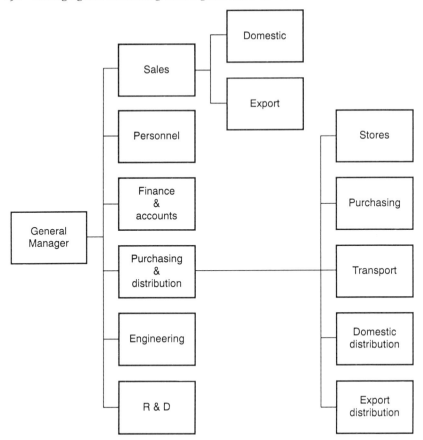

Figure 9.4 Commercial view

Any policies from the centre must also carry with them an inherent authority through experience and credibility. To ensure that this is so, policies and directives with regard to the channel are best worked out in co-operation with selected personnel at key levels from the channel, with people selected having the requisite credibility.

For instance, a channel member who is a distributor, is an independent entity. The relationship has to be developed on the basis of personal contacts and through interpersonal relationships on the one hand and on a legal/business framework on the other. A successful relationship can only result from mutual trust and leadership, through the knowledge and experience of both parties, and a tacit belief in their interdependence. The relationship with a distributor has to be based on the kind of 'partners-in-business' principle and the principle of 'mutuality'.

Managing interdependence

The channel members tend to specialize. Their roles are unique in some instances; manufacturers specialize in design, production, global marketing, national and international promotion, etc.; distributors who may be wholesalers or retailers tend to specialize in merchandising, personal selling, distribution, local promotions, among other things. This, naturally leads to operational interdependence among the channel members, arising because of the need for resources – money, people, skills and access to markets. Co-operation among channel members is essential in that the members need to find the means to undertake the necessary planning, exchange of information, sharing of the operational tasks and decision-making. The reward structure needs to be arranged in a mutually satisfactory manner so that each member can justify achieving the common goals on their own criteria.

Independent organizations wish to maintain their autonomy and this of necessity may lead to strain and sometimes to conflict. Managing interdependence requires some means of resolving conflict.

When a new distributor has been signed up, the following steps should be taken:

1. Send a notice of the fact, drafted jointly, to a combined list of customers.
2. Introductory training should be arranged for the distributor's staff on how to use the price lists, catalogues and samples supplied by the manufacturer; these items should be already prepared. All distributor staff assigned to sales and support should be trained adequately.
3. Provide past sales data to the distributor so that the business trends can be traced with regard to different customers and the sales campaign can be planned after considering their own data.
4. Any negotiations with common customers which are pending should be discussed with the distributor so that no time is lost during the changeover.
5. A written statement concerning the commission to be expected on the various deals should be available to the distributor.
6. While a preliminary objective is necessary for a manufacturer to set targets for the market, many distributors will hesitate to name a figure without more experience of the product line. It is better to ask for an educated guess without holding the distributor to it and to allow for overoptimism.
7. The form should be sent for the distributor's signature at the earliest possible time.
8. Distributors should know which person to apply to for what purpose and also who to appeal to in difficulty.

9. Joint calls are a good way to introduce a new distributor to your company products and methods.
10. Factory visits should be made at the time when the distributor wishes for them to help with the learning process.
11. Make sure all your distributors know about the new member and vice versa, through written communication; keep in constant touch during the early phases.
12. Acknowledgements of good performance and praise should not be stinted at any time.

The manufacturer must know what can be expected from the distributors and also what they expect in return. At the beginning of the relationship, the distributor expects to receive good vibrations regarding:

- the manufacturer's image and reputation with the customers
- the manufacturer's relationships with previous distributors
- the allotted commission
- the 'fit' of the products with the distributor's general line of trade
- basically, how well the personalities making the deal fit together.

Later, the reasons for the distributor's continuing commitment will be somewhat different, depending mainly on the profits that are expected to be made and the prestige, comfort or otherwise derived from the relationship. Distributors expect the manufacturer to take an interest in their main concerns and also to provide:

- marketing support, e.g. market research, A&P
- positive response to customers
- confidence that promises made will be kept
- new product development to supplement established product lines
- a commission policy which is fair for the industry concerned
- prompt and professional dealing in all matters regarding payments or commissions
- a sense of partnership
- a positive response to suggestions
- dependable support
- prompt action for correction of defects
- copies of all customer communications.

For instance, Nestlé issue a monthly magazine called *Communication Marketing* from their head office in Switzerland which has details of new products developed by its companies throughout the world.

In return, apart from the sale, the manufacturer should receive the following from the distributors:

- customer feedback
- advice on marketing in their territory
- answers to questions on market performance within reasonable time
- a fair share of time and selling effort
- a reasonable market share within a reasonable period
- investment in promoting the products
- refraining from selling competing products, especially if the distributor has been appointed on an exclusive basis
- prompt information regarding changes in key personnel
- a professional attitude to the relationship
- staff time for product training
- some assistance in the solution of joint problems.

Distributors tend to react negatively to long drawn out problems with the manufacturer, expectations of unethical conduct, bureaucratic demands, demands for instant response, a bossy attitude on part of the manufacturer, too much pioneering effort without adequate reward and requests for uneconomic services.

CULTURE PLAYS AN IMPORTANT PART

Culture has been defined as the total communication system including words, actions, postures, gestures, tones of voice, facial expressions, ways of handling time, space and materials, and ways of working, playing, sexual acts and defence. Culture also includes the conscious and unconscious values, ideas and attitudes that shape human behaviour and which are passed on from one generation to the next.

The cultural system of any people can only be understood fully when the person concerned is familiar with the history, society and culture of the people. If you are insensitive to an important aspect of the culture of the person you are dealing with, everything else about the relationship will be affected. Culture is built up as a consequence of learned responses to recurring situations. Eating habits, taste, preference for colours, attitudes to products, e.g. a disposable item, all are acquired through learning. All of these have an impact on the international marketing environment.

Some attitudes are universally applicable, e.g. music as an art form is part of all cultures. But music in the form of a 'commercial' is not universal. Through travel and communication, some attitudes are becoming international and perhaps universal. In understanding cultures, it is often helpful to apply Maslow's hierarchy of needs.

Misunderstandings are probable when two cultures meet; knowledge of one another's cultures will help to avoid them. A negotiator can create a favourable impression through such knowledge and gain advantages in negotiation. It is difficult for an international marketer, who moves from country to country marketing his goods, to be familiar with every culture that is met. The sales staff, however, who concentrate on one country for a period, have opportunities of assimilating the local culture during that period.

When a company has subsidiaries in other countries, it comes across problems of cross-communication. If the managers are sent out from headquarters, there are problems in communications between them and the local connections; if the managers are locally recruited, then problems exist in communications between them and headquarters. There also exist the problems caused by the subsidiary 'company' culture. Education modifies cultural responses and creates another dimension to these problems.

Where distributors are involved, the link persons and other personnel in a manufacturer's organization must remember that cultural insensitivity, arising from being wedded to one's own office culture and working practices, and lack of appreciation of the kind of problems faced by an entrepreneurial distributor can lead to an undoing of established good relationships. In many countries, distributor organizations live in an uncertain world where cost pressures and small volume demand can play havoc with retention of their existing business. The scale of their operation may not in any way compare with those of a manufacturer. Under difficult economic conditions, they may be forced to look for a product mix beyond that supplied by established manufacturers. Such distributors need careful handling.

Sometimes distributors feel that they are not treated by manufacturers as important customers; this can arise from a not uncommon view held in some companies that the distributors' role is mainly to sell the company's products. It must be remembered that if the distributors are treated as valuable customers and given adequate information on time, they in turn may treat their customers well and with the necessary degree of importance. This point was recently confirmed by Mike Eldon, the general manager of a distribution company in Kenya.

Language

Languages relate to the culture they originate in. Therefore they have distinctive vocabularies. It is also necessary to study the culture of the people whose language is being learnt. For example, flat tones and pauses between sentences can mean different things in different cultures and can be misinterpreted by people from another culture. The best way to overcome a language barrier is to learn to talk the language fluently. Most people will welcome a foreigner who tries to speak their language, however incorrectly. There are exceptions to this rule, like the French who dislike inaccurate use of their language.

Expressions and style

Within every culture, there is a wide range of permitted visual expressions and it is worthwhile learning to recognize them. For successful communication, the two parties have to adapt to each other's styles; otherwise the communication cannot be co-ordinated.

Edward Hall[3] has drawn a distinction between what he calls high context cultures, which depend heavily on non-verbal communication signals, and low context cultures, which depend more on verbal communication. While arguments are often expressed in terms of war in the Anglo-American culture, in Sweden, which has been neutral over many decades, consensus is preferred to confrontation. Broadly, interpersonal communication can be considered to include all activities which keep the negotiation going, regulate the interactions, help with the comprehension of messages or relate the context to the issues involved.

National differences

Every market goes through the standard adoption process before accepting any new product or idea: awareness, interest, evaluation, trial and adoption. Every innovative idea has to be examined for its cultural impact in terms of relative advantage, compatibility, complexity, partial or limited usage and communicability.

In establishing the perception of the market needs in a particular culture, it is necessary to fight against the cultural value judgement made by an unconscious reference to what James Lee[4] calls the 'self-reference criterion' (SRC). He tackles this issue by a systematic four-step approach:

1. Define the issue in terms of home country's cultural traits, habits and norms.
2. Define the issue in terms of the foreign country's cultural traits, habits and norms.
3. Isolate the SRC influence and examine the issue for any complication.
4. Redefine the issue without the influence of SRC and solve it for the relevant market.

In some European countries, like Germany and Italy, it is customary to overstate one's case; in Britain and in Scandinavian countries, the opposite is the case. Power relations usually decide who adapts to whom and they generally depend on the territory in which the negotiations are taking place. For example, in Scandinavian countries, it is necessary to remember that their culture firmly embodies concern for consensus. In the context of leaders and subordinates, initiatives by subordinates are welcomed in Scandinavia and the relations are sufficiently relaxed so that a subordinate will not resent the negotiator trying to go over his head to a superior. Some cultures, such as Swedish or Australian, do not encourage verbal self-presentation. Arabian culture, on the other hand, finds it acceptable behaviour.

Cultures broadly divide into high context or low context ones. Japan and the Arab countries are examples of the former. The position you occupy and the values you hold are vital in the high context cultures. In a low context culture such as Swiss–German or Anglo–American, explicit messages count, i.e. words carry messages. Other examples of cultural traits are given below.

High context culture

1. Everything in life must be dealt with in its own time.
2. Decisions are taken at the highest level.
3. A major purpose of negotiations is to allow all the people to get to know each other well. Negotiations are lengthy.
4. Competitive bids are infrequent.
5. A person's word is their bond.
6. Lawyers are very important.

Low context culture

1. Time is money.
2. Everything needs to be tackled in a linear order.
3. Decisions are pushed down to the lowest level.
4. Negotiations are conducted comparatively quickly.
5. Competitive bids are common.
6. A person's word is not taken for granted – it needs to be written down.

Negotiation

Successful negotiation in business requires:

- an awareness of the process of negotiation
- understanding and use of ways of influencing behaviour
- empathy for other cultures.

There exist various methods of cultural assessment which will help a negotiator in a foreign country. Some level of understanding of cultural differences and how they can interact is vital to success in negotiations.

Communications between citizens of different countries can break down owing to differences in expectations which arise from cultural differences. It is worthwhile studying the issues as seen from the point of view of the people being communicated with. Just negotiating towards set goals, such as higher profits, could bring problems in the future, if not in the present.

Negotiation often involves deception. In order to be successful, a negotiator should be able to recognize deception in others. As Desmond Morris says, to lie successfully, it is necessary to involve the whole body in the lying process; otherwise, the other party can recognize the lie via common body signals.

Trust is necessary in negotiations and therefore it is essential that the negotiators familiarize themselves with each other's cultures. They have to gauge each other's attributes, preferences and intentions in order to deal with each other. Interpretation of body signals is useful in this activity.

Personal relationships/personal ties are far more important in international business arrangements than mere contracts/legal considerations. Mutually beneficial trust between and empathy with business contacts are essential in international marketing. Most carefully prepared plans can go wrong, as there are many events/situations which can develop and which defy prediction, e.g. natural catastrophes, political problems, depressions, widely fluctuating exchange rates, changes in economic priorities.

PERFORMANCE EXPECTATIONS

General measures of performance

In a business situation, it should be possible to conduct a research into the sort of performance measures by which a business unit can be monitored for effectiveness and efficiency. Effectiveness is often made up of two elements:

(a) deliverables related to what the end-users demand of the channel members and
(b) stimulation of the latent demand.

Efficiency is characterized by

(a) productivity of the resources employed in generating and satisfying the demand for products and services, and
(b) profitability in terms of return on investment, growth of profits, etc.

In essence, productivity is a measure of physical efficiency and profitability is a measure of financial efficiency. Besides effectiveness and efficiency, equity is also cited as another important factor. This measures the extent to which channel members serve the disadvantaged or isolated customer groups such as disabled people or residents of remote/inaccessible geographic territory.

Performance criteria

The following variables, measured over a certain period, can give a proper quantitative assessment of distributor performance:

1. Number of new customers in the period
2. Number of new markets entered
3. Sales value in the period
4. Number of units sold
5. Size of orders
6. Number of deliveries made on time
7. Number of short deliveries made
8. Number of customer complaints
9. Accuracy of sales forecasts
10. Number of errors in order filling
11. Size of discount offered
12. Business gained from competition
13. Business lost to competition
14. Number of customers lost to competition
15. Number of customers gained from competition
16. Per cent of stockout units
17. Per cent of obsolete inventories
18. Per cent of bad debts
19. Number of customers paying on time
20. Unit warehousing cost
21. Unit distribution cost
22. Unit transportation cost
23. Other costs per unit

In a similar manner, certain qualitative measures can also help to assess the performance of a distributor:

24. Willingness to plan campaigns jointly with supplier
25. Ability to plan
    (a) business strategy
    (b) new initiatives
    (c) annual profit budgets
26. Ability to set

    (a)   sales quotas
    (b)   merchandising policy
    (c)   credit policy
    (d)   direct product profit targets

27. Degree of
    (a)   administration
    (b)   sales co-ordination
    (c)   product delivery co-ordination
    (d)   flexibility in dealing with market situation

28. Recognition of
    (a)   the supplier's goals
    (b)   the role of the distributor

29. Availability of information about:
    (a)   physical inventory
    (b)   product characteristics
    (c)   pricing
    (d)   sales promotion aids
    (e)   personal selling
    (f)   advertising and displays
    (g)   market conditions
    (h)   competition

30. Ability to keep up with new technology and to adapt distribution methods accordingly

31. Liaison with trade associations and consumer groups

32. The most important financial measures are:
    (a)   sales revenue (absolute level)
    (b)   profit generated (absolute level)
    (c)   return on investment %

The other measures can be ratio-orientated:

Net profits/Net sales (%)   This is what margin management is all about.

$\times$

Net sales/Total assets   A measure of asset management skills.

$\times$

Total assets/Net worth   Use of leverage.

$=$

Net profits/Net worth (%)   Return on net worth of the firm.

The financial ratios can also be viewed as a total system using a DuPont chart.

References

[1] Morris, M. and Sirgy, M. J., Applications of general systems theory concepts to marketing channels, *Educators Conference Proceedings 1985*, American Marketing Association, Chicago, 1985.

[2] Posner, Richard A. The next step in the antitrust treatment of restricted distribution, *University of Chicago Law Review*, Vol. 48, pp. 6–26, 1981.

[3] Hall, Edward T. Beyond Culture, Anchor Press/Doubleday, 1976

[4] Lee, James A. Cultural analysis in overseas operations, *Harvard Business Review*, March/April, 1966.

10 MANAGING AND MOTIVATING THE DISTRIBUTOR

In the previous chapter, various aspects were identified for establishing a good relationship and for making sure that both parties understood what was expected of each other. In this chapter, we consider the important task of ensuring that the relationship is maintained at the desired level and that the motivation to pursue the common shared goals remains at the level necessary for both parties to succeed.

THE VISION, MISSION AND OBJECTIVES

Channel objectives determine channel strategy. Making a major change in an established channel structure is difficult and often risky. Therefore it is desirable to set up the objectives properly in the first place. They should be dictated by the service level output which is desired by the ultimate consumer and the global vision and mission of the company in terms of long term return on investment, market share, absolute level of profits to be achieved and sales growth.

The specific objectives of any channel, apart from the global aspirations of the company, should be firmly based on the service outputs demanded by its customers. Different levels of these outputs may be required in different segments of the market and these need to be determined. The use of multiple channels catering for different segments of the market is common in marketing today.

Once the service levels are decided upon, then the market coverage needed has to be determined. This in turn determines the support which can be expected from the channel in the event of different coverage strategies. Here the company should also decide whether it needs to own the entire channel or parts of it and what the costs of full and part ownership are going to be in terms of possible consequences.

Three choices are possible: intensive, selective or exclusive distribution. These have been described already in Chapter 2 in the context of a distributor channel strategy. It is worth mentioning in this context that they are all possible in case of vertical or non-vertical integration although the costs may be prohibitive in case of full ownership of a channel specializing in intensive distribution.

Intensive distribution is generally used for products which are frequently bought and which need to be easily available, like newspapers and sweets. Selective distribution is usual for products which buyers like to choose with some effort, e.g. clothing. This type of distribution can range from expensive items which are almost exclusive, to items like cosmetics which are almost intensively distributed. Exclusive distribution implies a mutually dependent relationship between seller and re-seller and is used for large or expensive items such as farm machinery or very expensive clothes or jewellery.

It is appropriate to check and verify that the strategy adopted is in line with current circumstances when considering how to motivate a channel member. The channel structure and the type of distribution are also interdependent to some degree. A 'long' channel structure which possesses many intermediate wholesalers allows for greater spread and therefore more intensive distribution. Conversely, a 'short' structure has more direct channels and tends towards exclusive distribution.

It is obvious that the more intensive the distribution, the greater the sales in the short term. However, over a long term, adverse effects such as lower margins appear, followed by unwillingness on the part of the distributors to sell the product, consequent necessity of an increase in promotional efforts by the manufacturer and deterioration of the service levels. As a business executive once remarked 'you can take fifty years to build a brand and you can ruin it in three years through careless distribution'.

However, intensive distribution is successfully followed in the case of innumerable products through a well-formulated marketing programme which fulfils the requirements of distributors and consumers alike. The various factors should be carefully considered before deciding on a distribution strategy, in particular the relation between the products marketed and the last selling point for them.

MOTIVATIONAL TOOLS AND CONTROL AREAS

The following means of persuasion are available to channel members to influence the decision-making or behaviour of others.

1. Rewards: If A possesses some resource which B wishes to obtain and B believes this can be obtained through conforming to A's wishes, this

amounts to reward power. Specific rewards to channel members could include wider margins, granting of exclusive territories and various promotional allowances.

2. Coercion: This exists if B believes that A will punish anyone who does not conform to A's wishes. Coercion amounts to negative sanctions or punishment including reductions in margins, withdrawals of rewards granted earlier and slowing down of shipments. This brings less results over the long term than other tools and should therefore be considered as a last resort.

3. Expertise: This occurs when B perceives A to possess some special knowledge which would help B. Small retailers often rely heavily on their wholesalers for expert advice. However, once transferred, expertise is considerably reduced in power. If a business wishes to retain expertise over a long term, the following options are open to it:

    (a) It can ration its advice to small portions and keep back sufficient vital knowledge so that the others remain dependent upon it. This could be detrimental to efficient working of the channel as every member should work up to its capacity for the channel to function successfully. A member starved of vital information cannot do so.

    (b) A better though somewhat expensive option is to collect accurate information regarding market trends, threats and opportunities, and other ongoing matters which individual channel members would find difficult to obtain themselves. The benefits of this option can be high in terms of channel goal achievements.

    (c) Another way is for channel members to invest in specialized transaction expertise which is difficult to transfer to other products or services and so hinders the members from leaving the channel.

    (d) The ability of a channel member to acquire information which is necessary for another channel member to function efficiently confers power on the acquirer. For example, retailers hold a privileged position with respect to manufacturers because of their close customer contacts.

4. Identification: This occurs when B identifies with A or desires to do so. For example, given equal returns from two different dealerships, one may well choose that which one would like to identify with, perhaps the more prestigious one. Here the company reputation or image confers an advantage on the business.

5. Legitimacy: Results from B feeling that A has the right to exercise power over them. This would be the case between workers and their supervisor, for example. In a channel relationship, such a power may be assigned to the largest firm. Or the retailers and industrial suppliers may believe that they have the power since they are in contact with the

end-users and the others are not. However, the amount of power thus exerted is usually small.

In real life situations, all these powers are used simultaneously in most situations. Sometimes, the use of one power may enhance another power base; or the opposite may happen. Environmental conditions and the effect of such a use of power on them must also be considered in this situation. The norms of the channel systems also prohibit the use of some of these powers.

The degree of success that a channel member will have in influencing the behaviour of other channel members will depend on its leadership behaviour. When the channel members have common goals, the use of information exchange and/or recommendations will probably produce positive results. In other situations, promises, threats, legalistic strategies and requests are used with varying success.

An international business manufacturing paints, which is based in Italy, has the policy of treating its agents like its own employees. They are required to submit progress reports every month just like the company sales force. All these reports are fed into a computer and analyzed. The company management keeps an eye on the stocks bought by key customers and the price they paid. Any falling off in an agent's performance results in rapid identification of the problem and support provided by a senior staff member on the spot.

Focusing channels onto specific products and target markets – motivation of channel principals and sales force

Ensure that the traditional distributor attitude and priorities are recognized by you and dealt with. Distributors:

- always feel that a high price is charged by the manufacturer
- think that manufacturer's mark-up is high
- think that the manufacturer does not invest in the market

Avoid the traditional manufacturer attitude. The manufacturer:

- is interested in volume sales
- is interested in profits
- wants distributors to make stock investment

How to ensure that a manufacturer's product is majored

Check that the points in Table 10.1 are true.
For mutual benefit the relationship should produce:

- acceptable profit margins to the distributor
- acceptable volume and rate of growth to the manufacturer, at optimum profit margins

Distributor principal has:	*Distributor sales executive has:*
1. Quality product	1. Quality product
2. Reliable delivery dates	2. Reliable delivery dates
3. Fair profit margins	3. Technical information as and when required
4. Good communications, physical and written	4. *Ad hoc* bonuses, e.g. money, travel, trip to manufacturer's head office, etc.
5. Reasonable advertising and sales promotion support	5. Good communications with manufacturer's 'field' representative.
6. Willingness by manufacturer to assist with distributor's general problems	6. Fair evaluation of performance

Table 10.1   Factors affecting the majoring of a manufacturer's product

The manufacturer's 'link person' must try and assist the distributor in upgrading their entire operation. Allow the distributors to consult your financial director; let individual interested distributors have the use of the director's time for a day or two. Run seminars on relevant subjects, e.g. 'modern warehousing'. A distributor should be able to call on the manufacturer's experience when trying to solve any problem relative to their business.

Control systems

First and foremost, a system to establish an annual campaign plan must be introduced. This campaign plan should cover, as a minimum,

- the common goals to be achieved in the first year at least;
- what this would mean realistically in terms of the quarterly volumes of sales to the channel's customers and shipments from the manufacturer;
- the recommended price at which the product would be marketed;
- the price/discounts/terms of trading at which the manufacturer will supply the product;
- what this would mean in terms of market share;
- levels of sales and supporting staff resources to be deployed;
- a schedule of training to be provided by the manufacturer;
- promotional materials, campaigns, etc., to be undertaken by the manufacturer and the channel;

- specific actions to be taken concerning inventory/logistics, etc.;
- key event/action review calendar.

Secondly, regular monitoring and review sessions must be held to ensure that the performance is on course and that if needed, corrective actions are taken on time.

Motivation of the distributor

The link person or manager can do the following to motivate a distributor:

1. Attempt to categorise and understand the distributors' motives in terms of Maslow's hierarchy of needs: security, social needs, esteem, self-fulfilment.
2. Discover their wants as well as their needs; this will help your dealings with them.
3. Remember that monetary rewards serve many needs and are therefore the best rewards.
4. Bear in mind, however, that recognition, praise, promotion and successful achievement of a task can also be effective motivations and are sometimes more needed than money.
5. If people know that good work will earn a reward, this makes the reward more effective. The expectation should be clearly set out on a payment-by-results basis, with an appropriate bonus or commission scheme. Achievable targets and standards should be set. Praise should be bestowed when deserved at not too frequent intervals. The rewards and efforts required should be clarified. The penalties also should be stated, if targets are underachieved or if substandard results are recorded.
6. Paraphrasing what Douglas McGregor said in another context, conditions should be such that the members of the channel system should best achieve their own expectations by working for the success of the channel system as a whole. It is necessary to identify the needs of the members so that appropriate rewards can be devised and to agree targets and standards with all the members.
7. People can be motivated by the work itself if their needs for achievement and responsibility are thereby satisfied. This can result from:
   (a) giving people more responsibility where called for and more scope for variations in methods and speed of work;
   (b) giving groups a unit of work to perform, thus reducing specialization and increasing the sense of achievement and responsibility and the expertise;
   (c) relaxing overhead controls while setting targets and/or standards to make members accountable;

  (d) making available the necessary information so that members can monitor their own performance;

  (e) encouraging the channel members to join in planning and innovation.

8. Try to make sure that the group pressure is working for you by involving the members of the channel in decisions which affect them.

The link person's role can be likened to that of a master of ceremonies, who initiates the use of the available motivational tools, which are listed and illustrated in Figs. 10.1 to 10.4. As explained in Chapter 11, the link persons have to be self-motivated and display enthusiasm for their company, its products and its distributors. It is important that they appear self-confident. Their leadership, management skills and bond-building activities will then be able to play the necessary part in motivating the distributor principal and the sales force.

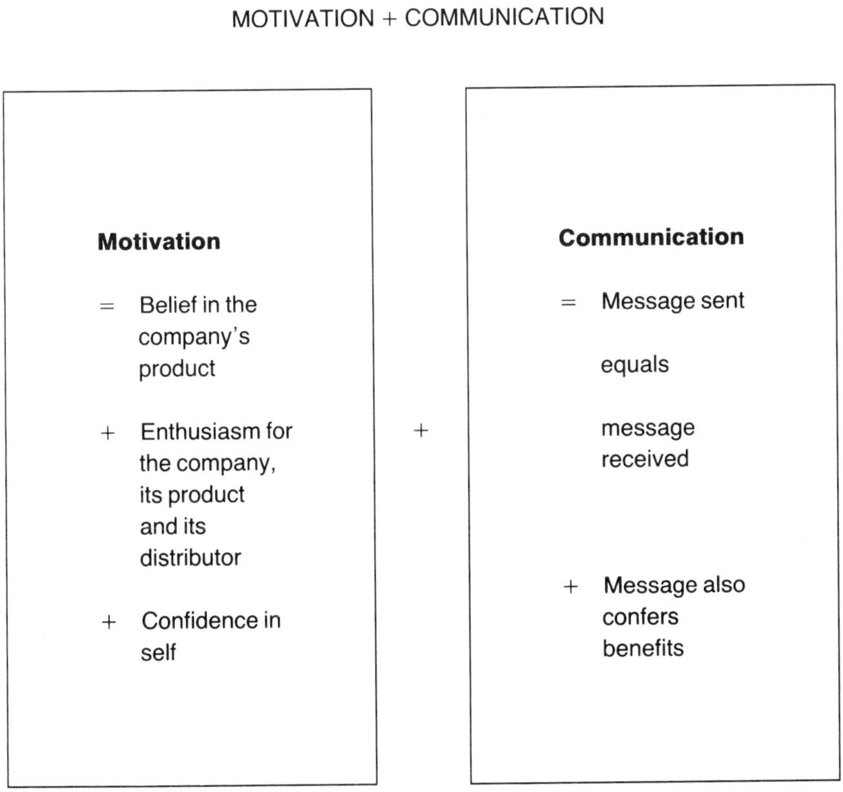

MOTIVATION + COMMUNICATION

Motivation

= Belief in the company's product

+ Enthusiasm for the company, its product and its distributor

+ Confidence in self

+

Communication

= Message sent

   equals

   message received

+ Message also confers benefits

Figure 10.1 The link person–likened to a master of ceremonies

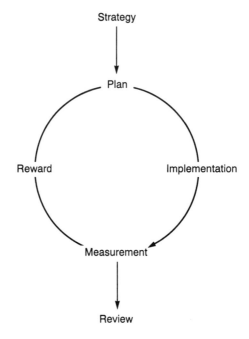

STARTS WITH

Strategy

Plan

Reward

Implementation

Measurement

Review

This process calls for an understanding of the relationship, mutual SWOTs, mutuality of benefits and a commitment to working together for common goals.

- A creation of the right environment – nature, scope and style of operation
- Realistic objective setting, review & control
- Joint development of campaigns

Figure 10.2 Motivation process

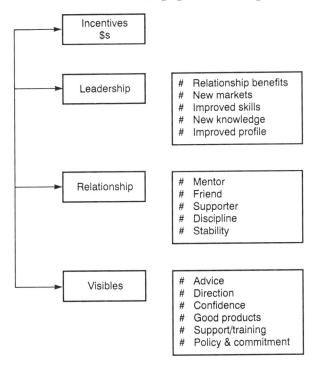

Figure 10.3   Motivational tools for a distributor principal

DISTRIBUTOR SALES FORCE

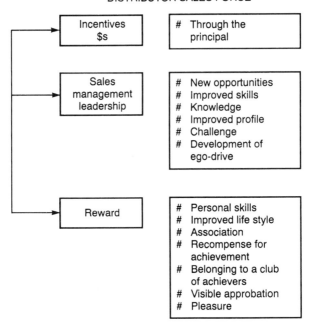

Figure 10.4 Motivational tools for a distributor sales force

Remuneration of the salesperson

Industrial selling

Industrial selling is distinguished from other kinds of selling by 'customer penetration'. As a rule, when distributing a product for resale, the sale is made by a salesperson to the buyer or the merchant acting as their own buyer. Rarely does the sales executive have to 'sell' both the buyer and the owner of the shop, though a smart person makes sure that anyone who sells their product understands its sales points. In industrial selling, however, it may be necessary for the sales executive to persuade several people before walking out with an order. First, the user of the product has to be sufficiently interested to suggest to their immediate supervisor that this particular product be specified when a requisition is next placed; since few workers are capable of effectively relaying a sales presentation, the sales executive must also 'sell' the supervisor. After the supervisor requisitions the product, the matter may go to the works manager or the engineering department for approval, if it is sufficiently important. Again, the salesperson has to make sure that these executives understand the engineering advantages of the product. After being approved by the engineering or operating department, the requisition may travel to the financial controller, who approves the budgetary expenditure and passes it along to the purchasing department.

The buyer or the assistant may or may not issue a purchase order at this point. After checking the price against competition, some similar product may be found which seems 'just as good' and may be cheaper. So, unless the sales executive is on the job, the requisition may travel back to its point of issue to ascertain whether the cheaper product may not be acceptable. This process is quite usual in industrial selling. In the case of equipment involving a considerable outlay of money, it may be necessary to 'sell' several executives and the board of directors. There are usually 'no people' in every organization, who may not actually have much buying authority, but who can, if not otherwise persuaded, wreck the sale.

Remunerating the sales effort

Remuneration of sales executives always provokes a great deal of lively discussion whenever the topic is raised. So it should – it is an important motivational factor as far as the salesforce are concerned. Companies use various methods to calculate the amounts paid to their salesforce, depending on their number or the products they sell or other factors. However, any method of remuneration must be of mutual benefit to both the sales executives and the company employing them; if either party feels that it is not getting a fair deal, then the association will eventually, if not immediately, break down. A sales executive who is dissatisfied with the remuneration, will leave the company. While a company that is unhappy with the salesperson's performance, in view of their total costs, it may discharge him. We will briefly examine the methods of remuneration in current use.

SALARY ONLY

A salary, however high, does not provide the incentive needed for extra effort when it is necessary. This arrangement is preferred by the salesforce when the salary is high,but the cost may be too high for the management to accept. It may be a good idea when large capital plant is being sold, but in that case the selling may well be handled by a senior employee, whose incentive would perhaps be an equity holding in the company.

HIGH BASIC SALARY PLUS BONUS ON TRADING PROFIT

This method is a little better than the previous one from the incentive point of view. But sales executives tend to be impatient people, and they are not usually prepared to wait for a year or so before knowing whether they are going to get a bonus. Therefore the advantage is slight. Also, too many intangible factors affect the bonus payments and many of them are not controlled by the salespeople. While the salesforce in the field may have done extremely well, the orders may be fouled up by a strike in the factory or an extra large payment may be made to a departing chairman, depleting profits; such happenings could cause justifiable dissatisfaction among the salesforce.

COMMISSION ONLY

This can create insecurity, especially with new recruits. If they have family responsibilities, and cannot obtain orders quickly enough, it can create dishonesty, which does not do either party any good in the end. If a company with a wide range of products pays its salesforce on a commission only basis, the sales executive will only sell what they wish to sell and are good at selling. Those products may not be the ones the company wants pushed. A salesperson doing well on a commission only basis can still feel insecure. If the performance is too good, the company may decide to take on someone else, thus effectively reducing their territory and their earnings. This naturally has a dampening effect on their selling capacity. A company cannot effectively control and direct the effort of a sales force paid on a commission-only basis except by harsh measures, which may be undesirable.

LOW RATE OF COMMISSION PLUS A 'LIVEABLE' BASIC SALARY

This method is the most widely used in industrial selling. This is quite satisfactory for a one product or one product range company, but problems appear when the company expands or increases the sales force. The sales executives are not interested in establishing new lines or in the expansion of the company's activities.

CONTINUOUS INCENTIVE BONUS SCHEME

The total remuneration should be made up of a liveable salary and a bonus, in a predetermined ratio, say 80 : 20. The company must have a master plan with its aims and expectations clearly defined. At the beginning of every financial year, the company should set out, in the form of an overall company sales target:

- the total sales target for the next twelve months;
- the target for each salesperson in that achievement;
- the share of the total sales target to be borne by each product range, particularly if a multiplicity of products are to be sold.

It is one of the functions of senior management to determine the target proportions carried by each product range and it is one of the sales executive's major functions to attain those objectives. It is vital that the salesforce sell the product range that makes the highest gross contribution to the company profit. Others may be easier to sell, so incentives should be tied to selling those lines which enhance the bottom line of the business and maximize the return on capital employed, which is the true measure of the company's success. The continuous incentive bonus scheme is designed to inform the salesperson exactly what is required of them in the year ahead and what their rewards will be if the objectives set are attained. This ensures that the goods are sold according to the overall company targets and in the right product range proportions. Every sales executive is given a mutually agreed sales target overall and by product range, and points are allocated to the targets set. For example, over a year a typical profile may be that given in Table 10.2.:

Product range	$	Points
A	40,000	20
B	30,000	15
C	20,000	13
D	20,000	13
E	10,000	10
F	10,000	10
G	10,000	10
General work		9
Total	140,000	100

Table 10.2 Setting sales targets by product range

In this example, nine points are allocated to general work. This covers punctuality, grooming, accuracy of records, etc. The percentage of target achieved, up to a maximum of 100 per cent, but not beyond, will qualify for that percentage of points allocated to the product group target; i.e. 75 per cent achievement of product range A target above qualifies for 75 per cent of twenty points, equal to fifteen points. In the case of general work, points received will be based on the recommendation of senior management.

At the end of the period, the points achieved per product range are added up and a total arrived at. A bonus is then paid according to a previous scale laid down, e.g. (for twelve months) it may be as given in Table 10.3.

	$
95 points and above earns	1500
85 – 94 points earns	750
75 – 84 points earns	375
74 and below earns	nil

Table 10.3 A bonus scale based on target achievement

It should not be necessary to point out that a sales executive does not qualify for a bonus unless all the product ranges are sold, not just a few. The executive should be kept informed of progress by the regular issue of progress information. This scheme combines flexibility with a fixed basic method and level of bonus payment. It can cope with changes in territory or in targets. Product range F may be more important than product range B, even though the target is lower; the profitability may be higher or it may be a new product. Therefore, the former may carry more points than the latter.

Note that

1. Sales should be equal to invoice sales less credits.
2. All sales targets must be achievable, for the system to work, so management must plan ahead with due care.
3. The scheme can be operated by the company over any time period, viz., twelve, six, three or even one month.
4. The scheme is not difficult to operate and makes use of paperwork, such as invoices, which should already be produced by the company.
5. Sales costs could be significant (total costs against net sales turnover). The cost depends on marketing objectives and other factors which should be considered before costing.

Finally, while remuneration is the most important motivational factor for sales executives, job satisfaction, security, etc., also count. Remember your salesperson's role:

> *to maintain personal contact with customers and buyers for the purpose of obtaining sales.*

RISK MANAGEMENT

Good management is all about anticipating events and planning for action before the events happen. This is where understanding the sorts of risks which are likely to arise is very important. The risks may be of one or more of the following types:

1. The usual product risks, political risks, economic risks, etc. that exist in any international marketing operation – these are not being explored here.
2. A chosen channel member may turn out to be a misfit. This is where careful planning and selection of the right partners is vital. A good channel member of yesterday may not be a good channel member tomorrow. A mutual understanding of the roles of the channel members and their responsibilities to each other is a must.

3. At least one channel member is not pulling their weight. The performance expectations must be made clear right from the start. Mutual monitoring of performance is vital to the continuing success of the 'venture'. Mutual reliance must be recognized. All campaign planning must be undertaken jointly so that no motivation is lost due to inadequate planning.
4. Breakdown of the 'relationship' – where independent members form a significant part of the channel, the relationships are based on individuals, their interpersonal behaviour, trust, mutual understanding of a set of common objectives and other objectives based on the needs of the parties concerned. 'Mutuality' of interest must be maintained to avoid the risk of damaging the position of the two parties.

In all these cases, rapid contingency planning is crucial to safeguard the company's position.

11 THE LINK PERSON – NEGOTIATOR, MOTIVATOR, MANAGER

The person managing/dealing with the distributor relations has an important role in the manufacturer/producer organization. In many organizations, this role is either misunderstood as a simple staff role or underemphasized by other functions, including in some instances by the top management. In this chapter, the role as a general manager–entrepreneur is defined and elaborated.

NATURE, SCOPE AND SPECIFICATION OF THE ROLE

General management

The general management responsibilities should include the setting of objectives for the markets concerned, planning for the short and the long term, implementation of the plans to achieve the company's performance in the relevant markets, and reporting on the performance and corrective actions, if any. In particular, the manager should cultivate:

- an organizational culture whose goal is success in the long term achieved through making the right decisions; good distributors thrive in such a culture;
- good teamwork among the various functions involved in distribution;
- commitment on the part of top management which is vital for good distribution;
- an awareness of the importance of the distribution function, which should be constantly stressed and reinforced through training sessions for the company staff.

Distributors admire a company where the top man is interested in ensuring that the company is sensitive to customer needs and distributor needs, and remains so. This interest is shown through general involvement in marketing, collection and assessment of information, and important marketing decisions. Other factors are successful market segmentation, emphasis on innovation and team-building.

Polaroid cameras achieved instant success because of the perceived benefits by the customers and distributors: the speed, ease of use, dispensing from packets and good quality pictures developed instantly at a reasonable cost.

Job specification – 'link person'

1. Scope:
    (a) to strive for **maximum sales with the required profitability** of the full range of the company's products, in all the relevant territories to achieve the assigned sales targets through:
        - routine field visits;
        - training, advising and motivating the company's distributors;
        - assisting the managers of overseas subsidiary companies and co-operating with them;
        - achieving 100 per cent sales promotional support from distributors and subsidiary company managers;
        - achieving goodwill for the company.
    (b) to achieve maximum consumer/industrial usage of all the company's products by training, advising and motivating distributors and customers, and by co-operating with the subsidiary company managers for the same ends.
2. Accountabilities:
    (a) The person will be accountable for an agreed target volume and value of sales from their territories and for the level of profit contribution as agreed/budgeted.
    (b) They will be the manufacturer's representative when on distributor territory; but will represent the distributor's perspective and interests when back on base.
3. The responsibilities will include:
    (a) maximizing the use of his time and effort for the benefit of the company;
    (b) maintaining full awareness of the company's marketing policies in the markets;
    (c) keeping up-to-date with distributors' correspondence, other than day-to-day matters, relative to orders, progress chasing, etc.;
    (d) keeping the company fully up-to-date regarding competitors' activities within their territory and keeping the distributors aware of the strengths and weaknesses of each significant competitor and of the company itself;

(e) keeping the company fully aware of customer (end-user) requirements in the territory covered;

(f) ensuring that the distributors maintain sufficient stocks of the products and spares to cater for customers' (end-users') needs;

(g) reporting on overseas visits in detail and submitting statements of expenditure incurred;

(h) co-operating fully with the subsidiary general managers – such managers carry 'line' status and the 'field man' acts in a 'staff' capacity;

(i) recommending marketing policy and sales and profit targets, for the territory covered and ensuring that such agreed policies are executed;

(j) displaying appropriate business and commercial leadership skills and using them as necessary to motivate and lead distributors to achieve improved performance;

(k) ensuring that the distributors have sales and technical information and sufficient up-to-date supplies of catalogues and literature, including product manuals;

(l) working 'in the field' with the distributor salesforce, training, advising and motivating, to win their confidence and to ensure their willingness to develop their selling techniques;

(m) evaluating distributors so that their performance is constantly measured against the market potential and trend;

(n) attending such conventions or committees as may be necessary for improving general knowledge as well as particular knowledge of the territory covered;

(o) making sure a newsletter is regularly sent to the distributors, perhaps every quarter, giving them sufficient information to help them improve their performance;

(p) if possible, publishing a monthly report of open negotiations and new orders for each distributor; this lets the distributors know the company is aware of their activities;

(q) making sure the commission report, which is an important document, is accurate and publishing it in time;

(r) trying to ensure that the company emphasizes its leading role in its industry through contributing technical articles/papers/lectures at the appropriate industry occasions and sending such contributions to the distributors for their attention;

(s) complementing advertising and promotion, which form a large part of the support activities expected by the distributors from the manufacturer, by direct mail, telemarketing, etc., as appropriate;

(t) trying for improvements in communication between the manufacturer and distributors by the use of the latest devices; these can be beneficial for their mutual relations;

(u) making use of sales meetings which play a positive part in the forming of a good relationship with distributors and in communicating with them.

4. Scope of authority. This includes:
   (a) full authority to carry out the sales policies as agreed;
   (b) relationships:
   - line: directly responsible to the . . ., for all distributor selling, merchandising and technical activities of the parent company and that of subsidiary companies
   - functional: co-operating and maintaining satisfactory and amicable relationships with all colleagues with whom their work or his responsibilities bring them into contact, either personally or by correspondence.

PERSON SPECIFICATION

The main characteristics are best stated as those of:

- an extrovert
- a commercially minded business executive
- a technical person, with a commercial training (industrial)
- a decision-maker
- a self-contained, reliable and adaptable person with empathy
- someone good at languages, aware of different cultures and with an international outlook
- a professional salesperson with experience including product knowledge and overseas marketing
- a motivator

As the job involves a lot of international travel and mixing with different cultures, which may involve the sampling of varied cuisines, success in the profession requires good health and stamina. Perhaps the phrase 'an international marketing professional with good health and a sound domestic background' sums it all up.

THE LINK PERSON AND PRODUCT MANAGEMENT

Companies offering multiple products may adopt a divisionalized structure on a product group basis, with different product managers dealing with the logistics of the finished products, their marketing aspects and the co-ordination of product-related services for the different product groups. Whereas, as far as the distributor in a specific market is concerned, the link person may be dealing with all the company products in that market. Two points arise in this respect.

1. The link persons have to co-ordinate the company's product offerings and the manner of their marketing and presentation, in order to give a cohesive and convincing perspective to the market-place, via the distributor. The mix has to be made attractive by compensating for the absence of incentive in one product or product group through extra benefits conferred by other product groups. This can involve the link person in dealing with different product managers in their company.
2. The link persons have to persuade the different departments and functions within the company to adopt policies to provide a uniform and efficient logistics and customer service. This may be a trouble-shooting role absorbing a good deal of time and resources.

The only way that the link person's role can be made effective is for the company firstly to recognize the need for the product management staff to ensure a good and efficient product service and second to practise the full marketing concept within the company.

ROLE OF PRODUCT MANAGEMENT

When product management in practised in a company, especially in the high technology field, the product manager has the main task of master-minding the introduction of new products, starting from the design concept, getting the product into a deliverable state and handing it to the sales force. It is important to keep abreast of the technological developments and market needs, the ease or the difficulty that will be experienced by the channels in marketing the product and to have a good knowledge of the competitive and competitor situations so that the product is adequately differentiated and made easy to sell. The product manager may not have the full knowledge and control of the specific markets in which the products may have to be sold to sustain its profitability and the returns for the company. However, when there is no link person involved, the product manager has an important part to play in shaping the product marketing strategy.

Pricing the product at the appropriate level is a matter to which the product manager has to give serious attention. In addition, many questions need to be taken into account in deciding on the pricing strategy. What stage in its life cycle has the product reached? Is the product an innovative new product which has very little competition? What are the chances of the product being copied or improved upon by competition? Is the market willing and ready to accept the new product? Or does the market have to be educated regarding the product and its benefits? What should be the response to competitive attack at the various stages of the product life cycle?

Training the channel operators and the sales force is also a crucial matter to which the product manager has to pay particular attention. As the product champion of the company with responsibility 'from womb to tomb', they must take account of all the implications for the channel before any product marketing decisions are taken. If the manager is also responsible for generating the ROI on the product investment, he has to keep an eye on the costs of the product, volumes of sales and manufacture, inventory levels, income to the company and the product life cycle and competitor actions which may affect the product sales performance. In addition, there is responsibility for:

- developing long and short term objectives for the product line;
- planning for the achievement of the objectives;
- sales support through proposals for customer inquiries, publication of applications, price lists and technical articles/papers, sales training programmes, regular field visits and a good departmental climate for the support of the channel network;
- evaluation of the distributors in terms of the product concerned;
- help in personnel training and development.

What a company usually offers is not just the core product but a host of value-added services and packages. It is through the total offering that a company differentiates itself from the other players. Product managers have an important part to play in shaping the total offering.

BUSINESS LEADERSHIP

The job of the link person cannot be complete without the recognition of the need to provide business leadership to the distributor channels. Most distributors will not be exclusive to the company. They might be distributing several companies' products, although the products themselves may not compete with each other. In order to get a distributor to major the companies' products, it is necessary to provide some business leadership to the channel structure.

A joint campaign should be planned between the two parties. A motivating start would be to enlist the distributor's interest and seek their views on the market-place by requesting their advice. It is important to establish a common perception of the target market, its potential and an agreed common goal to gain a target share of the business. As mentioned in Chapter 9 on 'Establishing a good relationship', the common understanding of the market should be based on independent confirmation of the market knowledge available to both parties.

In most businesses, Pareto's law applies: roughly 20 per cent of the customers are responsible for 80 per cent of the business. A typical distributor in a far-off market-place is not motivated by general statistics about markets and their structures. Specifics that matter concern ways of obtaining more business and approaches to key customers. As already mentioned elsewhere, let me repeat: the names of the top 20 per cent clients who yield 80 per cent of the business must be sought from the channel operator together with the target volume sales which can be reasonably expected in the planning year for each of those clients. The remaining can be a matter for estimation.

A pro forma joint campaign (plan) must, for all practical reasons, consist of at least the seven steps as listed in Fig. 11.3.

A part of the role of business leadership is to establish whether this business level is viable and economic from the manufacturer's point of view; if not, then renegotiate the volumes. While the target volumes are being established, one must not ignore the price at which the end customers will buy the products, i.e. the price which the market will bear. It must not be forgotten that this price also provides the profits for the distributor. Can the manufacturer and the distributor both compete profitably at that price?

It is important to stress that the views of a channel operator and their motivation are often coloured by the price at which the manufacturer supplies to them, as this is the main factor in determining their profit. This needs to be followed by an agreed plan for:

- developing the necessary means of gaining the access to the market;
- obtaining the resources needed for getting the business;
- having the right type, number and quality of skilled human resources and training them;
- carrying out the promotional campaigns.

ADVERTISING AND SALES PROMOTION

Advertising and sales promotion are complementary marketing functions with a common goal which is to increase sales and/or profit; they must be thoroughly co-ordinated for optimal effect. Advertising is information which is paid for by the customer in the end. It has to be realized that enlightened customers may question the value added by the advertising policy of a company, especially when they feel that the price paid for the total product package is too high or that the service provided is deficient in some way.

The objectives of advertising and promotion have to be clearly kept in mind when dealing with international markets. Advertising has to be planned and disseminated in a persuasive manner by identified sponsors through the various media. It is neither an art nor a science but a marketing communications tool, designed to transmit a specific message to a particular segment of the population which is the 'target audience'.

The categories are:

1. Consumer – where the companies try to influence the consumers directly through the media.
2. Trade – where the advertising and promotion is directed not only to the general public but also towards the trade.
3. Business to business:
   (a) industrial   – technical
   (b) professional – ethical
   (c) agricultural   – farmers
   (d) medical   – legal and ethical issues

Possible advertising classifications are:

1. Local/retail – advertising and promotion is localized and this falls rightly within the responsibility of the distributor.
2. Regional – advertising and promotion may be undertaken by the regional distributor and/or the manufacturer/supplier.
3. International – advertising and promotion is almost always undertaken by the manufacturer unless the international market is regionalized and master distributors are appointed. The manufacturer will have to co-ordinate advertising and promotion, and absorb a large part of the expenditure.

Advertising has existed from the time when exchange of goods or services or announcements of events began. The history of advertising is traced through the following:

1. It existed 2000 years ago at gladiatorial events and large public gatherings.
2. In the middle ages, artists painted signs advertising their own skills as well as the painted objects.
3. 1477 saw the first hand-pressed print advertisement.
4. During the industrial revolution, advertising was done on a larger scale,

using billboards, etc.

5. Press advertising began in the nineteenth century.

Summing up advertising as a marketing tool, its functions are to:

- identify products and differentiate them;
- communicate information about the product;
- induce trial of new products by new users;
- suggest repurchase by existing users;
- stimulate a product's distribution;
- increase the use of the product;
- build brand preference and loyalty.

The common goal of advertising and promotion is to lead up to a sale, by shortening the time and reducing the cost of the selling process, and by eliminating some of the steps leading up to the buying decision. Advertising cannot create repeat business for a product/service that does not satisfy the consumer. Industrial advertising not only provides information but also educates the reader. Freedom of the press is a spin-off of advertising and today advertising is very big business.

Advertising and sales promotion media

In many countries, advertising campaigns are mounted through:

- national/popular press
- trade and technical journals
- television and radio
- cinema
- billboards
- various directories, e.g. Yellow Pages

Besides regional campaigns promoting a company's image or brand, special campaigns can be linked to specific events, e.g. sporting events, special exhibitions.

Sales promotion can be a follow-up to advertising campaigns or connected to them at specific times dictated by marketing and tactical action programmes. For example, a sales promotion campaign can be initiated as a follow-up to the success of a country's team in the Olympics during which the company generally advertised its image and brands. Similarly, a sales promotion campaign can be initiated by the launch of a new product as part of a marketing strategy. In another case, a company faced by a fall in the orders book and a stock build-up may opt for a price promotion campaign.

Sales promotion campaigns can be mounted through or via the following:

- exhibitions
- show material
- packaging and finish
- in-store promotions
- plant visits/product training
- conferences
- consultants/beauticians
- bonus schemes (sales and counter staff)
- literature
- direct mail
- field sales aids
- premiums
- editorials
- advisory councils
- house journals and newsletters

Cost of advertising

A manufacturer decides on the sales forecast and then asks the question: What advertising and sales promotion do I need to help me achieve the forecasts? The plans should be first made and then costed. The cost should be related to the sales as a percentage; if it is within the allocated 'norm', it should be left alone. One must not start by saying 'We will allocate 5 per cent to advertising and sales promotion this year. Now let us see how to spend it.'

The faster moving the item and the greater the number of end-users, the larger the percentage spend. In industrial consumable products, for example, and only as a guide, 50 per cent of the appropriation can be on space advertising and the balance on sales promotion. (Overseas visits are not included in sales promotion.) Advertising and sales promotion within a market other than the domestic one is generally the distributor's responsibility. Exceptions to this rule are usually found in consumer products where an international brand leader may control this marketing function very tightly.

Assuming that the above rule holds, the costs incurred should be built into the price at which the products are sold in the territory. However, the manufacturer may help by:

(a) allowing a fixed percentage annually on all purchases made by the distributor, providing such an allowance is spent on advertising and sales promotion;
    or
(b) making available a fixed annual advertising and sales promotion amount available, providing that the distributor matches it on a 50/50 basis.

In any event, certain items for advertising and sales promotion will be provided free of charge by the manufacturer to the distributor, e.g. printing blocks, specific literature, exhibition materials.

COMMUNICATION CHANNELS

Effective communications

Basically, there are two points of view regarding what constitutes communications with consumers: a limited point of view that identifies communications with advertising, point-of-sale material, personal selling and public relations; and an extended point of view which recognizes that all aspects of a firm's marketing activities represent an opportunity for communication. The first view is unrealistic. What marketers say in advertising and customer relations may be belied by their actions; e.g. what the company do with the product, the package, the price or other aspects of their visible marketing activities.

'Effective communication takes place when the receiver of the communication perceives the message as conveying the benefit that was intended by the sender.' Mass communications are particularly prone to failure because of the lack of face-to-face contact between the sender and receiver, making feedback difficult. Feedback is essential for evaluating the effectiveness of the communication. In order to get good feedback, continuous independent market research is essential.

One advantage of personal selling is the scope for observing the buyer's reactions and obtaining immediate feedback. Feedback, if received and properly interpreted, provides a basis for evaluating the effectiveness of the communication and for making changes in it as needed. The marketer must initiate and maintain independent and continuing research to monitor consumer responses to their programme. Ideally, feedback occurs quickly and takes the form of questions requesting clarification or responses that indicate whether the intended message is being received. In practice, marketing feedback is often delayed and ambiguous when received. Corroboration is vital through face-to-face checks with the ultimate customers.

The difficulty of mass communications led Schramm to identify the essential conditions for all marketing communications. The message must:

1. Be designed and delivered so as to gain the maximum attention of the target.
2. Be conducted in terms of language which the target can understand in order to get the meaning across.
3. Increase awareness and arouse latent needs in the target customer and indicate that the product can meet these needs.
4. Confer benefits to the channel so that the channel member can reinforce it.

The following are the communications variables controlling the brand image for industrial goods.

1. The product itself: if it does not live up to the promises made, it will cause consumer dissatisfaction and disappointment. The product must be clearly differentiated from the products of its competitors.
2. The brand name: its role is well recognized.
3. The price: this is a well-understood basis for market segmentation and/or positioning a product.
4. The marketing communication: its main role is to communicate information regarding the brand and supplying it with psychological nuances that make it attractive to consumers.

Each is a vehicle for communicating various messages about the brand; they must complement each other to create a clear brand image.

Personal selling

Personal selling is the primary communication channel for many products and an important source of information about the market. The personal selling process has seven steps:

1. Prospecting and qualifying: An essential research activity to learn about the prospective customer and to estimate all the facts to determine whether the prospect fits in with the company's target, is appropriate for inclusion in the portfolio and has the resources to pay for the product.
2. Pre-approach planning: The next stage and also an important research activity to confirm the need and prepare for the face-to-face meeting.
3. Face-to-face personal contact: The customer is personally approached and an effort is made at building up a personal relationship.
4. Presentation and demonstration: The heart of personal selling where the central objective is to gain attention, hold interest and obtain action; the selling activity is two-way and involves answering questions.
5. Handling objections: Acknowledging genuine objections and countering arguments from buyers.
6. Closing the sale: Recognizing the buying signals and asking for the order without much further discourse.
7. Follow-up: Consists of checking that the buyer has received the product and is satisfied with its performance. This is critical for building customer loyalty and for repeat business.

Personal selling is expensive and requires research designed to ensure its effectiveness. The key elements to success are empathy, the ability to monitor customer reactions, feelings and attitudes, and adaptability, which is the ability to adapt to changing customer reactions as they occur.

Marketing communications

The only communication a producer has with the consumers is through the products and what is said about them. The message should therefore be clear, direct and unambiguous. It should be realized that all marketing activities can lead to opportunities to communicate with the consumers. While advertising and promotional activities are the obvious communications tools, their impact can be nullified by what is done in other fields, such as service.

An advertising message should be designed to gain the attention of the target audience and be couched in a way that is meaningful to the sender and the receiver; it should make the receiver realize needs which can be satisfied through ways suggested by the message. There are various theories about the way advertising can work. Some assume that the consumers make a rational decision of purchasing a product and the message should claim desirable qualities for the advertised product and offer proofs. Another basis is the influence of heuristic factors in consumer decisions. A third is concerned with emotional responses. Any or all of these factors may be used in advertising a product.

The advertising media, consisting of publications, radio, television and outside posters, convey most of the advertising messages to the consumers regarding widely distributed products. New media emerge from time to time. Advertising is generally handled by advertising agencies, co-ordinated by advertising divisions in large companies. It is necessary to have a media plan for comprehensive advertising because media define their own target markets and atmosphere, and the correct media should be identified and a campaign planned.

The media plan

The key to effective media operation is the media plan, which is subordinate to the overall marketing plan and is co-ordinated with other marketing activities. It is a vital element in advertising communications because it links the advertising message with the media in which the message will appear, the media in turn linking the source of the message (the producer) with the relevant channels and the final receiver, who is the ultimate consumer.

The media plan will depend on the product concept, the target market, the marketing channels, the budget available and the creative strategy. The media analyst, working within this framework, tries to select the combination of media – within the budget constraints and marketing requirements that offers the best chance for effective communication with the desired market. The media define their market in the sense that they attract certain types of people. On the other hand, specific media may allow the marketer to target their advertising message to a very specific audience.

Communications research

In a marketing economy, much of the marketing consists of communications. The marketer's communications with the consumers must be clear and unambiguous. All aspects of a firm's marketing activities represent an opportunity for communications. Despite the crucial role it plays in a competitive marketing economy, communication is little understood and much maligned. There is a need for communications research. Large amounts of company resources are directed into communications and it is the responsibility of marketing management to see that the expenditure is wisely made.

Advertising research can be divided into:

1. Budget research – concerned with the amount of money allocated for advertising.
2. Audience research – concerned with the frequency, coverage, efficiency and effectiveness of different media and combinations of media in delivering advertising messages.
3. Copy research – dealing with what is said and how it is said.

When advertising goals are divorced from marketing goals, the measurement problem becomes greatly simplified. The extent to which an advertising campaign builds awareness, provides knowledge, or creates interest in a product or brand can be measured through the use of appropriate survey questions, whereas its influence on sales is more elusive. While the function of advertising is communication, it is communication with a purpose: to influence consumer attitudes or to induce consumer action relevant to marketing objectives.

CROSS-BORDER COMMUNICATIONS

Good channel communication implies that both the receiver and recipient of any communication benefit from it. Effective channel communication occurs where the channel members and the manufacturer subscribe to it, both in form and content, and commit themselves to actions that flow from it. Such communication across borders, therefore, has to take into account the culture, customs and business behaviour in the recipient member territory – the sender must have total empathy with the receiver and the message must be compelling in that the receiver must realize that he cannot get the full benefits without acting on such communication received. The link person has an important part to play in ensuring that the distributors take an active part in implementing the cross-border communication policy.

The international marketing manager should carefully evaluate cross-border advertising goals to make sure that they are relevant to the marketing goals. Testing has to be done before committing major resources to a programme; it provides empirical support for judgements, reduces risk and eliminates or modifies questionable material. Evaluation is made after company resources have been committed for a programme or campaign, in order to determine if the company goals have been achieved. Both testing and evaluation can be delegated to a specialist manager; it is wise, however, to make sure that these assessments are made personally in conjunction with the link person and communicated to higher management along with recommendations for future improvements where needed.

Take the case of the Martini Rossi company. Having advertised Martini as 'the right one' for a number of years, the concept of the brand needed an update. The presentation was to convey the image of Martini as a pleasant, refreshing and smart drink for the young, well-to-do and professional classes, the common factor among all the people being an active, social life-style. The visual advertising and promotion campaign had to be designed for the different cultures in Germany, Italy and the United Kingdom, for example, without sacrificing the basic concept message. The German ads showed mountain ski scenes with Martini as a refreshing drink for skiers, emphasizing the German consumers' typical need to know more about a product and its use. The Italian ads reflected car racing scenes as a backdrop for a young couple drinking Martini, reflecting the love for this sport in Italy. The UK ads showed fantasy scenes, ballooning sequences over castles in midsummer, followed by drink parties. This targeting paid off; Martini sales increased and their brand image was clearly established.

SYNERGY AMONG CHANNEL MEMBERS

It is only through efficient interchannel co-ordination that the channels can attain their full potential in giving satisfactory service to the ultimate consumers and obtaining the best possible returns for the channel members themselves. The performance of the whole channel system depends upon its structure as well as on the actions of the individual members.

The link person (or persons if there are more than one) associated with the channel members in a region must be conscious of the need to achieve synergy between their actions. These actions must not be allowed to upset the agreed company image, adversely affect the brand image or position, or give cause for competitors to make inroads and grab market share. The key areas of co-ordination are:

1. Price image: If it is a quality product, do the prices quoted by the channel members diminish the quality image or imply unnecessarily a higher quality than the actual?
2. The level of service: Is the service level consistent with deliveries quoted/ achieved and in line with what is demanded by the customers?
3. Sales representation: Do the sales force and contact personnel deal with customers according to the best practices agreed with the channel members?
4. Advertising and promotion: Do all the channel members practise agreed advertising and promotion procedures?
5. Cross-border co-operation: Do the members co-operate with each other for the benefit of the whole network as opposed to benefits for themselves?
6. Customer perception of the network operation: How do the customers perceive the company, its products, its distributors, the service levels provided, the promotional programmes? Is the customer perception in line with or better than that envisaged in the plan?

MOTIVATION OF CHANNEL PARTNERS

Motivation starts with the manufacturer's link persons – it is very important that they believe in their company, its products, its policies, its people and the distributors. It is equally important that they have confidence in themselves and their ability to do things or get them done. Without this self-motivation, the manufacturer's staff will be transparent in dealings with the distributor and the latter will be able to detect gaps to exploit. This is best illustrated by considering the link person as performing the role of a conductor in an orchestra; this person leads, directs and gets all the players performing in unison and according to a prerehearsed plan.

The next important aspect starts with a strategy – a grand plan; without this, no one will be able to give directions to the distributor operations concerning what is expected of them. The campaign needs to be carefully planned and jointly worked out with the distributors so that they feel part of it and are fully committed to the campaign.

To gain the distributor's commitment, one needs to understand what makes them tick. What are their basic needs, higher needs and aspirations, and how do the objectives/goals of the company match with those of the distributor? What are their main strengths and weaknesses? For instance, these could be as follows:

1. Strengths:
    (a) good area sales coverage;
    (b) sound knowledge of 'buying influences' in the companies called on;
    (c) good local knowledge.
2. Weaknesses:
    (a) near lack of real sales objectives in a marketing plan;
    (b) multiplicity of product lines;
    (c) lack of technical knowledge of the product;
    (d) possible low calibre of sales personnel.

The advantages of distributors' strengths to a manufacturer are obvious. While their weaknesses can never be completely eliminated, they must be reduced to a minimum if a manufacturing company selling through distributors is to achieve volume sales at optimum price levels. The principal aims of a manufacturer in motivating a distributor must be to:

- impart a sound knowledge of the company's products to the distributor's salesforce;
- improve their overall knowledge of the field in which they are operating as well as improve their sales skills;
- stimulate and motivate the distributor principal and salesforce to devote more time on each call to the company's products.

Sales executives will 'major' a product in which they have faith and about which they feel confident.

The association with the distributors must be very close in order to achieve the above aims. They must respect and above all **trust** the manufacturing company implicitly. After obtaining the distributor's trust, the company must work in partnership together; the distributor should co-operate with the manufacturer in all matters, especially in increasing the sales-effectiveness of the sales force.

The method of operation of the manufacturer's export sales executives closely affects the training and motivation of the distributor principals and their sales force; a section titled 'field assistance' within the statement of sales policy, should ideally illustrate the manner of this operation and how the approach of the manufacturer will contribute to achieving the overall objectives.

Given the trust of the distributor, the link person/manager should be in a position to advise on the marketing plan, the size of his sales force (bearing in mind the total operation), the levels of remuneration for sales executives, and other relevant matters. Help should be given, if requested, in selecting and recruiting the sales force; it is in the company's own interests to do so.

A TRAINING PROGRAMME FOR CHANNEL MEMBERS ON TECHNOLOGIES AND PRODUCTS

There are some things you can be sure of in any industry:

(a) technology changes continuously;
(b) competitors will always try to get your customers and sell them their products;
(c) the people working in the industry are getting better qualified and are eager to advance themselves;
(d) innovation and competition, between them, will try and make your product obsolete faster and faster;
(e) return on your company's investment can only be obtained by making your channels work hard and get results well within the sales life cycle of the product.

The process of selling, supporting and staying ahead of competition needs all the channels members to be fully informed of the state of the art, the developments in technology, new and emerging applications, and ways of retaining competitive advantage. Just knowing is not enough – the knowledge has to be applied for the benefit of the customers.

The only way of achieving all these objectives is to have a continuous education programme, training sessions for updating the knowledge of products, their applications, the emerging technology and competition, and how to combat them and still deliver benefits to the customer. Keeping customers satisfied is the only way of making satisfactory profits.

Every business needs to have a continuous training programme for the direct sales force and support force, the independent channel principals and their sales force, and the after-sales service force. This can take several forms. It has to be kept in mind that the channel members in the territories will be reluctant to give up selling or income-earning time to spend it instead in a remote training place, which means the staff will be out of action for long periods, at a high cost. Means must be found to minimize out-of-station training programmes.

CO-ORDINATION OF HIGH TECHNOLOGY KNOWLEDGE AND PRODUCT EXPERTISE THROUGH CHANNELS

One of the key success factors is the extent to which all the members of the channel act in step with each other. The common aim is to get a share of the profitable business. This needs a good understanding between the members on the goals, strategies and actions to be undertaken to get 'a share of the cake' that is going. The co-operation in this venture can only be obtained if there is a common purpose with a common goal and if everybody subscribes to it.

This calls for trust and a pooling of the knowledge of the market, the product benefits and features, the applications, etc. Manufacturers generally tend to have good knowledge and expertise in the product areas but the other members of the channel, especially those who are close to the market-place, have access to what is actually happening in the market-place and how the available products are being used. The manufacturer needs this feedback and in turn, the manufacturer can inform the channel members of the product advancements and the kind of things needed for upgrade/ enhancement/development.

EVALUATION OF MUTUAL PERFORMANCE GOALS/OBJECTIVES

The evaluation should be made on the basis of:

- trend of new orders generated in comparison with other comparable distributors;
- the ratio of actual orders as compared to proposals;
- degree of attainment of agreed objectives;
- trend of market share performance over sufficient time compared with performances of similarly situated distributors;
- curves showing the new inquiries per month and total open proposals on a monthly basis;
- a check to see whether the compatibility profile, on the basis of which the distributor was chosen, is now changed in any way, and if it has, whether the distributor still fits the new profile as well as before;
- assessment of the degree of the distributor's commitment to the company, including enthusiasm in promoting their products, the degree of his co-operation and the feedback received.

It is an important role of the link person to evaluate the performance of both the manufacturer and the distributor in the market-place regularly. The purpose of this evaluation is not just to find out if the distributor has performed his obligations and/or to find fault with one of the parties. The object of the exercise is to improve the performance of the firm in the market-place. An effective and professional set of procedures must be introduced and kept up-to-date for such an evaluation.

ESTABLISHMENT OF EVALUATION PROCEDURES

Requirements of the manufacturer:

1. A manufacturer requires from the distributors volume purchases at optimum profit margins to himself. Such purchases, reflected as distributor sales, should show a growth pattern consistent with the national growth in the potential of the product.
2. The distributor's main marketing functions, i.e. sales, service, administration, advertising and sales promotion, must be constantly under surveillance at all times by the manufacturer. The most effective way of carrying out this surveillance is through regular contact by the 'field executive'.
3. A combination of this communication with the requirements contained in the Distributorship Agreement and/or the Statement of Sales Policy offers the basic means for measuring the success or otherwise of the distributor.
4. A manufacturer can never get perfection from distributors; and must learn to live with their limitations.
5. The manufacturer should conduct a self-evaluation before embarking on evaluating the distributor :
   (a) Is the product right for the market?
   (b) Are the prices right for the market?
   (c) Are deliveries being made on time?
   (d) Is the product being correctly promoted?
   (e) Is the distributor being supported properly and as agreed?
These are some of the questions that should be asked.
6. The market must be evaluated not only in terms of potential but also with regard to the trend. What percentage of the available market is the distributor obtaining? How does their performance compare with other distributors?
7. Evaluate the situation periodically, regularly and clinically at least once a year.

The link person should also evaluate the short and long term effectiveness and efficiency of the channel's performance. Such an evaluation concept leads to a number of questions as seen in Fig. 11.1.

It is also vital to keep an eye on the strategic return on investment from both the manufacturer's and distributor's points view. The key financial ratios must be monitored and interpretations sought for any divergence from the stated objectives. If the link person assumes the role of a business executive and treats the distributor principal as a colleague (which is certainly the case), a dialogue modelled on the lines of how Lord Weinstock

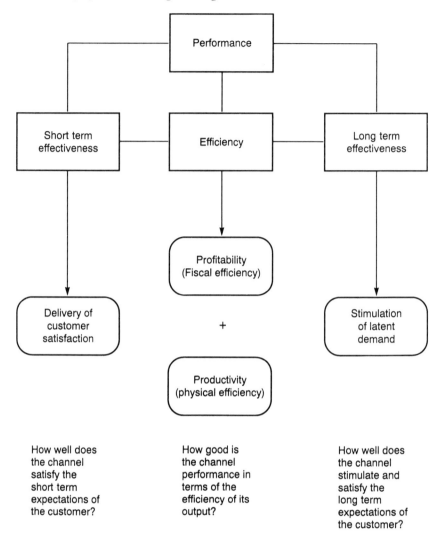

Figure 11.1 Channel performance

of GEC (UK) manages his subsidiaries on the basis of ratios will prove helpful. See Fig. 11.2 for an interpretation of the part played by key ratios in general management. See aso Fig. 11.3 for a joint plan.

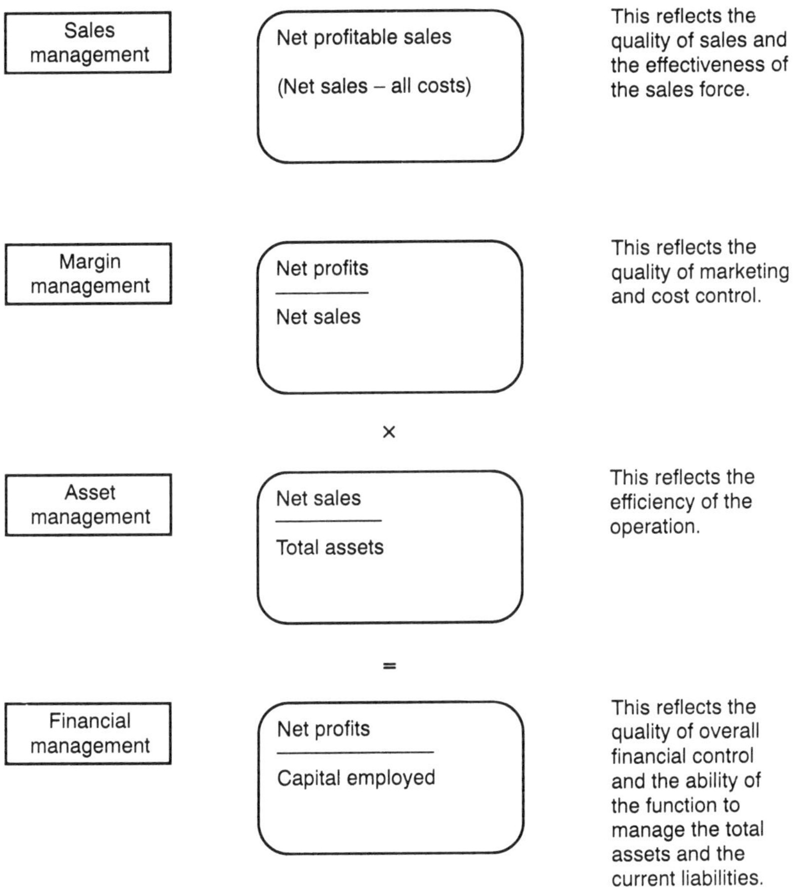

Sales management	Net profitable sales (Net sales – all costs)	This reflects the quality of sales and the effectiveness of the sales force.

Margin management	$\dfrac{\text{Net profits}}{\text{Net sales}}$	This reflects the quality of marketing and cost control.

$\times$

Asset management	$\dfrac{\text{Net sales}}{\text{Total assets}}$	This reflects the efficiency of the operation.

$=$

Financial management	$\dfrac{\text{Net profits}}{\text{Capital employed}}$	This reflects the quality of overall financial control and the ability of the function to manage the total assets and the current liabilities.

Figure 11.2 Strategic return on investment

JOINT CAMPAIGN WITH DISTRIBUTORS FOR THIS YEAR AND A PREVIEW FOR NEXT YEAR

The objective is to get a share of the 'cake' in terms of revenue and profit opportunity

Pass 1

1   Ask for distributor's advice on the market, competition and opportunity for the manufacturer

2   Target levels of business

Year 1	Qtr 1	Qtr 2	Qtr 3	Qtr 4	Year 2
Top 20% of customers	. . .	. . .	. . .	. . .	. . .
Others	. . .	. . .	. . .	. . .	. . .

Pass 2   Validate 1 and 2

3 Cost to the outlet	. . .	. . .	. . .	. . .	. . .
4 Recommended price	. . .	. . .	. . .	. . .	. . .

5   How to gain the share of the cake?
   (i)   How many sales people to deploy
   (ii) Product knowledge training
   (iii) Sales training and training on benefits to end-users/customers
   (iv) Motivational schemes
   (v) How and by what means the product should be promoted

6   (i)   What should the outlet do by way of actions?
   (ii) What should we do?

7   How and when are we going to review?

Figure 11.3 Joint campaign (plan)

DISTRIBUTOR EVALUATION – CHECK POINTS

1. Who is the company?
2. What is it?
3. What products of ours are handled by it?
4. What is the number of sales executives employed?
5. What have their purchases been?
6. What is their stockholding, in total and by product?
7. What is the calibre of their sales personnel?
8. What is their attitude towards advertising and sales promotion?
9. What is the amount of attention being given to our products?
10. What are the list prices/discounts applicable to our products?
11. What is the gross profit on our products?
12. What is the method of remunerating sales executives?
13. What is the sales and distribution policy of the company?
14. What are the standards of sales administration and after-sales service and what are the facilities offered?
15. Who are the distributor's main customers and major accounts?
16. Who and what is the competition?
17. What are the import duties and taxes on our products?
18. What is the state of the market and what is its trend?
19. Is the distributor paying for his purchases within the agreed credit period?

In general terms, consider the following:

- company
- products handled
- number of sales executives
- purchases
- stockholding, etc.
- operation of personnel, plant, advertising and sales promotion
- attention given to your line
- prices and discounts – your line – gross profit
- remuneration of sales executives
- sales administration/service facilities
- major users/accounts
- import duties and taxes
- market: current status
         trend
- competition: strengths
             weaknesses
- overall recommendations

PROFIT IMPROVEMENT FOR THE MANUFACTURER

In attempting to improve profits, the usual action taken by a manufacturer would be to increase sales volume without increase in fixed cost base and/or increase unit selling price. The effect of this on the distributor would be to increase inventory with the associated costs of funding and storage and/or reduce the margins. The following checklist is taken from a lecture delivered in 1991, by Phillip Day.

A checklist for profit improvement

Key areas where profits can be improved:

1. inventories
2. cost of supply
3. indirect cost
4. competition

Practical steps for profit improvement

1. From inventories:
   (a) extended credit terms;
   (b) bank funding – Letters of Credit and trust receipts;
   (c) shorter lead times for ordering;
   (d) more frequent deliveries;
   (e) faster deliveries;
   (f) interim storage and distribution;
   (g) richer 'mix' of products;
   (h) funding the safety stock cushion;
   (i) consignment;
   (j) buy-back.

2. From cost of supply:
   (a) volume discounts;
   (b) improved warranty terms;
   (c) price reduction coupled with reduction in support;
   (d) weak currency invoicing;
   (e) change invoice structure;
   (f) better packaging.

3. From indirect costs:
   (a) quicker account servicing;
   (b) sales force training;

   (c) advertising and marketing support;
   (d) systems support;
   (e) encouragement of parallel services;
   (f) market and product research;
   (g) management audit and assistance;
   (h) investment in distributor:
- direct investment (shares/assets);
- indirect investment (leasing/rentals).

4. In the face of competition:
   (a) increased marketing effort;
   (b) indirect sales force incentives.

What to do when a major problem is discovered:

1. Concerning old stock:
   (a) Confirm the product profile of last consignment with order control/dispatch.
   (b) Confirm this profile with identification of stock likely to be damaged when held in temporary warehouse.
   (c) Obtain authority to declare stock obsolete, pending investigation.

2. Replacement stock
   (a) Ascertain stock availability and time-scales.
   (b) Ascertain delivery channels and time-scales.
   (c) Consider terms of business:
- extended credit;
- consignment;
- impact of duties if free replacement.

3. Contacts with the dealer
   (a) personal visit
   (b) telephone call

Further actions

1. Review own position on:
   (a) storage facilities;
   (b) external packaging;
   (c) internal packaging;
   (d) dealer correspondence;
   (e) dealer warranty terms;
   (f) dealer credit terms;

(g) internal procedures for correspondence;
(h) major account customers;
(i) distribution funding;
(j) marketing assistance;
(k) buy-back policy.

2. Review the dealer's position on:
   (a) financial status;
   (b) marketing and selling policy;
   (c) order size and frequency;
   (d) stockholding policy;
   (e) physical stockholding facilities;
   (f) distribution methods;
   (g) other products;
   (h) internal systems.

12 RESOLVING UNSATISFACTORY SITUATIONS

It is not uncommon to find that a situation develops in a manner that is unsatisfactory to either the manufacturer or the distributor. In this chapter, an analysis is made of the main reasons why this sort of situation can develop and how one can cope with it.

CONFLICT MANAGEMENT – UNDERSTANDING THE FUNDAMENTALS

Channel members are generally chosen for their specialist knowledge; if the parts they play in the channel are also unique, their function is of added value. The division of labour among all the channel members, including the manufacturer, helps the operation to run more efficiently, but it also means that the members are interdependent. Therefore co-ordination is needed on various matters, such as planning of operations, dissemination of information and sharing of profits, among others.

At the same time, organizations like to show their independence and it is not uncommon for some of them to display their power now and again. In general, a manufacturer and the other channel members should be able to recognize this behaviour and respond appropriately to contain the whole situation for the benefit of the channel structure. However, in some circumstances, inappropriate behaviour can lead to conflict situations. As a rule, the greater the dependence of channel members on each other, the greater the possibility of conflict among them; even minor disagreements can blow up into large conflicts. First the parties become aware of some factor of discontent, then they work it up into a grievance and only afterwards does it lead to open conflict.

A channel participant needs to understand fully the strands of interdependence to be effective in managing the situation. The more the dependence, the more probable is the chance of conflict. Conflict management is all about the careful handling of any changes so that a smooth passage is assured. Conflict is likely to occur when one member finds another placing obstacles in its way, preventing it from realising its goals . The following are the main causes of channel conflict:

1. Incompatibility of goals among the channel members – for example, it is obvious that more profits for one member would mean less for the others:
   (a) Large manufacturers are interested in growth, whereas the numerous small retailers served by a large manufacturer are likely to want to maintain the *status quo*. The former may push for actions that promise faster growth while the latter tend to drag their feet.
   (b) In all channel systems, there are system goals, and individual operational goals and these may not always fit together. A certain amount of flexibility is necessary for the efficient operation of the channel, but it must be remembered that each business has its own distinct philosophy and interests, and these cannot be identical in any distribution system.

2. Definition of the market to be served by the various channel members, including the customers and the territory to be served, the services to be performed and the marketing techniques, are all likely trouble spots. If a channel member feels imposed upon in being asked to perform services that it does not have resources for, then trouble is likely. Also if the geographical territories overlap between channel members, this could cause friction. For example, car manufacturers sell most of their production through franchised dealers; they also sell direct to fleet operators and large rental and hire companies. If the latter sell their used cars in the territory of a dealer, this could be a cause for friction between the dealer and the manufacturer.

It is therefore necessary that:

- the territories are defined clearly;
- it is made clear who is to hold inventory and where;
- inventory is properly controlled at all levels;
- it is spelt out who is to provide service and cope with warranty claims;
- sufficient spare parts are made available wherever necessary in the distribution system;
- adequate financing is available wherever it is needed.

Different perceptions of the existing situation can cause trouble because the members are likely to respond according to their own ideas. Differing responses will probably mean frustration and conflict. The following are likely trouble spots:

1. Fixed ideas regarding the other channel members can exacerbate the situation, e.g. the supplier is out to make profits at the expense of the

retailer. Retailers are apt to think that supplying salespeople promise supplies without considering the level of production or possibility of delivery. On the other hand, suppliers feel that retailers do not try to sell their products and stock many lines in different priority orders, making it difficult for them to manage their affairs efficiently.

2. The right way to handle key customers, inventory levels, quality of distribution management and delineation of territories are among the most frequent matters for disputes.

Such perceptions are generally due to non-communication and differing goals and views.

Here is a case in point (this was narrated by Franscico Lafuente Bueno, Ingeneer and a Commercial Director in Spain). A European manufacturer was a leader in its market sector, its product line A containing well-known items with a large market share. They started a new line of products B which differed substantially from A and which were sold in a very competitive market. These two lines were sold through the same distribution channel. While product line B provided a better profit margin compared to A, a lot more effort was needed to sell them. The total market for B had been growing generally at a higher rate than the market for A at growth rates of nine and five per cent per annum respectively. At that point in time, line B of this manufacturer registered an overall growth rate of 30 per cent compared to that of A which was about five per cent in the last two years. Yet, line B only accounted for four per cent of the total turnover for the manufacturer.

The distributor in this case was a family firm which had excellent relations with the manufacturer. The firm, with a turnover of $20 million, was one of the main distributors of the manufacturer in the territory; product line A contributed 98 per cent of the firm's turnover. The distributor's turnover of product line B grew only by 6 per cent while other distributors were growing this line of business by about 30 per cent. The manufacturer felt that the distributor was not marketing product line B in the right way and was letting the competition get ahead in its territory. The distributor was not willing to put in further effort into product line B since the firm was doing well with the other line A.

First the manufacturer discussed the matter with the distributor in the new year, persuading them to pay more attention to line B, since the line was growing fast and had a better profit margin. The distributor agreed to increase efforts to sell B products and repeated this assurance at all quarterly review meetings. At the end of the year, however, the growth in sales for B for this distributor was 10 per cent as compared to a distributor average of 25 per cent.

Next, the manufacturer had a detailed on-the-spot survey of the territory prepared and proposed some marketing actions to the distributor, with help provided by the manufacturer. The distributor turned down the actions on the grounds of high costs but repeated assurances of paying more attention to B in the future. Six months later, the distributor's share of the B market had grown at 8 per cent as compared to the 25 per cent growth of the rest of the distributors. So the gap between the amount of line B the distributor ought to sell and what it actually sold, was getting wider and wider.

The manufacturer expressed dissatisfaction with the distributor's performance on the B front and said it would have to look for another distributor for the line in the territory if there was no improvement. This annoyed the distributor who threatened to give up on both the lines of the manufacturer if this happened. At the end of the next period, the growth rate for B was still 10 per cent for this distributor as compared to an average of 25 per cent. There was now a conflict between manufacturer and distributor on this point.

The manufacturer had another survey done on the territory and came to the conclusion that the distributor did not pay more attention to the B line because it could not do so rather than not choosing to do so. The owner of the firm was 60 years old and had two sons of 25 and 20 respectively, helping him, the first being in charge of administration and finance, and the second promising to be good at sales. The father was in charge of everything else and was not keen to take in outsiders as he wanted to pass on the family firm to his sons when he retired.

After considering all the facets of the problem the manufacturer offered the distributor another solution. The distributor firm would have two divisions to deal with the two lines, the father remaining in charge of A and the younger son being given the charge for B, with the older son being in charge of finance and administration for both divisions. The younger son being inexperienced, he would be given the necessary training in general management and marketing, by the manufacturer's staff to fit him for this responsibility. This solution would increase the turnover and profits of the distributor, his younger son could develop his potential fully and would be ready to take over the business of both lines when his father was ready to retire.

The distributor agreed to this strategy which was carried out as planned. The first year, product line B put on a spurt of 60 per cent increase in sales and this remained at 50 per cent two years later. The distributor had hopes of increasing its turnover over the next five years with 25 per cent of the total turnover coming from the B line products. The younger son was proving to be a good manager and as his self-confidence increased, he became more interested in the family business. The conflict between the manufacturer and distributor was thus resolved and the distributor remained grateful to the manufacturer for this solution. The moral of this story is,

> if the will to resolve something exists and if both parties realize that there could be mutual benefit in the resolution, then there can be a way out.

THE EFFECT OF POWER FACTORS

A channel system works because its members derive adequate benefits from their membership and the members in turn provide unique services to the system thereby adding value to it. In other words, the system functions effectively when each member is able to attain their own objectives through its membership of the system while the whole distribution system achieves its objectives through employing the members.

Conflict occurs when there is any imbalance between the various members' objectives and/or those of the whole system. On the other hand, some friction is necessary to ensure stimulation of the members. This motivates the channel members to adapt themselves to new situations, to innovate and to grow. It is necessary to prevent the conflict from causing any irremediable harm either to individual members or to the system. For this, active conflict management is necessary. It is a major task of channel management, to use conflict constructively and to prevent it from degenerating into harmful situations. Power is needed for this purpose as well as for the definition of channel roles.

A channel member has to possess sources of power such as reward, coercion, expertise, etc., in order to be able to control other channel members. These power factors react with each other. Excessive rewards may make the recipients feel that the rewarder is foolish and thus reduce his power in another way. The usual effect of reward is positive and that of punishment negative.

It has been found that the use of coercion generally increases channel conflict. Conversely, co-operation flourishes where the leader makes use of non-coercive power in the main. The more powerful the leader, the less use is made of power. The potential for positive reward increases dealer satisfaction even without the actual bestowal of a reward.

Economic power has a more direct effect on the ability to exercise influence than any other kind of power. On the other hand, the use of this power is likely to turn the 'influenced' channel member against the wielder of such power. Whereas the use of non-economic power may be seen to be beneficial in getting the channel member to conform to the leader's ideas.

It is therefore necessary to study the effects of use of both economic and non-economic power on channel members and use them carefully in a balanced mix to influence the members in the way the leader wishes. In conflict management, the ability to combine/flex the mix of powers gives one a 'win-win' situation. See Fig. 12.1 for a comprehensive list of powers which can be exercised by a channel leader.

ACQUIRING POWER POSITIVES

A properly managed channel operates more efficiently and provides increased satisfaction to all its members. This satisfaction can result because of four different factors:

1. Product – satisfaction with the quality and quantity of the products.
2. Finance – satisfaction with the available margins and returns.

The ability to combine/flex the mix of powers gives the basis to achieve a 'win-win' situation.

REWARD

EXPERTISE

ACCURATE INFORMATION

SPECIAL KNOWLEDGE

SPECIALIZED TRANSACTION

RELATIONSHIP

REPUTATION

IMAGE

LEGITIMACY

IDENTIFICATION

SUCCESS/FINANCIAL

LEGAL

PENAL

INTRINSIC

Figure 12.1   Conflict management

3. Help – from the manufacturer for joint promotion programmes, etc.
4. Intercommunication – between the manufacturer and the other channel members, handled by the former's representatives.

Satisfactory performance in the channel has been shown to co-exist with general high level of satisfaction among the channel members, though it is not clear which is the cause and which the result. However, effective channel management promotes both and increases the chances of survival of the channel.

One member of the channel system should be willing and able to assume leadership, using its power sources to cope with the varying aspirations and aims of the different channel members, and to impose such rules and restrictions as will enhance the efficiency of the channel. This control is essential to ensure performance levels in the channel. Control can be exercised through the leader's power to forecast future events and to obtain desired results in its channel relationships. Such control is generally the outcome of channel leadership and depends on the power commanded by the leader and the willingness of the members to be so led. Therefore the leader has to exercise discretion in the exercise of power and not exceed the level of tolerance of the various members. Channel members may be more willing to tolerate exercise of powers by the channel leader if past decisions of that leader have contributed to their performance.

Certain powers are specific to the category of the channel member. For example, the manufacturer may control the pricing in some markets and the retailer the inventory level.

Many factors will influence the success or otherwise of a channel leadership. The activity of other competing channels, possible alternatives, environmental factors and the leader's efficiency in the control of his own resources, can all affect this outcome. In the end, success depends on whether the channel performs well or not. Good performance results from effective channel control and the general level of satisfaction with the channel relationships among the channel members.

STRATEGIC MEANS FOR NEGOTIATION OUT OF CONFLICT

The following seven means are in common use.

1. Common goals: The adoption of common goals is almost always desired by all parties to the dispute as an ideal way of solving conflict. The difficulty lies in discovering goals which will result in the combatants subordinating their own separate goals to the achievement of this common goal. An outside threat can supply such a goal. The conflict may sometimes recur when the threat is removed.
2. Diplomacy: It is common to find individuals or teams employed for the purpose of diplomacy in channel management, especially in non-integrated systems. Their functions include help in shaping the policies, negotiating with those channel members that the diplomats are concerned with, gathering and disseminating information. It is essential that the status of diplomats be high enough to impress their power on the channel member they hope to influence. Inherent diplomatic skills, displaying sensitivity, are vital for success.
3. Exchange of personnel: A two-way exchange of personnel can be of immense help in promoting the ability to see each other's viewpoints. It gives the participants a broader view of the complexities of the whole

system and increases their commitment to making it work. This exchange is effective when it involves people who are uncommitted and whose role is perceived as important in channel co-ordination.

4. The introduction of new elements: The process of introducing new elements into the policy-making and decision structure of an organization after adequate consultation with channel members, in order to increase its stability, requires the establishment of a mechanism for the exchange of information, help and requests among the channel members. This device has been successfully used in some cases but it can raise legal issues or lead to dissatisfaction if no real heed is paid to the information provided.

5. Trade associations: The membership of such associations helps to air common problems at meetings as well as obtaining help through common experience and joint presentations. Even limited interaction through such membership is of help.

6. Third party mediation: This may be used for the settlement of a dispute. It has to provide new insights to the disputing parties as to the consequences both of continuing disputation and of a successful resolution of the conflict. The status of the mediator can influence the settlement of the conflict. Openness among the disputants should be encouraged as this helps them reach a common goal.

7. Arbitration: This can be made legally compulsory or it can be voluntary. However, legal decisions in one case may not apply to other cases where the circumstances are different and their value is therefore limited.

To be able to resolve a conflict, it is important to recognize how the conflict arose and what part was played by the key factors: interdependence, scarcity of resources, actual performance, perception of power and behaviour. The relationship of these factors is explained in Fig. 12.2. The best way of managing conflict is to use all of these possible methods and combine them into a suitable and effective policy. For example, 3M, which is noted for its marketing proficiency, uses eleven different ways to manage its distribution system and obtain information regarding all aspects in the system:

- association involvement
- dealer advisory council
- business planning partners programme
- fieldwork
- personal letters
- market needs conference
- branch co-ordinators' conference
- national office study
- market needs research

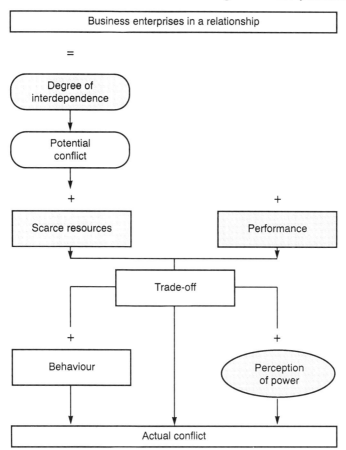

Figure 12.2 Field of conflict

- individual distributor conferences
- informal mini-councils

Pressure for profit

One of the perennial issues which crops up in the relationship between a manufacturer/supplier and a distributor is the pressure from the distributor for 'more profit'. Only two options appear to be open to the manufacturer by yielding to the pressure, reduction of the price to the distributor (or an increase in the discount enjoyed by the distributor) or an increase in the end-price which can jeopardize the competitive position of the company's products or services.

Generally, the top management deals with these negotiations and neither alternative is attractive to them. Management specialists or consultants are often called in this situation. After full investigation, a more desirable alternative can usually be found which leaves both participants in a win-win situation.

From the distributor's viewpoint, to put it simply, profit is income less costs. The two alternatives above deal with an increase in the 'income' part of this equation. However, the profit can equally well be increased by decreasing the costs. The manufacturer can often help in this by improving support to the distributor without materially increasing his own costs.

The manufacturer has, as a rule, developed efficient operating procedures, information systems and working methods for staff. These can be used by distributors internationally after suitable adaptation. Distributors themselves are unwilling to invest sufficiently to evolve their own procedures to that pitch of efficiency and often end up with minimal systems and procedures and thence a suboptimal support operation. If the manufacturer's own procedures, systems and methods are made available to the distributors or they are developed centrally, this can help distributors to increase their profits without adversely affecting the manufacturer's own position. Such assistance can be provided in many ways. The following are just two examples of this, quoted by John Wellemin, an international customer service consultant.

A UK manufacturer of diesel engines found that he was losing market share in some West African markets. His own distributors were dissatisfied with the amount of profits they made on his products and were not promoting them sufficiently. As a result, engines manufactured in other countries were taking an increasing share of the market. On close study of the circumstances, it was found that the end-users were demanding improved after-sales service support from the distributors which they found increasingly expensive. The manufacturer ran his own after-sales support organization in United Kingdom and in certain other countries, and had already developed efficient procedures, systems and methods for this purpose. These had been offered to the distributors world-wide but not 'sold' to them sufficiently, so that some distributors did not take up the offer under the impression that their own organizations were too small to profit from them. Now an effort was made to convince the distributors of the advantages of using these procedures, by showing the reduction in costs in distributor organizations who had adopted them elsewhere. This worked over a period of time so that the after-sales service in that particular market improved and the manufacturer's market share rose again.

A Japanese manufacturer of business equipment had European headquarters in Germany and marketed products through local distributors. In the former West Germany, he had six distributors strategically located in the major business and industrial centres. These distributors provided the manufacturer with data based on different parameters which made comparison between them difficult. The manufacturer negotiated with the distributors to standardize their data base and reporting procedures. They would have to change their procedures for the whole of their product base, which included products from other manufacturers as well and this made the process difficult. However, the manufacturer had a good reputation in his field and the distributors agreed to this proposal. The proposal consisted of providing each distributor with a standard information system package, making relevant hardware available to them and training his staff to utilize the system, learn the interpretation of the terminology, etc. All the distributor had to do thereafter was to send the required data to the manufacturer in the required form at stated intervals. This data was analyzed by the manufacturer for the whole of the country and detailed information was sent to the distributor regarding his own operation, comparing his performance with the average for the country. This approach meant the manufacturer could streamline the whole operation, improve the efficiency of his distributors by stressing their strengths and weaknesses, and increase profits and market share. The results were so satisfactory that the decision was taken to expand this approach throughout Europe.

PROBLEM-SOLVING AND REMOVAL OF BOTTLENECKS

There are many problems in establishing and managing international marketing channels. It is necessary for an international marketing manager to be aware of the problems that are likely to occur in the initiation, development and management of international trade and so plan accordingly. Let us examine this topic from the point of view of a situation involving distributors.

The first question is the objective of the operation from a business and a marketing point of view. If the supplier/manufacturer firm is not clear about this, how can it convincingly develop an idea of what the distributor should do? The next difficulty is in finding the 'distributor', although several directories now exist to help in this task. As stated in Chapter 9, it is worth repeating that, even after finding the distributor, rigorous criteria have to be applied to:

- the financial strength
- the connections
- the businesses represented
- the quality of the facilities, personnel, etc.
- the match between skills needed for the manufacturer's product coverage and the skills available within the candidate.

Problems can also arise in the development and management of the distributors. It is all the more necessary to choose distributors very carefully, as many countries have protective legislation to make it difficult to terminate the relationship easily in case of difficulties. The trading practices, the economic structure and cultural conditions of the host country can mean constraints on available channels.

Distributors in less developed countries, in particular those who are small, are not keen on innovation or large inventories, owing to the risk involved and the capital investment or the effort needed. Motivating foreign intermediaries can be difficult. Financial motivation may not work in certain cultural conditions. Some form of control is essential for the international marketer over the foreign channel members.

Existing arrangements between industry and intermediaries can restrict or block access to certain markets. All these difficulties and many more account for the increase in integration into manufacturing by these intermediaries, and into wholesaling and retailing by manufacturers. This in turn will form new financial barriers for new entrants into international trade. In all of these cases, it is necessary for an international marketing manager to have a problem-solving process in place so that the process can be put into effect quickly.

Such a process should enable the manager concerned to scope and define the problem clearly in an unemotional manner with an articulation of the root causes as to why the problem arose in the first place and its effects. The process should also enable identification of the issues involved and the critical success factors which must be met for a viable resolution of the issues. The process should facilitate the identification of possible options which might bear fruit and the means of implementing the options. Subject to an acceptability test and an examination of the risks and rewards, the manager should be able to put into action a remedy for the removal of the bottleneck or an appropriate solution to the problem.

Problems can arise from a failure to:

- keep the product up-to-date
- assess the market potential accurately early on
- anticipate the market trends correctly
- judge competitors' actions and their SWOTs
- appreciate seasonality, regional differences and peculiarities
- implement a good communication policy
- establish an appropriate advertising and promotion budget
- test-market new ideas in time
- differentiate between short term tactics and long term strategy
- follow-up on long term policies
- integrate all relevant marketing activities
- gain top management backing at an early stage.

A regular systematic global marketing audit to assess the specific market conditions, competition, overall performance of the company; a viable and acceptable plan of corrective action to improve the position in each of the key markets; a budget and an implementation programme are essential prerequisites for successful problem-solving.

13 UNSATISFACTORY PARTNERS

Unsatisfactory situations are one thing, but having unsatisfactory partners is another thing altogether. An unsatisfactory situation can probably be remedied with some effort and adjustment on the part of both parties, but an unsatisfactory partnership can be the result of something incapable of remedy. So it is important to enquire how the dissatisfaction arose in the first place.

CRACKS IN RELATIONSHIP

Cracks in relationships appear when the expectations of one party fail to materialize and when the relationship, whether personal and/or organizational, begins to deteriorate. The main causes may not be apparent – the surface reasons may be just manifestations of an unhappy situation. A dispassionate appraisal of the situation, an understanding of the symptoms and an analysis of the root causes are essential for mapping out remedial actions.

It is necessary to be clear about the importance of the relationship from strategic, operational and tactical points of view. The nature and the seriousness of the situation will depend upon the extent of the breakdown. Possible remedies may exist. However, if no remedies are possible then the only way out is to sever the relationship without jeopardizing the long term goals of the business. Whenever there is a mismatch between the needs of various parties and their expectations are not met, one needs to ask a key question, 'How are the needs of the various parties to be balanced?' The situation is well reflected by Fig. 13.1, which represents an adaptation from the idea developed by A. J. Proudman[1]. Frank Bradley uses a similar model in *International Marketing Strategy*.

The most important thing is to make an audit of the current distribution objective and the distribution operations, and see how these match the overall marketing objectives set for each chosen market. Any deviations indicate the absence of certain key factors which contribute to a successful

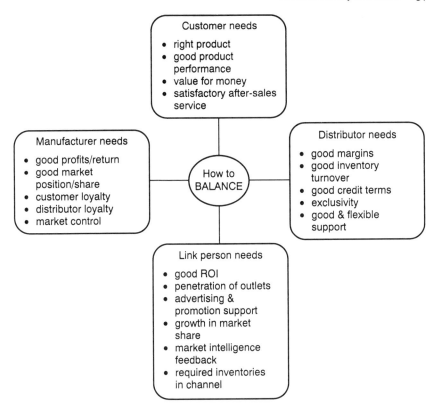

Figure 13.1 Balancing members' needs

distribution strategy. This analysis would be a starting point to establishing the gaps in distribution. As already explained in Chapter 2, a number of causes might create a gap:

- the marketing objective may be flawed;
- the strategy may be unclear or ill-defined;
- the distributor may not have understood the role of the supplier or his expectations;
- the manufacturer and the distributor may not have clearly defined what they expect of each other and established a common basis and agreed mutually beneficial objectives;
- the channel members may have developed incompatible objectives since the start of the relationship and this fact may have escaped the attention of the link person;
- there may be lack of sufficient margin for both parties;
- the product may not match the market needs;

• despite amicable discussions and reviews, a concrete action programme may not have been agreed.

UNSATISFACTORY PARTNERSHIPS

If things are really bad, termination may be the answer; but before embarking upon the final act, it is worth examining the implications.

All distributor or agency agreements are bound to end sometime. The majority of terminations are instigated by the manufacturers for genuine business reasons. However, the distributor is apt to see it as an unjust act that deprives him of well-earned profits and takes away the opportunity to earn interest from a considerable investment in developing the market within the assigned territory for the manufacturer's products. Therefore the likelihood of a tussle at the time of any termination is high. The payment provisions are the likely ground for the dispute and the probability of an acrimonious dispute is really high in case of verbal or improperly executed agreements.

If the agreement is terminated for a proper cause defined in the contract, then the case may be settled by arbitration. Unless a properly drafted 'non-waiver' clause is included in the agreement, the distributors may successfully claim that the company has waived its right to terminate for that cause by ignoring or condoning a previous omission.

Some modern contracts are considered to stipulate that the manufacturer is paying for the services of the distributor and/or certain key persons on their staff in order to obtain purchases of his product in their territory and for other named activities, and if these services are no longer available, the relationship is not of value to the manufacturer. If the distributor proposes to replace named key persons by others and the manufacturer disapproves, it will then be necessary to put forth valid reasons for non-acceptance.

Terminations are generally effective as soon as a written notice is given. It may be advisable to smooth the path by generous payments of commissions without insisting too much on the letter of the agreement.

Legal provisions vary. Europe has a plethora of protective national laws. These are in the course of being harmonised. In general, the provisions of agency law in the Netherlands is likely to be followed. A notice period can be one month if so specified, otherwise four months is the norm and a compensation of one year's commission or profit is normal. Belgium has an over-protective law allowing as compensation for agents and distributors, a value equivalent to any increase in goodwill, any expenses incurred in developing the business for the principal and compensation for employees discharged as a consequence of termination.

In Switzerland, a minimum period of one month's notice is required for terminating an agency agreement and agents are entitled to a compensation of a year's net profit from new clients gained for the principal.

In the Middle East, the provision is according to the prevailing Islamic law for resolving conflicts. Most Far Eastern laws are on the basis of common law principles. Japan, Korea, India, Malaysia, Singapore, Thailand – all provide for a termination period of a few months and compensation for termination without just cause.

Termination without cause is usually allowed to either party upon written notice of such intention, but such cases are even more likely to cause confrontations. Previous communication offering explanations and compensation may prevent costly litigation. Unless the notice period is shorter than stipulated in the agreement, there is no legal action available to the distributor. Even a shorter than stipulated notice period may not bring enough damages to justify legal action. However, various countries have passed laws to protect their nationals from such actions and these laws can help distributors to recover substantial damages if they can prove wrongful dismissal.

In Latin America, a maze of laws exist. A typical example of such legislation is the following part of Puerto Rican statutes called 'Dealers' Contracts' which states:

> *Notwithstanding the existence in a dealer's contract of a clause reserving to the parties the unilateral right to terminate the existing relationship, no principal . . . may directly or indirectly perform any act detrimental to the established relationship or refuse to renew said contract on its normal expiration except for just cause.*

Note that under this law a manufacturer cannot refuse to renew a contract except for 'just cause'. An earlier section defines just cause as 'nonperformance of any of the essential obligations of the dealer's contract or any action or omission by the dealer that **adversely and substantially affects** the interest of the principal in promoting the marketing or distribution of this product'.

Another part lays down substantial damages for termination without just cause. Yet another part stipulates a liberal interpretation of this law and denies a waiver for it.

It is entirely possible that a foreign distributor may not have to conform to the termination provisions of the agreement signed, because in many countries it may be considered a matter with wider, national implications and be dealt with under protective laws which discriminate against foreign companies. It is necessary to consider the implications of any agreement entered into with foreign entities and to get expert legal opinion before entering into any agreement.

Moreover, termination involves many other aspects apart from the legal one. Termination is desired usually because of unsatisfactory performance on the part of the distributor or the commercial agent; but other causes are possible, such as change in corporate policy, a wish to sell direct through branch/subsidiary or company mergers or acquisitions.

It is necessary to understand that in selling in foreign markets, a good distributor is a rare animal; so one must work closely with a good distributor to ensure that sufficient profits are earned on the deal. Mostly there is a spread of the good, the mediocre and the bad. It is usually impossible to change a bad or mediocre distributor into a good one. The best approach is to accept what you have for the time being, but keep up a continuous search for good people. At the same time, remember that each market is different, legally, economically and culturally, and has to be dealt with in different ways. It is essential that you should be able to get rid of unsatisfactory distributors quickly without fuss and expense; at the same time, it should be done with the full knowledge of the possible consequences. Termination is vital if the performance is unsatisfactory. International companies have to terminate a large number of agreements in order to be successful. Their reputation in this field, in turn, helps them to succeed.

Generally speaking, the foreign distributor represents the company as well as sells its products. It is better to make sure that the legal agreement spells this out, because by claiming that they acted as your agent, extra damages can be claimed upon termination. Watch out also for protective laws which classify the distributor's staff engaged in selling your products as your staff and entitle them to a generous compensation upon termination. While such laws were intended to ensure fair treatment for the distributors, in many cases, they serve to encourage poor performance by protecting such performers.

A distributor's interest in a competitor's product and offer of advantageous terms can also become a cause for conflict. A case in point is that of the Compaq Computers which experienced a costly channel conflict in early 1989. Their relations with Businessland, the largest publicly quoted computer store chain, were getting worse since 1986. This chain accounted for 7 per cent of Compaq's revenues and was a key customer. However, about one-third of their sales consisted of IBM products and IBM started to give them preferential treatment over their other dealers while the argument with Compaq regarding preferential treatment and pricing was going on, thus fuelling the conflict. IBM also offered its dealers incentives for promises of extra sales. Businessland tried to use this deal to extract concessions from Compaq. However, while IBM had the policy of negotiating separate terms with each of its dealers, Compaq had always held to a straightforward policy of equal treatment for all dealers and this had helped it to succeed. Instead of bending this policy in favour of a key customer, Compaq took the courageous decision to sever the relationship. They also publicized the IBM arrangements, hoping to arouse other IBM dealers into demanding similar terms and thus leading IBM into loss of profits.

DISSOLUTION OF THE RELATIONSHIP
AS A FINAL RESORT

What to do

1. Evaluate the performance of the distributor and the territory according to a planned schedule following the criteria already described in Chapter 11.
2. Ensure that the legal/contractual situation allows for appropriate actions to be taken in the event of a distributor failing to perform despite being given the necessary notice for remedial action to be taken.

How – and how not – to end a partnership

> **Remember:** It is easier to **hire** than it is to **fire**.

Normally a distributor is 'fired' because of unsatisfactory performance. Before committing yourself, check:

1. Does the agreement allow the action?
2. Does the law prevalent in that territory allow it?
3. Has the distributor failed because you failed them in some way, e.g. late deliveries?
4. Does the distributor owe you a lot of money?
5. Have good relationships been established with major customers?

There must be valid practical reasons for removing a distributor; otherwise, a distributor can take a manufacturer to court for damages. A messy removal can prove very expensive. A manufacturer may have to show '**just cause**'. Often the laws of Puerto Rico are good to remember. Courts generally favour the small firm and the local firm.

It can often happen that overseas distributors have friendly contacts with company representatives. They may take their dismissal personally and deep feelings can be aroused. It is best if the matter of termination is handled politely and in low key in order to maintain the company image locally. Reasonable payments should be made to keep things smooth, if possible. Customers should receive an explanation about a friendly parting of the ways and major customers a letter or visit. Continuity will need to be maintained by prompt signing of a new contract with a new distributor. Replacements should be investigated and decided upon before termination.

Once the decision is taken to 'fire' the distributor and problems have been anticipated and taken care of, use the following checklist:

1. Check if you have done everything correctly to help you market through your distributors.

2. Get good legal advice. (Engage a good lawyer in the country of the distributor and decide on the terms of payment beforehand. A six to nine-month contract enables the principal to judge the distributor's performance. The shorter the contract, the smaller the indemnity to be paid. A periodic written evaluation of the distributor's performance is of help in proving breach of contract. This should be sent to the distributor by registered post or some legally provable method.)
3. Line up, as discreetly as possible, an alternative distributor before making the break. Move quickly.
4. Get your major customers on your side.
5. Practise good human relations – try to save the old distributor from being humiliated.
6. Try for an amicable 'parting of the ways'.
7. Transfer the stock held by the old distributor to the new distributor.
8. Remember that there are **competitors** out there. Check your:
    (a) marketing strengths
    (b) product technical features
    (c) product – sales pluses
    (d) method of distribution
    (e) sales force calibre and size
    (f) method of remuneration
    (g) prices and discounts
    (h) advertising and sales promotion
    (i) after-sales service
    (j) financial situation
    (k) major weaknesses.

Reference

[1] Proudman, A. J. 'Distribution channels: Analytical aspects of the marketing system', p. 15, *The Quarterly Review of Marketing*, Winter, 1976.

14 FUTURE TRENDS IN DISTRIBUTION

It is worth exploring how distribution is likely to be affected by the changing scenario of world events and the trade issues as they develop.

THE EUROPEAN COMMUNITY TRADE ISSUES

The industrial trends for the 1990s, as regards Europe, are inseparable from the trend towards internationalization. A global economy is being evolved at several inter-related levels:

1. Economic policy – the commitment stemming from the 1987 Louvre accord for international co-ordination is likely to continue.
2. Deregulated financial markets increasingly influence economic policy.
3. World trade increased by about 7 per cent in 1989. In 1992, as this book is being written, the world trade is experiencing a severe downturn and the winds of recession can be felt everywhere. The much delayed agreement on the General Agreement on Tariffs and Trade (GATT) has not helped the situation either. The continuing deliberations of the GATT/Uruguay round will decide whether there is going to be a slide into protectionism and bilateralism.

One thing is certain – diverse pressures will continue to lead companies into international alliances so as to secure the critical size to compete in world markets. These global corporations need to be strong and lean, with enough management muscle to cope with its international division of labour.

The European Single Market is one of the most ambitious of regional groupings within the international economy; there are similar groupings emerging in North America and the Far East. The competitiveness of nation states is under severe strain.

New technology is changing the terms and conditions of competition. The emphasis is shifting from production processes to product design as consumers demand more sophisticated and stylish products. Research and development is becoming more important in these circumstances and larger markets are needed to finance this growing expenditure. Alliances help to spread the risk. With product lives becoming shorter, the pressures are building up to reduce the time gap between conception and the finished product. With production spread over vast distances, these distances have to be reduced through sophisticated communication systems.

Products are becoming so complex that it will soon become impossible for a single company to encompass expertise in all the technological aspects required. Increasingly, manufacturers will be specialist designers and assemblers of components made by subcontractors from all over the world. As competition becomes based on knowledge, industry will have to become more closely involved with education and training policies. Growing environmental concern will affect most industries.

ICI recently promoted their reputation as an innovative and environmentally sensitive company among the industry and trade alike; they marketed a new water-based car paint and substitute for car wax polish, both of which substantially reduced the overall noxious emissions from car paint and polish which pollute the atmosphere. This solved a problem for car manufacturers because the car finish is now a selling point for quality cars. This discovery has also opened up profitable opportunities for ICI with new uses being found for the paint.

Heinz were considering how to promote their image as a caring company through a series of charity promotions. They decided to do so and to celebrate the hundredth anniversary of the first Heinz sale in Britain by promoting a sponsorship appeal for the WWF. Heinz have a corporate policy of sponsorship which is not always linked to their advertising and promotion campaigns.

The break-up of the Soviet Union and the opening up of Eastern Europe could have a wide-ranging impact on industry as defence systems adjust to changed circumstances. The Organization for Economic Co-operation and Development (OECD) and International Monetary Fund growth forecasts predict a gradual slowing down of growth, with the United States at the bottom of the table, Japan at the top and Europe in between. The economic improvement in Latin America could mean improved prospects of trade there; the events in Eastern Europe could open up new opportunities; while the East Asian grouping around a more balanced Japanese economy also promises well in terms of world trade.

There is a risk in inflation continuing at around 4 per cent. If this is compounded by another oil crisis as predicted by some, matters could be serious for growth in the EC countries. Further defaults by developing countries and possibly by the United States are probable early in the new decade. These and the old financial wreckage will have to be handled carefully if a crisis is to be avoided.

During the last decade Japan tripled its share of world stock market capitalization to 45 per cent and increased its net external assets from nought to $350 billion. Japan has been spending more on capital investment in real terms than the United States and over twice as much per person as the US. It does, however, need to deregulate and drop its protectionism. A start could be made through opening farm markets, freeing the land market and enforcing anti-monopoly legislation more rigorously.

EFFECTS OF ECONOMIC AND MONETARY UNION

The Single European Market (SEM)

This was originally conceived as 'the creation of a growing unified market that utilizes to the full the resources available to it', ['Completing the Internal Market', White Paper from the Commission to the European Council, June 1985.] covering goods, persons, services and capital. In some ways it attempted to create a market similar to that of the United States by stipulating that a manufacturer in any member country should be able to sell products in any other member country. In some other ways, it tried for more liberalization, for example, in seeking to approximate taxes and freeing financial services from trade barriers. But little was heard about common monetary and economic measures until the Delors Committee Report in 1988. The pressing question was whether the programme was intended to help the consumers or the producers of Europe. The Treaty of Maastricht signed at the end of 1991 is being tested within the nation states making up the Community and already questions are being raised. Opinions remain divided.

Disagreements over most points have held up the various measures proposed by the European Commission. The twelve countries that are included in the Community and the thousands of businesses that are housed in those countries naturally have different priorities and perspectives, and these need to be reconciled before any progress can be made.

The removal of trade barriers was considered a main priority, a symbol of the envisaged united Europe. The ability to live in and work in any member state was another measure to promote the idea. The taxation proposals were made for the same reason, calling for value-added taxes in two bands, a standard 14 to 20 per cent band and a lower 4 to 9 per cent band for essential goods plus single rates of excise duties for goods such as alcohol or tobacco. As a matter of fact, different indirect taxation levels do not impede trade in other federations, such as the United States. The fear was that the prospect of a wave of consumers freely crossing frontiers in search of bargains in selected goods would prevent the member states from agreeing to remove all frontier controls. When France, Germany and the Benelux countries agreed in 1989 to free their borders by 1990, the Commission replaced its original taxation proposals by setting minimum allowable rates and letting market forces deal with the different tax levels.

The originators of the SEM idea realized that psychological and cultural barriers inhibited cross-European trade as much as actual trade barriers. Therefore a lot of emphasis has been placed on making a psychological impact through publicity. The various national businesses have to think of themselves as part of a European market and act accordingly. It has pushed multinationals into considering Europe-wide marketing policies and retailers into European growth through acquisitions and joint ventures.

The progress so far

The need for unanimity hampered all progress for a long time. In 1986, the Single European Act allowed majority voting and weighted majority voting in a number of important areas. It also advocated the mutual recognition of national standards and regulations as a way forward for free movement of goods which did not need technical regulations. Later this was extended to services including financial ones. In the area of motor vehicles, the fear of Japanese competition successfully exploiting the unified market has held back both the adoption of Community-wide approval for components and the consensus on national quotas for Japanese imports. Members have been afraid of standards falling to the lowest common denominator in such areas as health and safety, and this has delayed agreement in other areas. An emphasis on better environmental standards in some areas of the Community will also hinder the freer movement of goods.

For consumer products, the expansion across SEM is comparatively easy. For industrial products, it will be far more difficult. National specifications are applied to industrial goods and whereas external suppliers can try for sales, their goods may not be preferred even though they are cheaper. The difficulties facing businesses trying for rationalizations and mergers because of company organization and differences in language, culture and consumer attitudes still remain unchanged. Most governments insist on mergers having to be in their national interest. Economic reasons sometimes make opportunities outside EC more attractive to European businesses. EC's merger directives will help clarify the position and make mergers and acquisitions easier in the Community. The progress made so far is uneven and the process should be considered as evolving continuously over many years instead of being completed by the beginning of 1993.

Europe in 1993

The situation in the Community in 1993 will depend largely on the way the following issues are resolved:

1. The goals of free competition which will benefit consumers and pro-motion of global European companies which will benefit producers of goods and services are contradictory, at least in the short term. What degree of importance is to be attached to each of them?
2. Are European companies to be the main beneficiaries of the SEM? How will this affect the relations of EC with the rest of the world?
3. Should SEM aspire to be more than just a barrier-free trade area in terms of economic and political co-operation and introduce further measures making more impact on people and businesses?
4. Will the creation of SEM mean more liberalization or just some amount of regulation which will be common to all members?
5. How far will Brussels take over power from national governments and in which areas?

There has been some degree of acceptance on the part of member govern-ments that the Commission has taken over some powers from them and is likely to take over more. The European Commission is continually strug-gling against national governments over non-conformance with some EC law or regulation. Many member countries can now face and accept the idea of monetary and economic integration and reduction in sovereignty in favour of the SEM. The vision of a politically and economically united Europe which can successfully compete with the US and Japan inspires many people. The volatility of foreign exchange markets is seen as deterring many would-be European businesses, and a Central European bank and a common currency are seen as remedies.

The attitudes of the member states vary widely on the relevant issues. At one end are the United Kingdom and Denmark who sometimes tend to see the Single Market solely as an aid to exporting to Europe. Then there is Luxembourg which considers itself completely a part of the Community. France and Germany try to protect national interests but they also bow to compromise in the wider interests of the Community. Italy, Belgium, Netherlands and Ireland are in favour of greater unity because they feel either internal disunity or small size precludes them from national power. Portugal and Greece wish for the removal of regional disparities and Spain is moving from this position to the Italian one.

The disparity of opinion on the Social Charter, for example, is typical of the national interests. Germany and some other high cost countries are generally in favour of this charter which seeks to equalize working conditions across the EC; the countries which benefit most from their low labour costs, because businesses prefer them as manufacturing locations, are against it. The opposition of the UK government has been on the basis of the Conservative party policy and the UK businesses are not keen to increase the cost attributable to labour.

Businesses in the United States and Japan have long feared that the consolidation of the Single Market would mean some degree of protectionism against foreign companies and have therefore increased their investments in Europe rapidly in recent years. The EC members themselves as well as the Commission are deeply divided over this issue. It can be said that too much protection would damage European businesses even more than foreign businesses since the former depend heavily on exports outside Europe. It would be possible to introduce protection through:

- setting standards and regulations so as to favour European companies;
- not freeing public procurement to non-EC bids;
- rules against dumping and similar other rules to make non-EC businesses establish themselves in the EC to obtain equal treatment;
- insistence on reciprocity – on 'equal access' being granted to EC firms if access is granted to non-EC firms.

There is great divergence over the encouragement of free competition. The car industry is a typical example. It is afraid of Japanese competition and would like protection until it becomes competitive. There has been opposition to Japanese companies having subsidiaries in the EC and thus evading the quota system by producing cars there with a sufficient number of locally manufactured parts.

However, although economic reasons may cause opposition to foreign participation, they can also work the other way. The Italian telecommunications equipment firm Italtel chose AT&T for its partner in future enterprise instead of one of a number of European companies which had tried for the partnership.

The idea of reciprocity has shifted from 'equal access on equal terms' in 1988 to the present, when the Commission proposes to take action on a sector-by-sector basis. As far as foreign companies are concerned, American companies are treated better than others, especially Japanese companies. This is due to a number of reasons, historic, cultural and economic. However, in order to make progress on public procurement directives covering public utilities, the Commission has lately proposed that discrimination should be allowed against contractors or consortia who source over half of the value of their contract from outside the EC. The Japanese and Far Eastern businesses are right to press on with establishing bases in the EC in order to evade protectionist measures. A sufficient percentage of the components will have to be manufactured inside the EC and their R&D activities also will have to be conducted locally.

There is a group of countries, consisting of the six founder members of the EC (France, Germany, Italy and the Benelux countries) plus Spain, that wish for further integration, while the others are not so happy with the idea. The economic systems of the six founder member states are sufficiently similar for them to view the idea of harmonization with equanimity. These core countries are getting impatient over the lack of progress towards further integration. This split may mean that a core of EC countries may proceed further with integration while others stay on the periphery as a free trade area; otherwise the progress on the implementation of the measures considered in the White Paper will be very slow.

The countries of the European Free Trade Association (EFTA), consisting of Austria, Finland, Iceland, Norway, Sweden and Switzerland, have also been very anxious over the Single Market proposals. They have far more at stake than any other country because over 70 per cent of their exports are to the EC countries. EC measures regarding employment, visas, investment, etc., will also affect them deeply. Most EFTA countries are either proposing to apply for EC membership, or have already done so. Already an agreement has been reached to integrate the economic and trade aspects and form an European Economic Area to include the eighteen into a new trading bloc with effect from 1993.

Owing to the break-up of USSR and the opening up of Eastern Europe in general, the fear of being in the middle of a war between the superpowers has receded. This in turn will affect the defence industry and thence quite a few other industries. The developments in the Eastern part of Europe may well have far-reaching effects on the Community's future.

Distribution in SEM

The European marketing and distribution systems are undergoing a thorough technological transformation. Home videotext will permit ordering of products direct from the manufacturer, thus revolutionising traditional distribution channels, while ensuring greater market transparency. An agreement exists on the compatibility of videotext equipment in the Community.

The function of international physical distribution expends most of its energy in overcoming barriers which would deny a marketing opportunity to the company. Its success in choosing the best option from available alternatives depends on the marketing policy and the choice of the markets most suited to the products on offer. Barriers to trade are represented by tariffs, prohibitions and quotas of various kinds which distort costs or make it difficult for the company to enter the market. The Single European Market aims to remove most of these in its territory.

Companies used to marketing through a particular set-up nationally may find it difficult to conduct marketing operations in countries where no such set-up exists. For example, no self-selection stores of the type of Boots in Britain exist in the rest of the common market. National restrictions may exist on selling certain products in certain ways, such as medicines in self-selection stores.

Many countries have legal restrictions which concentrate ownership of industry and distribution in the hands of their own nationals. This will no longer be possible in the Single European Market. Exclusive agreements may prevent competitors from marketing through certain outlets which are dominated by powerful companies. This kind of agreement will be difficult to enforce legally in the new Europe.

The cost of transport is expected to decrease substantially in the Single Market. Monetary Union, when it comes, will lead to reduced exchange risks as all countries peg their currencies within the Exchange Rate Mechanism in the immediate term. Moves towards a single currency and unified monetary control and fiscal policies will lead to minimization of risks associated with transaction, translation and accounting exposures. Trading from the point of view of currencies and accounting will become easier and the export manager will have a few less problems to overcome.

As has been mentioned elsewhere, the distribution systems vary between industries and between markets. Highly developed markets usually have short distribution channels with multiple-dominated systems. In long channel structures, the goods spend a long time in the system while a large number of intermediate transactions take place. Long channels are less easily controlled by the suppliers. It also requires a larger sales force to activate the system sufficiently to make the goods move through the system. Short channel systems are more controllable and use less stock which stays in better condition and reaches the end consumer more quickly. They do require a more efficient distribution system and the effect of any shortfall in stock is quickly felt in the market. Many companies are already beginning to investigate the warehousing, storage and distribution arrangements within the European Community. For instance, is there a case for siting the main storage and distribution centres in two or three places in ideal central locations so that all the major requirements for delivery of products can be cost-effectively managed for the benefit of everybody? Where should these be located? How can the existing infrastructure and transportation systems be best utilized? These and similar questions are occupying the minds of the distribution strategists of many companies in the European Community.

Management needs to formulate a proper strategy for physical distribution in order to take advantages of the new order from their own viewpoint. Physical distribution absorbs a large proportion of costs in getting the product to the market and it is worthwhile to use resources in order to maximize its efficiency and minimize its costs.

IMPACT OF SOCIAL, ECONOMIC AND CULTURAL CHANGES

Every company needs to examine the implications of the relevant EC directives and measure the impact on the business development strategy. The relevant directives/regulations relate to:

- deregulation and competition policies
- common European standards
- EC price harmonisation policy
- EC social policy
- EC safety and health standards

The following publications can be used for reference:

1. *Common Standards for Enterprises* – document published by the Commission of the European Communities[1]
2. *A Guide to Working in a Europe Without Frontiers* – document published by the Commission of the European Communities[2]
3. *Company Law and Competition* – prepared by S. J. Berwin & Co (the United Kingdom CBI Initiative)[3]
4. *Croner's Europe* – published by Croner Publications[4]

The changes in Europe that are taking place and the pace of economic, social and political integration have created certain preconditions for the integration of business activities in the EC countries. Each company needs to examine the pressures for regionalizing the headquarters activity and the role of the 'channel'. For example,

1. Are there benefits to be gained by a single European headquarters from which the total European activity is co-ordinated?
2. What are the benefits of continuing with subsidiaries? What is the role of the subsidiary in each country? How does this role differ in countries where distributors also play an important part? Why do we need different sales forces located in different countries?
3. What is the role of the distributor in each territory? Should we have stocks of our products in each territory? Can benefits be gained by locating the logistics, storage and distribution centres in a few central locations rather than having some or all of them in each territory?

4. As trade barriers are lifted, what is the anticipated customer buying attitude in terms of where and when to buy our products? Would the independent channel members remain content to operate in their current restricted territories? What will be the consequences of merger/acquisition moves among distributors?

OPPORTUNITIES IN THE ENLARGED EUROPE

The removal of a plethora of non-tariff barriers such as customs barriers, differing product standards and public procurement limited to national suppliers should give industry a vastly enlarged and improved competitive arena to do business in. They can make better use of their resources and exploit their strengths and the new opportunities in this enlarged market.

Economies of scale in the enlarged Europe could make significant reductions to costs. The competitive pressure should motivate companies to re-organize more efficiently so that they can cope with reduced prices from increased competition. This should also generate more innovation in processes and products.

Lower material and transport costs together with the possibility of using the best production locations from the point of view of labour and capital as well as transport will help companies to become cost effective. The businesses will also have a larger pool of skills to draw on in an integrated Single European Market.

Increase in efficiency will make up for any decrease in profit margins due to increased competition in the market-place. High technology companies are expected to benefit substantially from this new climate, from better opportunities for co-operation in R&D projects and help from the Commission in this field.

THE SINGLE MARKET: EMERGING STANDARDS

A European group which manufactures lifts has estimated that the costs generated as a result of the differences in technical standards from country to country accounts for almost 10 per cent of their manufacturing costs. The costs of telephoning in Europe are 8 per cent higher due to differing procedures for testing and approving telephone exchanges. The application of the principle of reciprocal trust will mean that a product legally manufactured and marketed in one member state can automatically be sold freely in another member state with different standards in force. By 1993, any product which can be sold in the member state of its origin, will be readily marketable in other states. The barriers are being tackled in the following ways:

1. New barriers will be avoided through measures already in force.
2. Harmonised European standards are to be introduced through the Community's New Approach to Technical Harmonisation, agreed in 1985. Directives will be limited to setting the essential requirements for health, safety and environment, the technical details being worked out by the various bodies dealing with European standards. The directives provide for total harmonisation, so that all products which comply with these requirements will carry an EC mark and can circulate freely in the rest of EC. The relevant European standards will replace the corresponding individual national standards. Some member states have reached bilateral agreements on mutual recognition of test laboratory accreditation and calibration.

Two non-political organizations, CEN (European Committee for Standardization) and CENELEC (Committee for Electro-Technical Standardization), are responsible for setting the standards and regulations. They rely on representations from manufacturing concerns to help them in their work. Industry should not see European standards-making as a reactive process to which it responds by manufacturing to a new standard. It should take an active part in influencing the setting of these standards from an early stage, through the appropriate bodies. Those countries and industries which are active in the production of European standards will give their countries/ industries a competitive advantage.

Three basic concepts must be held in mind to understand the changing Euro-norms. First are the national regulations set by the governments. Second are national standards evolved by industry, supposedly voluntary but often quasi-mandatory because they satisfy the national regulations. Then there is certification, by which a product is shown to meet regulations or standards.

To begin with, there was an effort by governments to decide by unanimous vote on new European standards. That took too long. So the Commission decided to trim the law-making back to only those safety attributes needed to assure a product the right to be sold in any EC country.

Two basic product directives have so far been agreed for toy safety and pressure vessels. They were relatively easy to agree upon. For more complicated products, the procedure appears doomed as a quick route to freer Euro-trade for various reasons:

1. The Commission is finding it hard to make government officials regulate in terms of aims (the machine should not catch fire) rather than descrip-

tions (the machine should be made of fireproof materials in such and such parts).

2. No adequate certification system exists to prove that goods meet European safety regulations. Even if rules exist, the mutual trust does not.

3. A basic European safety regulation does not in practice ensure an open market for goods. A machine tool may be deemed safe to be brought into Germany but not to be installed there because it is incompatible with German usage regulations.

4. Euro-standards do not in practice replace national ones, but are incorporated into them. The national standard-setters can add additional requirements. Again, an item may have right of entry but little chance of sale.

5. Smaller European countries fear that European standard-making will be dominated by Germany, France and the United Kingdom, who are the major standard-setters in the EC.

6. Some of these difficulties are bedeviling the 'machinery directive', the most ambitious product directive yet. This hopes to lay down the law for industrial machines which together have an annual turnover in EC of 120 billion ECUS.

7. There are arguments over how much detail it should contain and how the machines should be certified; and it is already spawning other directives about how they should be used.

All the European government can do is limit its own responsibility and involvement to considerations of safety, and hope that European industry sees that the balance of its advantage lies in co-operating rather than hindering. Luckily, in high definition television, in mobile telephones, in computer standards, there is mounting enthusiasm within European industry for agreeing standards beforehand instead of arguing about them afterwards. The feeling of being in one boat and surrounded by tough outside competition is taking hold.

THE SINGLE MARKET: PRODUCT MARKETING IMPACT

The following points should be kept in mind while considering the implications of the European Single Market:

1. All products must comply with the new EC standards set by the Commission. Descriptions of a product must not vary among the EC countries for the same products – consumers must have access.

2. Products may have to be differentiated to appeal to the different market perceptions which will inevitably be there, given the various cultures in the Community.
3. After the creation of the European Single Market in 1993, the prices will not be able to vary too much within the market owing to the spread of communications and easier transport across borders. Harmonisation of prices will be necessary to comply with the Community competition policy.
4. The terms offered to the distributors will have to be based on the principle of 'no unequal prices for equal services', in order to comply with the EC legislation concerning fair competition.
5. Satellite and overhead broadcasting will increase awareness throughout the whole Single Market and test marketing will have to be done on carefully selected bases.
6. Selective distribution has to conform to community regulations concerning competition and resale price maintenance.

EASTERN EUROPE

The ending of the 'cold war' and the removal of the formal barrier between East and West have released the aspirations of the peoples in Eastern Europe and their demand for expertise, know-how and products from the West have increased substantially. However, there is a long way to go before the Eastern countries can afford to pay for what they need from the West.

The infrastructure within the Eastern economies, the transport systems, the financial systems and the management processes of the economies will have to be radically altered to match the aspirations of their people. There is the realization that a move towards a market economy is the most effective way of attaining the goals which the Eastern Europeans wish to attain.

Time is not on their side to go through the processes of development in terms of technology that the West went through – it took several decades to get where we are today. One of the main ways of reducing the time needed towards progress to a market economy is to adopt modern technology quickly and readily. This opens up opportunities for the high technology businesses of the West to help Eastern Europe to modernize, to improve their economies and to enhance the social and economic life of the people. The opportunities are there for those who can invest in these countries, who are willing to take some risk in the short term to reap benefits in the long run and who are prepared to enter into various kinds of joint venture, co-operation or commercial trading relationships with local enterprises.

In this context, the various countries have different levels of risk associated with them because their political systems and the liberalisation and democratisation of the institutions and the societies are at different levels. Hungary, Poland and Russia are at the head of the list.

Most of the other EC member states would like to see the further expansion of the Community to counterbalance the influence of unified Germany. Many of the Community members think that rapid integration of the existing community is necessary so that attention can be concentrated on further expansion. The admission of East Germany to the EC folds has prompted the other Eastern bloc states to consider application for either EC membership or associate status such as the EFTA countries enjoy at present. The latter would mean preferential treatment with regard to tariffs and possible participation in EC initiatives, with R&D for example. While this would mean cheaper imports from Eastern Europe would be competing with EC products, it would not change the present situation substantially. Those imports have already been making their way to the EC markets through East Germany, which has now become a pipeline for trade with the former Eastern bloc countries. At the same time, the heavy investment made by West Germany in the eastern part was expected to give the other EC members time to catch up with Germany.

Cheap labour would no longer benefit Greece, Spain and Portugal when there are other options in Eastern Europe. This may fuel further demands from poorer EC members for protection against full integration. However, investment in Eastern Europe is slow at present due to lack of skilled labour, political uncertainty and lack of the necessary infrastructure. Later on, the local markets in the Eastern European countries are expected to absorb much of the products they are now exporting and their consumer markets are expected to expand rapidly.

A company wishing to invest in Eastern Europe should ponder the following points:

- the country or countries which should be considered and in what order;
- the products or services to be manufactured or marketed there;
- the extent of the company involvement in those product markets;
- the timing of the venture;
- the organization to be created to address the new market.

ACTION FOR THE 1990s

Today, more than ever before, understanding competition is vital to survival and success. When a business gets complacent and does not react quickly to the moves of its major competitors, the chances of its recovering its position are diminished. Companies must devote more energy to monitoring competition, evaluating competitors' strategies and developing appropriate responses.

It is worth bearing in mind that in the high technology world, some companies which ignored 'global marketing' are being pushed aside in their domestic markets by strong and competitive global companies. Every company must review its international channel strategy from a global point of view at least once a year.

Product life cycles have been getting shorter and shorter owing to various pressures. It is often difficult to know when a product has reached a plateau and is about to decline. When the decline does come, it can degenerate into a rapid fall. It is essential to plan and develop quick responses to status changes in product life cycles. Chance only favours the prepared mind.

Yesterday's channel may not be the appropriate channel for tomorrow. Every company should undertake a review of its channel strategy and examine whether there are viable and more profitable alternatives for the emerging world order.

Culture plays an important part in each national market – international companies and their channel management practices must either respond to the influence of the national culture or try to change it. Changing the influence of a culture is a mammoth task and time may not be on their side. So the former is the more beneficial route. Having people who know and understand the local culture is an important aspect of channel management.

Channel structure varies from country to country. Certain changes in the pattern can be brought about through market development. Good channel management means early recognition of this potential and taking advantage of the opportunity to innovate and gain competitive advantage. Avoid the most common mistakes of exporters.

1. If you are starting a new operation, don't fail to get good export counselling.
2. Develop a channel strategy as part of your international marketing plan before exporting.
3. Make sure that your top management fully understand what is involved and give their commitment to the plan. 'Distribution', Peter Drucker once said, 'is the darkest continent of business'. Many top managers have never ventured to sell anything abroad.
4. Take care and apply due diligence before selecting an overseas distributor.
5. Getting orders is the most important task – never fail to chase for business.
6. Don't ignore your export markets when the domestic market booms.

7. Treat international distributors as important contributors and not as second class channel members.
8. Make sure your warranty and service messages are clearly understood in overseas markets.
9. Don't fail to explore alternative routes to the markets.
10. Motivation of channels is the key to managing them.
11. Physical distribution management is a critical factor to the success of overseas marketing.
12. Do not expect the channel to have a long term orientation – long term direction is part and parcel of the manufacturer's channel leadership role.
13. Develop a mission for your business which includes the channel – without it you don't have a mission.
14. Determining service output levels is a prime responsibility of channel management.
15. Success in channel management can only be achieved if you know how to manage conflicts.
16. Channels only do what is inspected; they do not do what is expected.

References

[1] Nicholas, Florence and Repussard, Jacques. *Common Standards for Enterprises*, The Commission of the European Communities, Luxembourg. 1988.
[2] Seche, Jean-Claude. *A Guide to Working in a Europe without Frontiers*, The Commission of the European Communities, 1988.
[3] Berwin, S. J. & Co. *Company Law and Competition*, W. H. Allen & Co Plc, London, 1989.
[4] *Croner's Europe*, Croner Publications, London.

APPENDIX 1

A specimen distribution agreement within the EC

Caution *Use this specimen only if authorized by your legal advisers to do so. There are established practices, customs and procedures followed in certain types of industries, products and jurisdictions – local laws and customs vary in each country, state or territory.*

The following must be treated as a specimen only and it is provided on the understanding that the author and/or publisher is not engaged in the provision of legal, accounting or other professional service.

SPECIMEN DISTRIBUTORSHIP AGREEMENT

This Distributorship Agreement is made on

between   (1)

('the Company')

and   (2)

('the Distributor')

whereby it is agreed as follows:

1. **Interpretation**

  1.1   In this agreement, except as far as the context otherwise requires,

    'Guaranteed Turnover' shall mean

    'The Products'   shall mean

    'The Territory' means

    'The Trade mark/Know-how' means

    'The Statement of Sales Policy' means

1.2   Clause headings are for convenience only and shall not affect or be deemed to affect the construction or interpretation of the terms and conditions of this Agreement.

2. Appointment of Distributor

2.1   The Company hereby appoints the Distributor and the Distributor accepts the appointment as authorized distributor of the Products in the Territory with effect from the date hereof until   ; subject always to termination in accordance with the provisions of Clause 7 hereof. Thereafter this appointment will be deemed to continue for successive periods of 12 months commencing on 1 January   unless terminated by three months' written notice by either party.

2.2   The Company reserves the right to sell to and serve directly a certain list of named customers/accounts and the Distributor accepts this reservation of the Company.

3. Duties of the Distributor

3.1   The Distributor warrants that at the date of this agreement that it complies/will comply with and satisfies/will satisfy the Distributor requirements as set out in Schedule.

3.2   The Distributor shall use best endeavours actively to promote and extend sales of the Products throughout the Territory.

3.3   The Distributor shall have no authority:

- to offer for sale or accept any order for the Products on behalf of the Company or,
- to pledge the Company's credit or,
- to enter into, execute, acknowledge, deliver, cancel or amend any contract or any agreement, bond or other instrument whatsoever or contract any other rights or obligations on behalf of the Company or,
- to represent the Company or,
- to act as the Company's agent in any way whatsoever and shall not in any way hold itself out as having any such authority.

3.4   The Distributor undertakes to place such orders with the Company for the Products as will ensure that the Distributor has adequate stocks as defined in the Statement of Sales Policy from time to time to provide a reliable (to the reasonable satisfaction of the Company) supply of the Products to the customers of the Distributor.

3.5   The Distributor undertakes to adequately report as defined in the Statement of Sales Policy on matters which affect or may affect the sale of the Products in the Territory.

3.6   During the period of this Agreement the Distributor shall not without the prior written consent of the Company, manufacture or distribute or promote products which compete with the Products.

3.7   During the period of this Agreement the Distributor undertakes to purchase the Products only from the Company.

3.8 The Distributor undertakes to comply in all respects with the Statement of Sales Policy, issued from time to time by the Company.

4. Conditions of sale

All sales of the Products by the Company shall be subject to the Standard Conditions of Sale of the Company set out in Schedule   hereto and as amended from time to time by the Company.

5. Trade marks/know-how

The Distributor acknowledges that it has no rights to use any trade mark used by the Company or know-how of the Company in connection with the Products, except in accordance with the Company's instructions.

6. Confidentiality

During the period of this Agreement and for a period of three (3) years thereafter the Distributor shall treat as confidential and shall not disclose to any third party any information (whether technical or otherwise) relating to the Products, or the Company's affairs or businesses or method of carrying on business made available to it by the Company and shall not use such information except for the purpose of this Agreement.

7. Termination

7.1   Without prejudice to its rights under Clause 2 hereof, the Company shall be entitled to terminate this Agreement immediately by notice in writing if the Distributor shall not have remedied any breach of any of the terms or conditions of this Agreement within thirty (30) days after being called upon to do so in writing or if the other party shall become insolvent or go into liquidation provided that any termination shall not entitle the Distributor to any payment of compensation but subject thereto shall be without prejudice to the rights or claims of either party which may have arisen prior to or on account of such termination or to the provisions of Clauses hereof.

7.2   In the event that the Distributor shall not in any one fiscal year of the Company achieve the Guaranteed Turnover or in the event that no timely agreement shall be reached with respect to the Guaranteed Turnover for a particular year, the Company shall be entitled to terminate this Agreement immediately upon written notice to the Distributor.

7.3   Upon any notice of termination given pursuant to this Agreement and without prejudice to any other rights of the Company the Distributor shall at the written request of the Company return to the Company forthwith all stocks of unpaid Products supplied; failing which the Company shall have the right to enter upon the Distributor's premises during normal working hours and without notice to reclaim the same.

8. Assignment

The Distributor shall have no right to assign, transfer or in any way dispose of the benefit (or any part thereof) of this Agreement without the prior written consent of the Company.

9. Complete agreement

The terms and conditions of this Agreement shall replace any previous terms and conditions between the Distributor and the Company relating to any of the Products.

10. Variation and waiver

10.1   No waiver by either party of any provision of this Agreement shall be binding unless made and expressly confirmed in writing.

10.2   Any such waiver shall relate only to such matter, non-compliance or breach as it expressly relates to and shall not apply to any subsequent or other matter, non-compliance or breach.

10.3   If any provision of this Agreement is held invalid as a matter of law, such invalidity shall not affect the other provisions of this Agreement, all of which shall remain in full force and effect.

10.4   The Schedules   and   and the Statement of Sales Policy attached hereto are by this reference incorporated in and made an integral part of the present Agreement.

10.5   Any modification of the present Agreement, excluding Schedules and   and the Statement of Sales Policy hereto, shall have to be made and confirmed in writing by the parties hereto.

11. Governing law

The construction, validity and performance of this Agreement shall be governed by the laws of   and the authoritative text shall be that in the English language set out herein. Any disputes arising in connection with the present Agreement or further agreements resulting thereof shall be finally settled by arbitration in accordance with the rules of the   and such proceedings held and located in

12. Notices

12.1   Any notice required to be given to either party hereto shall be in writing and deposited by hand at or sent by recorded delivery mail or telex to the address of that party as set out below or such other address as may from time to time have been notified in writing by the party in question to the other.

12.2   In the case of notices to the Company

For the attention of:

12.3   In the case of notices to the Distributor

For the attention of:

As witness, the hands of the authorized representatives of the parties, the day and year first above mentioned.

Signed by:

For and on behalf of
(the Company)

Signed by:

For and on behalf of
(the Distributor)

SCHEDULE A:
STANDARD CONDITIONS OF SALE

As presented under Schedule

APPENDIX 2
A second specimen distribution agreement within the EC

Caution   *Use this specimen only if authorized by your legal advisers to do so. There are established practices, customs and procedures followed in certain types of industries, products and jurisdictions – local laws and customs vary in each country, state or territory.*

   The following is provided as a sample information and it is furnished on the understanding that the author and/or publisher is not engaged in the provision of legal, accounting or other professional service.

SPECIMEN DISTRIBUTORSHIP AGREEMENT

An AGREEMENT made the   day of   19
BETWEEN XYZ Limited, a company incorporated in   and having a place of business at   (hereafter called the Company) of the first part, AND Alpha Beta Company having a place of business at
(hereafter called 'the Distributor') of the other part.

WHEREAS XYZ is desirous of appointing the Distributor, and the Distributor is desirous of being appointed to be XYZ's Authorized DISTRIBUTOR for the sale of the 'XYZ' branded products described in Schedule 'A' hereof (hereinafter called 'the Products')   in (hereinafter called 'the Territory') on the terms herein set forth.

NOW IT IS HEREBY AGREED

1. **Appointment of Distributorship**

1.1   XYZ hereby appoints the Distributor to be its Authorized Distributor for the sale of the Products in the Territory.

1.2   The Distributor fulfils the qualifications listed in Schedule C (Distributor requirements') and wishes to be appointed as an Authorized Distributor of XYZ Company.

2. **Terms of appointment**

2.1   The Distributor shall be deemed to be an independent contractor and, save as may be provided herein, shall meet all its expenses in connection herewith, and shall not in any way represent itself as being the agent of XYZ.

2.2   The Distributor shall use its best endeavour to promote the sale of the Products throughout the Territory and shall employ such technically competent sales and technical staff as may be reasonably necessary to that end.

2.3   The Distributor shall not manufacture or distribute in the Territory during the term hereof any goods which compete with the Products without the prior agreement of XYZ given in writing.

2.4   The Distributor shall not sell any of the Products outside the Territory without the Prior agreement of XYZ given in writing.

3. Pricing policy

3.1   In consideration for the Distributor's undertakings under Clauses 2 and 5 hereof the Distributor shall have the right to purchase the Products from XYZ at the prices set out in Schedule 'A' hereof, as may be amended by XYZ by giving   days' notice in writing from time to time.

3.2   The Distributor shall be free to fix such resale prices for the Products as it thinks fit, but shall not fix those prices so high as may inhibit the sale of the Products. the Distributor shall keep XYZ informed of the prices and the discounts at which it resells the Products in the Territory.

3.3   Except it be otherwise agreed in writing, all prices quoted by XYZ shall be CIF (specified location).

4. Sales in the territory

XYZ undertakes not to sell any of the Products (being products sold under the brand name 'XYZ') directly in the Territory but nothing herein contained shall prohibit XYZ from selling the Products to other distributors outside the Territory.

5. Distributor's stocks and reports

5.1   The Distributor shall maintain such stocks of the Products, including as appropriate spare parts for the Products, as may be reasonably necessary to enable it to comply with its obligations hereunder, being not less in total value at any one time than   or such other value as may be agreed in writing from time to time, save that the Distributor shall not be deemed to be in default of this requirement if any reduction in stock below the agreed value is caused by exceptional sales by the Distributor or by failure of XYZ to supply any of the Products or by any Government export, import or other restriction.

5.2   The Distributor shall send to XYZ, at intervals not less frequent than one in each period of   months, or at such other times or intervals as may be agreed in writing from time to time, reports of any competition and potential competition by other manufacturers and sellers in the Territory which may affect the sale of the Products.

6. Technical information and training

6.1   XYZ shall keep the Distributor informed of such changes in the Products as XYZ may make from time to time which, in the opinion of XYZ, may be of interest to the users of the Products.

6.2   XYZ shall provide the Distributor, without cost to the Distributor, with such quantities of advertising matter as, in the opinion of XYZ, may be reasonably necessary to enable it to carry out its obligations hereunder.

6.3   XYZ shall provide such training for the Distributor's sales and technical staff as, in the opinion of XYZ, may be reasonably necessary to enable it to carry out its obligations hereunder. Such training shall be provided at XYZ's place of business recorded above, or at such other place as XYZ may decide. XYZ shall make no charge for this training and shall meet the reasonable accommodation charges of the staff. The Distributor shall meet all other costs including remuneration and travelling.

7. Conditions of sale and terms of payment

7.1   All Products supplied to the Distributor shall be subject to XYZ's Standard Conditions of Sales set out in Schedule 'B' hereof, as may be amended by XYZ by notice in writing from time to time.

7.2   Nothing contained herein, or in any Schedule hereof, shall be construed as an offer by XYZ to sell any of the Products, and all offers to sell the Products shall be the subject of separate correspondence. XYZ reserves the right to withdraw any reference to any Product.

7.3   Unless otherwise agreed in writing, the Distributor shall arrange for payment to be made to XYZ for all Products supplied to the Distributor, or to order, against shipping documents in London.

8. Minimum order value and allowance

8.1   The Distributor shall purchase from XYZ in each period of twelve months beginning on the first day of April (hereinafter called 'the Period') products to a minimum total net value of   or such other value as may be agreed in writing from time to time.

8.2   If in any period the total purchases of the Products by the Distributor exceed the minimum total value agreed for the Period and provided the Distributor produces evidence to XYZ which, to XYZ's satisfaction, demonstrates that the Distributor has complied with its undertaking to promote the sale of the Products then, subject to such Exchange Control or other permission as may be requisite, XYZ shall make an allowance to the Distributor equal to two per cent of the nett FOB price (excluding packing) of the Products sold to the Distributor during that period. This allowance shall be made by way of credit not to be offset against the purchase price of Products sold to the Distributor, or in such other way as may be agreed in writing.

8.3   If this Agreement comes into effect on any day other than the first day of April in any year, the minimum order value, and any allowance to be made thereon, shall be calculated on a time/proportional basis to the next thirty-first day of March.

8.4   If this agreement is terminated by XYZ at any time and for whatever cause, other than on the thirty-first day of March in any year, the allowance shall be calculated on a time/proportional basis until the date of termination.

9. Patents

In the event of any claim being made or action being brought against the Distributor in respect of infringement of   patents by the use or sale of goods supplied hereunder, the Distributor is to notify the Company immediately and the Company shall be at liberty with the Distributor's assistance if required, but at the Company's expense, to conduct through the Company's own lawyers and experts all negotiations for the settlement of the same or any litigation that may arise therefrom; subject to such notifications and provided that no such goods, or any part thereof, shall be used for any purpose other than that for which the Company supply them, the Company will indemnify the Distributor in respect of any such claims.

10. Termination provisions

10.1   This Agreement may be terminated at any time by either party giving to the other not less than three months' notice in writing, but such notice shall not be given to expire earlier than

10.2   This Agreement may be summarily terminated, by either party giving notice in writing to that effect, if at any time one party is in breach of any conditions hereof and that breach remains unremedied one month after receipt by the party in breach, of notice of the breach by the other party.

10.3   XYZ may summarily terminate this Agreement by giving the Distributor notice in writing to that effect, if by the end of any period the Distributor had failed to comply with the minimum order value condition set out in Clause 8 hereof.

10.4   This Agreement may be summarily terminated, by either party giving notice in writing to that effect, if the other party goes into liquidation, or becomes bankrupt, whether voluntarily or otherwise, or suffers a Receiver or Manager of its business to be appointed, or makes any composition with its creditors. If either party suffers any of these it shall immediately give notice thereof to the other.

10.5   Termination hereof, by whichever party, and for whatever cause, shall be without prejudice to any other right either party may have against the other at that time.

11. Repurchase of stock

11.1   If XYZ terminates this Agreement at any time and for whatever cause, the Distributor shall have the right to require XYZ to repurchase from the Distributor such stock of the standard Products as catalogued at the time of termination which, at that time, are in the ownership of the Distributor, and which at that time, are listed in Schedule 'A' hereof, and which are in good resaleable condition. The price to be paid by XYZ under these conditions shall be the price at which those Products were sold to the Distributor plus all costs of carriage, insurance, packing, duties and taxes appropriate to those Products.

11.2   If the Distributor terminates this agreement at any time for whatever cause XYZ shall have the right, if it so desires, to repurchase from the Distributor such stock of the standard Products as catalogued at the time of termination which, at that time, are in the ownership of the Distributor, and which at that time, are listed in Schedule 'A' hereof, and which are in good resaleable condition. The price to be paid by XYZ under these conditions shall be the price at which those Products were sold to the Distributor plus all costs of carriage, insurance, packing, duties and taxes appropriate to those Products.

12. **Previous agreements**

This agreement is in substitution for, and to the exclusion of all former Distribution Agreements entered into between the parties or between the Distributor and the former owner of the XYZ Products business, XYZ Products Limited.

13. **Arbitration and legal construction**

13.1   All questions and differences whatsoever which may at any time hereafter arise between the parties hereto, touching the meaning, construction or effect of any matter herein shall, if the parties are unable to resolve the same between them, be submitted to arbitration to the International Chamber of Commerce, and any award made in accordance with this provision shall be binding on both parties.

13.2   This Agreement shall be construed in accordance with English Law and the authoritative text shall be that in the English language set out herein.

Signed, for and on behalf of XYZ Limited

Director

In the presence of

Signed, for and on behalf of Alpha Beta Company

Director/Partner/Proprietor

In the presence of

XYZ Limited

SCHEDULE 'A'

Date:

PRODUCT   DISCOUNT

SCHEDULE 'B'
STANDARD CONDITIONS OF SALE

1. General

All orders are accepted and executed on the understanding that the Purchaser is bound by the following Standard Conditions of Sale. Where there is any inconsistency between these Standard Conditions of Sale and any Conditions which the Purchaser seeks to impose these Standard Conditions of Sale shall prevail.

2. Validity of quotations

The Company reserves the right to refuse the Purchaser's acceptance of a quotation unless such quotation is stated to be open for a specific period and is not withdrawn in such period.

3. Prices and discounts

The published prices of and the discount applicable to the Company's products are those ruling on the date of publication and are subject to alteration without notice. VAT, where applicable, will be added by the Company to its invoice.

4. Carriage

Unless otherwise specified by the Company goods are delivered carriage free to any part within the United Kingdom. When special delivery arrangements are requested special rates will be charged. Price for delivery of goods for export, will be CIF (location specified) or FOB (UK location) with the purchaser being responsible for insurance and freight charges.

5. Special orders

All orders for tooling, non-standard, not included in catalogues are considered to be 'Special Products' – the production of which is undertaken on the understanding that the Purchaser will accept under or over delivery to the extent of ten per cent at the price quoted per unit.

6. Payment

Unless otherwise agreed by the Company in writing, the goods shall be paid for in cash or by banker's cheque by the last day of the month following the month in which delivery was made. The Company's prices are net and not subject to any settlement terms.

Where a credit account is desired for a new account, a Bank and two trade references may be required.

7. Default

The Company shall have the right to discontinue delivery and also at its discretion to determine the contract in respect of any undelivered goods if the Purchaser defaults in payment.

8. Packing

A charge is made when it is necessary to despatch goods in crates or cases but this amount will be credited in full on the return, within one month, of the crates or cases in good condition carriage paid. No charge is made for any other form of packing and no credit will be allowed for its return.

9. Loss or damage in transit

Clear receipts should be given only if goods have been examined, as an unqualified signature may react to the disadvantage of the Purchaser if the consignment should become the subject of a claim. In the event of short delivery or damage in transit, it is essential that the Company's despatching depot and the Carriers be advised within seven days of receipt of goods. Irrespective of condition of packing, goods and packing should be held for inspection by Carriers before return. After inspection, Carriers should accept goods or return to sending depot, carriage free.

The following details should be sent to the company:

Advice note no.

Condition of package

Carrier's name

Date consignment received

Date Carrier advised

Extent of damage or shortage

In the event of non-delivery, Carriers and the Company's despatching depot should be advised within fourteen days of the date of invoice. The Company will not be responsible for goods lost or damaged in transit unless the above conditions are observed.

10. Liability for delay

Any times quoted for despatch, repair or replacement are to be treated as estimates only and the Company shall not be liable for failure to despatch, repair or replace within such time unless the Purchaser has suffered loss thereby and the amount payable in respect thereof shall have been agreed in writing as liquidated damages, in which case the Company's liability shall be limited to the amount so agreed to be paid. In all cases, whether a time for despatch, repair or replacement be quoted or not, the time for despatch, repair or replacement shall be extended by a reasonable period if delay in despatch, repair or replacement is caused by instructions or lack of instructions from the Purchaser or by industrial dispute or by any cause whatsoever beyond the Company's reasonable control.

11. Defects after delivery

The Company will make good, by repair at the Company's option, by the supply of replacement, defects which, under proper use, appear in the goods within a period of six calendar months after the goods have been delivered and arise solely from faulty design, materials or workmanship. Provided further that in respect of parts or components not of the Company's manufacture, the Company will give the Purchaser a guarantee equivalent to the guarantee (if any) which the Company may have received from the supplier of such parts or components in respect thereof but not so as to impose on the Company in respect of such parts or components a liability greater than that imposed on it by the aforesaid period of this clause. Save as aforesaid and as provided in Clauses 9 and 10, the Company shall not be under any liability in respect of defects in goods delivered or for any injury, damage or loss resulting from such defects or from any work done in connection therewith and its liability under this clause shall be in lieu of any warranty or condition implied by law as to the quality or fitness for any particular purpose of such goods.

12. Return of goods

In no circumstances may goods supplied against a firm order be returned without the customer having first applied for and obtained the written consent of the Company. A handling charge amounting to not more than 10 (ten) per cent of the invoice value of the returned goods may be deducted from any credit allowed where it is established that the reason for their return is not subject to the provision of Clause 9 or Clause 11 hereof or through any error on the part of the Company.

13. Descriptive matter and illustrations

All descriptive and forwarding specifications, drawings and particulars of weights and dimensions issued by the Company are approximate only, and are intended only to present a general idea of the goods to which they refer and shall not form part of a contract.

14. Legal construction

These General Conditions of Sale shall be construed in accordance with the law of England and if any question, dispute or difference shall arise between the parties in respect of their interpretation or their rights or duties heretofore, the same shall be referred to a single arbitrator in London in case the parties can agree upon one. Otherwise it shall be referred to arbitration in London under the provision of the Arbitration Acts or any relevant statutory modification or re-enactment thereof.

XYZ Limited

SCHEDULE 'C'

Date:

Distributor Requirements

APPENDIX 3
A specimen Agency Contract within the EC

Caution Use this specimen only if authorized by your legal advisers to do so. There are established practices, customs and procedures followed in certain types of industries, products and jurisdictions – local laws and customs vary in each country, state or territory.

The following must be treated as a specimen only and it is provided on the understanding that the author and/or publisher is not engaged in the provision of legal, accounting or other professional service.

SPECIMEN AGENCY CONTRACT

COMMERCIAL AGENCY CONTRACT

1. Messrs: (Principal)
of
entrust
Messrs: (Commercial Agent)
of
with their sole Agency for the Territory
for the sale of the following Products:

2. The Agent shall endeavour to obtain business for the Principal and is bound to serve the interests of the said Principal to the best of his ability. He will do his best to provide all information necessary for the purpose of promoting business, and especially inform the Principal immediately about every order received. He may not deviate from the prices, delivery and payment conditions of the Principal without his consent.

3. The Principal will provide the Agent with all necessary samples as well as printed and advertising matter free of charge, customs duties and carriage. The samples remain the property of the Principal, provided that they are not intended for consumption, and will be returned by the Agent on request and at the expense of the Principal.

4. The Principal will supply the Agent currently with all information of importance for the conduct of business, furthermore he will inform him without delay especially

of the acceptance or refusal of orders. He will also inform the Agent without delay, if there is a possibility that he can only accept orders to a limited extent.

5. The Agent will be supplied with copies of correspondence with firms in his Territory and of all invoices.

6. The Agent is only entitled to collect money from the customers in the case of express authorization.

7. The commission will be   % (in words   per cent) of the invoice amount for all business, both direct and indirect, transacted with customers in the Territory mentioned under Clause 1 above. The Principal will furnish the Agent with a statement of commission due upon all deliveries made during the month/quarter of the year not later than the 15th of the following month. The commission, to which according to such statement the Agent is entitled, falls due on the day the statement is forwarded.

8. The Agent's claim to commission expires only in respect of any delivery for which it is certain, that the customer will not pay; commission amounts that have already been received by the Agent will be taken into account in the next commission statement.

9. The Agent is also entitled to commission if it is certain that the Principal has failed to complete a transaction or has not executed it in the manner agreed upon. This shall not apply if the Principal can show that he is not responsible.

10. The Principal will reimburse the agent for the following expenses:

11. All claims that might be brought against the Agent because of a violation of a patent, a utility model, a trade mark or a copyright shall be the exclusive responsibility of the Principal. He has to make available to the Agent the necessary advances of the costs of the case, and at the Agent's request to advance them and to give all such information as may be required for the defence of the case. The Principal has also to reimburse the Agent for his own expenses. He warrants to the Agent his compliance with those legal provisions for the protection of end-users in force in the contractual Territory relating to the nature, labelling or packaging of the products. The Principal shall be exclusively responsible for all claims and obligations arising in the event of violation of such provisions.

12. The contract shall come into force on   and shall be valid for a fixed period until   or for an indefinite period (please cross out where not applicable.)

13. Where the contract has been agreed for a fixed period, it shall be extended for the same period provided that notice of termination shall not have been served, by registered letter, at least six months from the end of a calendar quarter.

14. Where the contract has been agreed for an indefinite period it may be terminated by either party thereto giving, by registered letter, six months' notice on the end of a calendar quarter.

15. In other respects the law valid at the domicile of the Agent is applicable to this agreement.

16. Any disputes arising out of or in connection with this agreement shall be decided by the court in the area of which the plaintiff has his residence or registered offices.

17. Amendments and supplements to this contract must be confirmed in writing in order to have validity.

(Signature of principal)

Place: Date:

(Signature of Commercial Agent)

Place: Date:

APPENDIX 4
A specimen distribution agreement outside the EC

Caution *Use this specimen only if authorized by your legal advisers to do so. There are established practices, customs and procedures followed in certain types of industries, products and jurisdictions – local laws and customs vary in each country, state or territory.*

The following must be treated as a specimen only and it is provided on the understanding that the author and/or publisher is not engaged in the provision of legal, accounting or other professional service.

SPECIMEN DISTRIBUTION AGREEMENT (XYZ Company)

1. Parties

This AGREEMENT is made and entered into at   as of
the   day of   , 19   ,
by and between   (1)

                                        (hereinafter referred to as 'the Company')
and   (2)

                                        (hereinafter referred to as 'the Distributor')

2. Recitals

The Company manufactures and sells industrial ABC machines, parts of machines, installation accessories and other products herein specified.

The Distributor desires to engage as a distributor of the Company in selling the Company's Products (except as excluded in Paragraph 3.3) to industrial and commercial users thereof in the Territory defined in Paragraph 3.1.1.

NOW, THEREFORE, for and in consideration of undertakings and covenants set forth in this Agreement, it is agreed as follows:

3. Terms and conditions

3.1   Appointment of the Distributor

3.1.1   The Distributor and the Company hereby agree that the Distributor shall have the right to sell and service the Company's Products as defined in Paragraph 3.3 hereof in the following area,   hereafter referred to as 'Distributor's Territory':

(Alternative: The Company hereby grants a licence to the Distributor to sell and service the Company's Products as defined in Paragraph 3.3 hereof in the following area,   hereafter referred to as 'Distributor's Territory'.)

3.1.2   The Distributor shall have no right to appoint sub-distributors for the Company's products without the Company's prior written consent.

3.2   Termination

3.2.1   This agreement shall be and remain in full force and effect for years after the date it bears. The term may be extended for additional one year terms upon written consent by both parties. If either party shall at any time violate any of the terms or provisions of this Agreement, the same may be terminated at any time thereafter by the other party upon thirty (30) days' written notice. The failure of either party to avail itself of any default shall not be deemed to be a waiver of any subsequent default. In addition, either party may terminate this Agreement, with or without cause, at the end of its original term or at any time during any continuation of the term, by giving the other party at least three (3) months' prior written notice by registered mail of the date on which the termination shall be effective, and this Agreement and all rights hereunder shall terminate on the date specified in the notice. The Distributor shall not be entitled to indemnity for any damages or loss of profits incurred as a result of any termination.

3.2.2   Upon termination of this Agreement, the plan for settling accounts and closing the business relationship between the Distributor and the Company shall be as follows:

3.2.2.1   The Company shall have first option, but not the obligation, to purchase all or any part of the Distributor's inventory of the Company's products as are new, in good merchantable condition and then in the Company's product line at the Distributor's landed cost not to exceed the Company's then current price to the Distributor, plus freight and duty. This option of the Company must be exercised within sixty (60) days after the Distributor submits to the Company a fully priced, itemized inventory listing.

3.2.2.2   At the request of the Company, the Distributor will return to the Company all manuals, books, sales data, sales help and similar material supplied to the Distributor by the Company, and a list of all persons, firms and corporations to whom the Distributor shall have provided the Company products during the term of this Agreement. The Company will bear the freight costs of returning these items.

3.2.2.3   The Distributor will immediately discontinue the use of all of the Company's trade marks, service marks, insignia and copyrighted materials.

3.2.2.4   At the option of the Company, the Distributor shall assign to the Company or its nominee all unfilled orders or contracts for the Company's products which the Company shall see fit to accept. If necessary import licences and payment guarantees (such as letters of credit) are received by the Company from the Distributor prior to the termination of this Agreement, the Company shall pay the Distributor a sum equal to   per cent (%) of the discount applicable to the products in Appendix B to this Agreement on such orders or contracts within ninety (90) days after the products are shipped.

3.3   Products included

3.3.1   Except for those classes of machines, parts and other products which are identified as excluded in the list of products appearing in Appendix A, the Company agrees to sell to the Distributor and the Distributor agrees to purchase from the Company all industrial ABC machines manufactured or sold by the Company, which bear the Company's brand name, trade mark or trade name and all parts of said machines and associated parts that the Distributor may require, need or use as a Distributor for such products within the Distributor's territory (collectively defined as Products). The prices shall be the Company's list prices as the same may be fixed from time to time by the Company (less the discounts defined in Appendix B), or in cases where list prices are not published by the Company, then at prices as fixed by the Company from time to time.

3.4   Company obligations

3.4.1   The Company will, in good faith, attempt to accept and fill the Distributor orders in a timely manner and will, in good faith, attempt to furnish the Distributor with its requirements to the extent that such products are available without denying other distributors their proportionate share. All orders must be made or confirmed by the Distributor in writing and once accepted by the Company cannot be cancelled without the Company's written consent. Any expense of cancellation will be borne solely by the Distributor. The Company will deliver Products to, or the direction of, the Distributor only within the Distributor's territory. In the event of termination of this Agreement by either party, the Company shall not be required to accept any orders received between the date of notice of termination and the effective date of termination which in the Company's sole opinion cannot be delivered before the effective date of termination, except that in the event that either party shall termi-nate this Agreement for violation of its terms by the other party, the Company may at its option cancel as of the date of notice of termination any orders of the Distributor on hand but not shipped.

3.4.2   The Company warrants that all Products sold under this Agreement are free from defects in material and workmanship which would render such Products unserviceable or unfit for their ordinary recommended industrial or commercial use. The foregoing warranty is in lieu of and excludes all other warranties not expressly set forth herein, whether express or implied by operation of law or otherwise including, but not limited to any implied warranties of merchantability or fitness. The Company shall not be liable for incidental or consequential losses, damages or expenses, directly or indirectly incurred during the sale or selling or use of the Products, or from any other cause relating thereto and the Company's liability hereunder in any case is expressly limited to replacement (in the form originally shipped or supplied) of Products not complying with this Agreement or, at the

Company's election, to the repayment of or crediting the Distributor with, an amount equal to the purchase price of such Products, whether such claims are for breach of warranty or negligence, and including without limitation, loss of future income.

Any claim by the Distributor with reference to Products sold hereunder for any cause shall be deemed waived by the Distributor unless the Company is notified in writing within thirty (30) days from the date the Distributor discovered, or should have discovered, any claimed breach. Any Products claimed to be defective may be returned prepaid to the Company's plant for inspection in accordance with return shipping instructions which the Company shall furnish to the Distributor upon receipt of the Distributor's notice of claim.

In addition the Company agrees:

3.4.3   From time to time to train members of the Distributor's staff without charge to the Distributor in the servicing and repair of the Company's Product at training centres established by the Company, the Distributor to bear all transportation and living expenses incurred by his staff in connection with such training.

3.4.4   To pay the Distributor commissions on Products but only where all of the following conditions are met:

(1) the sales are reported to the Company within twelve (12) months from date of sale,
(2) the Company sells directly to purchasers in the Distributor's territory other than the Distributor, and
(3) the Distributor can demonstrate, through documentary evidence, that the sales resulted in large part from the efforts of the Distributor. These commissions shall not apply to goods manufactured or sold by the Company (a) which are imported into the Distributor's territory by parties other than the Company without its consent or (b) which are sold under a brand name, trade name or trade mark other than that of the Company. Except for this commission, the Distributor recognizes that its only compensation shall be the profit it derives from resale of the Company's products. The applicable commissions appear on Appendix C to this Agreement.

3.4.5   To repurchase from the Distributor Products, at the Distributor's option, in accord with the Company's then current policy regarding returns from the Distributors.

3.4.6   To bear the cost of any litigation which Company may deem desirable to initiate for the protection of Company patent rights in the Distributor's territory.

3.5   The Distributor's obligations

The Distributor agrees as follows:

3.5.1   Energetically and faithfully to extend the sale and service of the Company's Products.

3.5.2   Not to manufacture, sell or solicit orders, without the prior written consent of the Company, for any competing machinery or parts of machinery.

3.5.3   Any settlement of claims for defective Products undertaken by the

Distributor shall be for the Distributor's own account, unless previously authorized in writing by the Company.

3.5.4   To solicit or canvass only customers or potential customers who reside or do business in the Distributor's territory defined in Paragraph 3.1.1 hereof.

3.5.5   Not to maintain stocks nor to set up establishments for the sale of the Products of the Company outside the Distributor's territory.

3.5.6   To establish an organization or department with proper supervision for the sale service of the Company's Products.

3.5.7   To employ a sales and service force of sufficient size and training to cover thoroughly the market for the Company's Products in the Distributor's territory.

3.5.8   To maintain a suitable place of business for the storage and sale of the Company's Products.

3.5.9   To carry at all times a sufficient stock of the Company's Products to ensure prompt supply for all probable demands, and permit inspection of such stock at any reasonable time by agents of the Company.

3.5.10   To maintain a shop with a trained staff for the service and benefit of its customers where the Company's Products may be adjusted, repaired and put into workable condition and to keep a supply of spare parts on hand for this purpose.

3.5.11   To advertise, to the extent reasonable, through publications, exhibits at trade shows and otherwise.

3.5.12   To deliver all Products returned to the Company's shipping plant and to pay the freight, insurance, duties, warehouse and other charges for these goods.

3.5.13   To provide the Company with such information pertaining to the industrial ABC machine business to the Distributor's territory and the Distributor's business as the Company may reasonably request from time to time.

3.5.14   To protect the Company against and to indemnify the Company for any damages alleged or assessed against the Company by reason of any acts or failure to act of the Distributor, or by reason of any agreement, statement, representation or warranty made by the Distributor.

3.5.15   The Distributor understands that the Company is subject to laws of
                                 which restrict or prohibit payments of any kind to
government officials, political party or candidates for public office (in any country) in order to obtain business or other forms of favourable treatment. In this regard, the Company's policy is to forbid any employee, agent, or independent distributor from making any such payment directly or indirectly on the Company's behalf or which might in any way favour the Company, except as otherwise expressly provided in its 'Statement of Policies Regarding Payments, Contributions and Gifts, Directly and Indirectly to Government Officials, Candidates for Office and Political Parties', a copy of which is attached hereto as Appendix D. The Distributor agrees that in all transactions involving the Company or its Products the Distributor shall not offer or make any such payments and shall otherwise abide strictly by the Company's Policy Statement as if it were itself the Company, or as said provisions may be amended or

supplemented from time to time and forwarded to the Distributor, (except that nominal payments need not be preceded by approval from the Company nor reported to the Company unless otherwise requested). Failure to abide by such provisions, as they may be amended or supplemented from time to time, shall be grounds for immediate termination of this Agreement at the option of the Company.

3.5.16   Not knowingly to sell machines, parts and other appliances to parties building machines or parts in competition with the Company's Products.

3.5.17   Neither directly nor indirectly to be interested in, nor permit any of its agents, associates or employees to be interested in any patent or application for letters patent on any mechanism made, used or communicated to the Distributor by the Company.

3.5.18   To co-operate fully with the prosecution of any litigation which the Company may deem desirable to initiate for the protection of the Company's patent rights in the Distributor's territory.

3.5.19   Not to divulge to any third parties during the term of this Agreement or thereafter, any information relating to technical data, market data and other information which constitutes the confidential intellectual property of the Company; and to hold such information in strictest confidence except for disclosures required in the performance of the Distributor's duties pursuant to this Agreement.

3.6   General terms

3.6.1   The relationship between the Company and the Distributor established by this Agreement is that of vendor and purchaser, that is, of principal and principal, and not that of principal and agent. The Distributor therefore acknowledges that it is granted no authority to assume or create any obligation or responsibility, express or implied on behalf of or in name of the Company, or to bind the Company in any manner whatsoever. In all its dealings with third parties, the Distributor shall clearly disclaim that it is acting as an agent for the Company in any capacity. The Distributor shall bear all of its own expenses for its operation and staff, except for such items as the Company shall by prior written agreement undertake to pay.

3.6.2   For the term of this Agreement only, the Company hereby grants to the Distributor a non-exclusive licence to use the Company's trade marks, service marks, insignia and copyrighted materials solely in connection with the Distributor's business conducted pursuant to this Agreement and in accordance with the conditions set forth herein and the written instructions and procedures as may be prescribed by the Company from time to time.

3.6.3   The Distributor acknowledges that the Company is the sole and exclusive owner of such trade marks, service marks, insignia and copyrighted materials, and the Distributor will not claim rights of ownership therein nor attempt to register the same. The Distributor agrees that no such trade mark, service mark or insignia of the Company shall be used by the Distributor as part of its corporate or other business name.

3.6.4   The Distributor may not use the Company's trade marks, service marks, insignia and copyrighted materials for advertising or promotional purposes unless the same shall have been previously approved in writing by the Company.

3.6.5   Payment of all Products ordered is to be made in (name of currency) through a bank approved by the Company, to the Company' offices at
unless otherwise agreed in writing by the Company. All payment or credit terms which are now or may be granted in the future by the Company on purchase orders placed by the Distributor are granted with the express understanding that at any time and from time to time prior to final delivery of any order, the Company has the right to modify, change or withdraw credit or payment terms and to require as a condition for further shipment, or for release of Products already shipped, such guarantee or security for payment as it sees fit, or to require payment in advance of any amounts due or to become due to the Company on such orders.

3.6.6   Insurance for fresh water damage, theft and pilferage, marine, marine war risk, fire and other damage will be arranged by the Company on all shipments. The Distributor will reimburse the Company in an amount equal to any premiums paid for such insurance by the Company.

3.6.7   Title to goods and risk of loss shall pass to the Distributor upon delivery of the goods to the inland carrier at the Company's premises. Neither the purchase of insurance nor the terms of payment in any letter of credit, nor the parties' agreement as to any shipment term shall in any way alter the parties' express agreement in this paragraph as to passage of title and risk of loss.

3.6.8   This Agreement and its benefits and duties shall not be assigned by either party without the written consent of the other, provided that the Company shall have the option at any time to have its duties undertaken and benefits received hereunder by any subsidiary or affiliate business entity. The Agreement shall be binding upon and inure to the benefit of legal representatives, administrators, executors, receivers, assigns or successors of the whole business of either party.

3.6.9   The Company shall not be liable for default in delivery or delays in shipment for any cause beyond its reasonable control, including but not limited to:

(a) fires, floods or other casualties;

(b) wars, riots, civil commotion, governmental regulations or martial law;

(c) the Company's inability to obtain necessary materials from its usual sources of supply;

(d) shortage of cars, trucks or other transportation facilities, or other delays in transit;

(e) existing or future strikes or labour troubles affecting production or shipment, or matters involving the Company's employees or employees of others, and regardless of the responsibility or fault on the part of the employer;

(f) other contingencies of manufacture or shipment.

3.6.10   The parties shall endeavour to resolve amicably any and all disputes arising under this Agreement. In the event that any such dispute (including disputes as to the interpretation of this Agreement, and the performance hereunder) cannot be so settled, it shall be finally settled by arbitration in accordance with the Rules of Conciliation and Arbitration of the International Chamber of Commerce (ICC). The arbitration proceedings, if any, shall be held before a three member arbitral tribunal in   and shall be conducted in the English language.

3.6.11   The authentic text of this Distributorship Agreement is in the English language and shall be controlling in the event a question of interpretation or construction should arise. The Company shall not be required to provide, accept, or act upon any document which is not in the English language. The Company shall not be required to use any weights, measures or other descriptive terms which are not expressed in the English language or which are not in general use in   .

3.6.12   This Agreement contains the entire understanding between the Company and the Distributor and supersedes all previous agreements and understandings, verbal or otherwise. No modification of, addition to, or deletion from this Agreement shall be binding upon any party unless it is in writing, is expressly stated to be a modification of, addition to, or deletion from this Agreement, and is signed by an authorized representative of the party against whom the modification, addition to, or deletion from is attempted to be enforced.

3.6.13   The validity and applicability of the entire Agreement shall not be destroyed by any finding by any tribunal that any particular provision is invalid or inapplicable. Instead, in the event that any provision or provisions are found invalid or inap-plicable, the remaining provisions shall continue in full force and effect as if such invalidated provision had not been included in the Agreement and the parties shall co-operate on replacing such invalidated provision with a valid one which comes closest to the essence and purpose of such invalid provision, both from a legal and economic point of view.

3.6.14   All notices required or permitted by this Agreement shall be writing, and service shall be deemed completed if made by registered air mail, ten days after the date of posting a properly addressed and prepaid envelope or wrapper containing such notice. The respective addresses of the parties for service of notices shall be the addresses indicated on the signature page of this Agreement. The address of a party may be changed from time to time, provided that such party provides written notice of such change to the other party in the manner aforesaid.

3.6.15   This Agreement shall be construed, executed and enforced exclusively according to the laws, including conflict of law rules, of
The Distributor and the Company agree that any disputes not resolved by arbitration shall be tried exclusively by courts located in

Signed, sealed and delivered by the respective parties, in duplicate, all at the place and on the day and year above written:

Signed on behalf of:

Witnessed by:

Signed on behalf of:

Witnessed by:

APPENDIX A

XYZ Company Distributorship Agreement

Excluded Products referred to in Clause 3.3

APPENDIX B

XYZ Company Distributorship Agreement

Discounts referred to in Clause 3.3

APPENDIX C

XYZ Company Distributorship Agreement

Commissions referred to in Clause 3.4.4

APPENDIX D

XYZ Company Distributorship Agreement

Statement of Policies Regarding Payments, Contributions and Gifts, Directly and Indirectly to Government Officials, Candidates for Office and Political Parties

APPENDIX 5
A specimen statement of sales policy within the EC

Caution   *Use this specimen only if authorized by your legal advisers to do so. There are established practices, customs and procedures followed in certain types of industries, products and jurisdictions – local laws and customs vary in each country, state or territory.*

The following must be treated as a specimen only and it is provided on the understanding that the author and/or publisher is not engaged in the provision of legal, accounting or other professional service.

SPECIMEN STATEMENT OF SALES POLICY

The Company's business idea is to leverage its knowledge and reputation in   for the purpose of achieving a leadership position among   in the target market   by furnishing them with the highest quality   . We will differentiate ourselves from the competition with the best technical support and delivery of these quality products.

As a declaration of faith, we believe that a distributor network is the mechanism which will best help us in ensuring that the needs of this market-place are constantly and efficiently served and satisfied.

This belief is the basis of the following Statement of Sales Policy and is reflected in every aspect of our relationship with our Distributors. It is the purpose of the Statement of Sales Policy to translate this belief into action in the way of guidance, support and assistance to all our Distributors.

Definition of a distributor

A Distributor is defined by us as a business enterprise which buys or imports goods and services; stocks goods and perhaps adds value; resells; and distributes or delivers to customers on its own account and at its own cost.

To qualify as a Distributor of   , the Distributor must fulfil the following basic requirements:

1. Reputation and integrity in the market-place

The Distributors must have a reputation and a presence in the community which is complementary and consistent with the   position.

2. Inventory

The Distributor must carry   weeks of inventory of our top selling products, inventory being measured in terms of the forecast agreed future volume of sales. These are the products which will be promoted actively. We will build future expectations upon the service and quality level of these products. In addition, any inventory must be handled, stored and maintained in a clean, efficient and organized manner according to conditions as specified by the Company.

3. Delivery

The Distributor should have the willingness and the ability both within his organization and within his geographic area of responsibility to process orders and arrange for despatch within   hours of receipt of the order.

4. Receipt of orders

The Distributor must, wherever it is technologically possible, maintain toll-free telephone numbers for the purpose of accepting orders from the end-users. These toll-free numbers must be staffed during normal business hours with the commitment made to have them answered by an individual knowledgeable enough to handle the order in an expeditious manner.

5. Telex/telefax

The Distributor should have a telex and/or a telefax which, among other purposes, will allow it to forward orders, as well as requests for technical assistance, to the Company in an expeditious manner.

6. Performance criteria

The Distributor will meet the performance criteria as specified by the Company under the section 'Performance Criteria' of this Statement of Sales Policy.

7. Financially viable

The Distributor must conduct business in a way which meets or exceeds generally accepted business practices and thereby establishes an on-going, financially viable business capable of meeting the terms and conditions of supply of products included in this Agreement.

8. Recognition

The Distributor must be recognized as a Distributor by other members of the distributive organization.

Method of distribution

Sales through and not to the Distributor
This common aim and community of interest is the basis of our close association and co-operation with our distributors. It is our firm intention that the majority of the Products sales should be routed through the distributor network of the Company.

As to the sale of other products in the Territory arranged by the Distributor for the Company, the account will provide eligibility for the Distributor of the 2% finder's fee, based on any transacted business so arranged within the first year beginning on the date of contact between the Company and end-user.

The products

The Products included as a part of this arrangement are those listed in and appear in   under the following sections:

In addition, any new products not appearing in this catalogue but introduced via   are included as a part of this Agreement. New products may be added from time to time. A minimum of   days notice will be given by the company so that the distributor can organize matters such as inventory prior to launch, adequate training for the sales force etc.

The Company reserves the right to modify the specifications of or to withdraw from sale generally any or all of the Products without incurring any liabilities towards the Distributor.

Whenever it becomes necessary for us to withdraw any product(s) from our mix, every attempt will be made to announce any such changes in advance to allow depletion of stocks and to advise end-users of that particular product's withdrawal from the mix.

Prices, discounts, terms and warranty

Prices
Details of recommended selling prices are published from time to time. The latest price list can be seen under Schedule   . This recommended selling price allows you, the   Distributor, a reasonable margin of profit when purchasing at Distributor's terms from us. Contrary to clause 3 of the Standard Conditions of Sale, prices and currency transactions are in

The published prices of and the discounts applicable to the Company's products are those ruling on the date of publication and are subject to alteration without notice. While every attempt is made to hold selling prices, it becomes necessary to increase prices from time to time. Whenever practical, at least thirty (30) days' notice of any impending increase will be given to distributors.

Price changes will normally take effect on a specified date. Any orders we have on hand for immediate despatch, or any orders in the past dated on or before the effective date which also specify immediate despatch, will be despatched at the former prices. Any orders on hand at the time of a price increase specifying a deferred despatch date will be subject to the prices relative at the date of despatch.

Discounts
The Distributor discount applies to the recommended selling prices. For all products as identified in Schedule   , a   % discount applies. Accounts dealt with by the Company and arranged by the Distributor as described in this Sales Policy under the section 'Method of Distribution', will not be eligible for the   % discount but will provide eligibility for the Distributor of a 2% finder's fee based on any transacted business so arranged within the first year beginning on the date of contact between the Company and the end-user.

Terms

Terms of payment are strictly net cash within one month following the end of the month of the relevant invoice. Payment is to be made in the currencies specified   . All Products supplied to the Distributor are subject to the Standard Conditions of Sale as set out in Schedule

Warranty

The Company does not expect the return of goods for credit unless it is a justified warranty claim. We are, however, prepared to consider sympathetically any request made by a Distributor experiencing over-stocking problems. Depending upon the situation, a credit arrangement subject to a possible restocking charge may be applicable.

Any expressed warranty herein is based on the carrying out of proper handling procedures and storage conditions of the Products as provided by the Company.

The Company will keep the Distributor informed of any product changes that the Company may make from time to time which in the opinion of the Company may be of interest to the end-users of the Products.

Distributor training

Field assistance

It is the Company's intention to provide adequate and satisfactory pre- and post-sale technical support to the Distributor and its customers in the event of enquiry, complaint or request for advice or assistance. The majority of this support will be provided from the Company's place of business but may from time to time involve the visiting of selected customers accompanied by a Distributor's salesperson.

The Company will, at a minimum of every eight (8) weeks, arrange for a representative to personally visit the Distributor for the purpose of working with the Distributor's salespeople, determining levels of inventory, explaining current and upcoming market communications and sales promotions, introducing new products and deleting products that are less than satisfactory, as well as, discussing any other subjects of interest.

Product training seminars

The Company shall provide from time to time product training seminars of a duration no longer than two (2) days for a Distributor's sales staff. Such training shall be provided at such places as the Company may decide. The Company will make no charge for this training. The Distributor will be required to meet hotel costs and travelling expenses for personnel attending such seminars.

Marketing assistance

The Company primarily advertises and promotes its Distributors, itself and its products via a comprehensive direct mail programme. Included in this programme are:

Performance criteria

In the initial years, on a time/proportional basis, performance criteria will include

Guaranteed Turnover at 19   price of:

Year   Turnover

'Guaranteed Turnover' shall mean such aggregate value of sales of products to the Distributor during each fiscal year of the Company as shall have been agreed between the parties in advance of such fiscal year. The Company's fiscal year starts on   and ends on   (both days are included in the year).

Other performance criteria include those listed as basic requirements in the 'Definition of a Distributor' as set out in this Statement of Sales Policy, as well as, any condition which must prevail to maintain a viable distribution contract as set forth in the main body of this Agreement or the Standard Conditions of Sale or the Statement of Sales Policy.

APPENDIX 6
A specimen licensing agreement

Caution *Use this specimen only if authorized by your legal advisers to do so. There are established practices, customs and procedures followed in certain types of industries, products and jurisdictions – local laws and customs vary in each country, state or territory.*

The following must be treated as a specimen only and it is provided on the understanding that the author and/or publisher is not engaged in the provision of legal, accounting or other professional service.

Specimen   **PART-MANUFACTURING LICENCE AGREEMENT**

AN AGREEMENT made this   day of
BETWEEN Blue Co. of
                                              (hereinafter called 'Blue')
acting by A Blue a member of its Executive duly authorized to sign this Agreement
on its behalf of the first part and Green of   (hereinafter
called 'Green') of the second part WHEREAS

(A) By an Agreement of even date herewith (hereinafter called 'the Distributor Agreement') Blue has appointed Green the sole distributor in the United States of America (hereinafter called 'the Territory') of **Jet** machines manufactured by Blue.

(B) For the purposes of the sale of **Jet** machines in the Territory special castings not included in Blue's manufacturing list at the date hereof will be required.

(C) Blue and Green have agreed that Green should manufacture such special castings and assemble the same with the other parts required to make up the **Jet** machines supplied by Blue.

(D) Blue is the registered owner of United States patents (hereinafter called 'the patents') registration no.   dated   and registration no.   dated   covering the manufacture and assembly of Blue **Jet** machines.

(E) Blue is the owner of Blue **Jet** machine standards, designs, design standards, standard procedures, manufacturing drawings, processing information, material specifications, heat treatment, technical data and information relating to the manufacture and assembly of the Blue **Jet** machines (hereinafter collectively called 'the know-how').

(F) Blue has agreed to grant Green an exclusive licence under the patents and the know-how to enable it to manufacture the special castings and assemble the same into Blue **Jet** machines.

NOW THIS AGREEMENT WITNESSETH and IT IS HEREBY AGREED as follows:

1. 'Special Castings' means castings not included in Blue's manufacturing list at the date hereof manufactured in accordance with the know-how.

2. Blue hereby grants Green subject to the terms and conditions hereof an exclusive licence under the patents to manufacture special castings and to assemble and sell Blue **Jet** machines in the Territory.

3. (a) FORTHWITH upon the execution of this Agreement Blue shall supply Green with so much of the know-how as shall enable Green to manufacture special castings and assemble Blue **Jet** machines.
   (b) Blue hereby grants Green an exclusive licence to use the know-how supplied under subclause (a) above in the manufacture of special castings and the assembly of Blue **Jet** machines.
   (c) The know-how shall at all times remain the property of Blue, shall be treated by Green as confidential information, and shall be returned to Blue forthwith on the termination of this Agreement.
   (d) Any modification in the know-how made by Blue which is in the opinion of Blue relating to the manufacture of special castings and the assembly of Blue **Jet** machines shall be disclosed to Green.

4. (a) Blue hereby grants Green the right and licence to use the trade-mark in connection with Blue **Jet** machines which it sells in the Territory and Green agrees that all Blue **Jet** machines sold by it in the Territory shall be marked in accordance with the instructions of Blue and, if so instructed by Blue, with a suitable legend indicating that they are made under licence from Blue.
   (b) Green agrees that without prejudice to the provisions of the Distributor Agreement it will only use the mark on the Blue **Jet** machines, that it will completely cease utilizing the mark or any colourable imitation thereof after the termination or expiration of this Agreement. Green agrees that it will not during the term of this Agreement, or thereafter, claim ownership of, or any interest in, the mark as the result of its use under this Agreement.

5. (a) Green agrees that it will at all times maintain in the manufacture of the special castings and assembly of the white **Jet** machines the highest quality of workmanship possible in order to procure a quality of product that is substantially equal to the quality of products manufactured by Blue.
   (b) Green agrees that the manufacturing facilities and processes utilized for the manufacture of the special castings and the assembly of the Blue **Jet** machines shall be open to the inspection of Blue at all reasonable times.
   (c) If, at any time during the continuance of this Agreement, Blue shall consider the quality of the special castings manufactured by Green to be

unsatisfactory, Blue shall so notify Green and Green shall consult with Blue in an effort to improve the quality of said products so as to meet the approval of Blue. If, after such consultation, Green fails within six months to improve the quality of special castings manufactured hereunder to a level acceptable to Blue, then Blue shall have the right to terminate this agreement forthwith upon the expiry of such period of six months by serving notice in writing to that effect on Green.

6. (a)   Green shall pay to Blue royalty in respect of each Blue **Jet** machine sold at the following rates:

In respect of each Blue **Jet** machines US$ per casting

(b)   Royalty shall accrue upon the sale of each Blue **Jet** machine and a Blue **Jet** machine shall for the purposes of this Agreement be deemed to be sold

(i)   when the invoice relating thereto is despatched by Green or

(ii)   when the same is delivered or

(iii)   when Blue received payment in whole or in part therefore, whichever shall be the earlier.

(c)   Upon the date hereof and upon each subsequent anniversary of the date hereof Green shall pay to Blue the sum of US$.   Each such payment shall respectively represent a minimum royalty in respect of each year of the term of this Agreement from the date hereof, shall be set off against royalty due in respect of Blue **Jet** machines sold by Green in the year to which the payment relates and shall in no circumstances be repaid in whole or part to Green by reason of the royalty payable to Blue by Green pursuant to subclause (b) above in respect of any year during the term of this Agreement falling short of such sum of US$.

(d)   Within 15 days of expiry of each quarter of the year ending 31st March, 30th June, 30th September and 31st December Green shall deliver to Blue a statement of the number and the selling prices of the Blue **Jet** machines sold by it during the preceding quarter and of the royalty payable to Blue under this Agreement in respect thereof. At the same time as delivering such statement Green shall pay the total amount shown to be payable in such statement except to the extent that the whole or part of such total sum has been covered by the minimum payment made in advance under subclause (c) above in respect of the year covering the relevant quarter.

(e)   Royalty payable hereunder shall be paid in US dollars at the rate of $ /£1 sterling clear of all deductions.

(f)   Green shall keep proper books of account relating to the sales of the Blue **Jet** machines and Blue shall be entitled upon reasonable notice to inspect the books and records of Green to check the amount of royalty payable hereunder.

7. (a)   In the event that Green shall make or discover any improvement relating to the manufacture of the special castings or the assembly of the Blue **Jet** machines it shall forthwith give full information and details thereof to Blue and all such information shall become the property of Blue.

(b)   If any improvement disclosed to Blue pursuant to subclause (a) hereof shall be patentable the invention involved shall be, or shall be transferred to Blue so as to become, the property of Blue and Blue shall be entitled at its discretion to institute and pursue patent applications both in the Territory and in any part of the world in respect thereof and any patents granted in consequence of such applications shall belong to Blue absolutely.

8. Green hereby covenants:
(a)   Not at any time during the term of this Agreement or after the termination thereof to dispute the validity of the patents.

(b)   To give notice in writing to Blue of any infringement or threatened infringement of the patents which may come to its knowledge.

(c)   Not to use the special castings otherwise than in conjunction with parts supplied to it by Blue in the assembly of Blue **Jet** machines.

(d)   Not to sell special castings to any person, firm, corporation or government outside the Territory, and to procure that all special castings sold by it will not be sold outside the Territory whether as separate equipment or part of other equipment.

(e)   Not to assign the benefit of this Agreement or any interest therein or grant any sublicence under the patents or under the know-how to any other person except with the prior written consent of Blue.

9. Blue hereby covenants not to grant a licence under the patents or under the know-how for the manufacture of special castings or the assembly or sale of Blue **Jet** machines in the Territory to any other person.

10. This Agreement shall subject to Clause 11 hereof remain in force for a period of five years from the date hereof terminable at the end of that time or at any time thereafter by either party giving to the other six months' prior notice in writing.

11. (a)   Blue may by notice in writing determine this Agreement forthwith if Green shall (in the reasonable opinion of Blue which opinion shall be final and conclusive) fail to observe or perform any of the conditions of this agreement.

(b)   This Agreement shall *ipso facto* cease and determine without compensation to Green and without any notice or other act by either of the parties hereto upon the termination, howsoever caused, of the distributor Agreement.

12. This Agreement shall be governed by and construed in all respects in accordance with the Laws of   and for this purpose the parties hereto submit themselves to the jurisdiction of the courts of

13. In the event of any dispute between the parties arising hereunder or in connection herewith the same shall be referred to a single arbitrator appointed by the parties hereto or failing agreement as to such appointment by a single arbitrator nominated by the President of the Law Society.

IN WITNESS whereof the parties to this Agreement have hereto set their hands the day and year first before written

FOR AND BEHALF OF BLUE CO.

WITNESS

FOR AND BEHALF OF GREEN CO.

WITNESS

APPENDIX 7

A specimen job description of a Manager for Distributor Relations – XY Products Company

Primary function

The Manager for Distributor Relations is responsible to the International Marketing Director for the operation of the Company's distributor programme in the various territories.

He is directly charged with executing the distributor policy of the Company, while, at the same time, maintaining the relationship between the Company and its distributors that will ensure a pleasant and profitable operation for all concerned. This also entails working with and advising the field sales organization on the proper handling of the Authorized Distributor organization.

Responsibilities and authority

1. *Management responsibilities:*

1.1 Develop and direct the Company's distributor programme to achieve maximum results from this marketing channel, consistent with the policies established by the International Marketing Director.

1.2 Formulate and administer the Company's distributor policy under guidance from the International Marketing Director and in co-operation with the Distributor Policy Committee.

1.3 Establish and maintain a continuous review of both short and long term plans for the expansion of company sales through the wholesale distributor organizations.

1.4 Select and direct the Authorized Distributor organizations within the limits set by the International Marketing Director.

1.5 Under the guidance of the International Marketing Director, co-ordinate the company advertising and sales promotion activities whenever pertaining to the distributor programme.

1.6 Collaborate with the Product Managers in the establishment of sales quotas for the Authorized Distributor organizations consistent with their capabilities and in line with the Company objectives.

1.7 Collaborate with the field sales organization, through the General Sales Manager, to ensure that maximum sales of the Company's products are achieved through the distributor organizations.

1.8   Ensure that all periodic or special reports desired by the International Marketing Director or other members of management are presented as required and on time.

1.9   Approve all expenditures and credits to the distributor organizations, whether they arise due to return of material for credit or for promotion allowances or due to sales policy decisions.

1.10   Maintain an effective system of control over activities such as distributor meetings and conventions, distributor training programmes, promotion meeting allowances, etc.

2. *Marketing responsibilities:*

2.1   Establish distribution policies and channels of sale; establish policies and procedures for the selection and removal of authorized distributors in accordance with the policies laid down by the International Marketing Director.

2.2   Advise and assist the field sales organization in the proper execution of the distributor policy.

2.3   Supervise the execution of the distributor policy to guarantee maximum benefits to the company without jeopardizing the respect and relationship between the Company and the Authorized Distributor organizations.

2.4   Assist the headquarters advertising departments in the editing and distributing of the house magazines for the Authorized Distributor organizations.

2.5   Write 'Distributor Memo' monthly for insertion in the relevant wholesaling magazine.

2.6   Establish and co-ordinate a distributor training programme with the Student Training Co-ordinators.

3. *Product planning responsibilities:*

Obtain from the field sales offices regular and periodic reports on competitors' products, promotion programmes, merchandising programmes to keep the International Marketing Director and the Product Managers abreast of competitive situations involving the Company's products sold through the distributors.

4. *Miscellaneous responsibilities:*

4.1   Maintain close contact and supervision with all personnel under his jurisdiction, to ensure proper understanding of their problems and to assist in their training.

4.2   Ensure that annual expenditure budgets are prepared and submitted for approval on time; when approved, keep expenditures to budget.

4.3   Submit for approval of the International Marketing Director salary recommendations of subordinates, in accordance with established procedures.

4.4   Handle special assignments including participation on committees and projects, involving other organizations outside the normal scope of his activities, as directed by the Vice President-Marketing.

Relationship to others

International Marketing Director:

The job holder is accountable to the International Marketing Director for the fulfilment of his functions and responsibilities. He will also act in an advisory capacity to the Vice President on any matter to which he is assigned.

General Sales Manager:

The job holder will maintain close liaison with the General Sales Manager so as to know the sales objectives and work closely with the field marketing organization towards meeting the objectives.

Product Manager:

He will work closely with the Product Manager to ensure that maximum co-operation is achieved between the distributor organization and the Product Managers.

Market Research Manager:

He will collaborate in the market research projects involving the Authorized Distributor organization or merchandise sales through this media.

Advertising Manager:

He will collaborate with the Advertising Manager on all advertising and sales promotion projects pertaining to the distributor organization.

APPENDIX 8
Distribution survey questionnaire

SURVEY ON MANAGEMENT & MOTIVATION OF DISTRIBUTORS

Please answer each of the questions by ticking the appropriate boxes or writing in brief statements where indicated. Do a similar exercise for the leading company in your industry and for each of your most important competitors. A comparison between the answers to such a survey would indicate possible areas of beneficial enquiry.

Q1 How many products and services do you offer to your target market?

	1	2–5	6–10	11–20	21–40	41–80	80+
NUMBER of PRODUCTS NUMBER of SERVICES							

Q2 What proportion of products and/or services are sold into various markets?

		PRODUCTS			SERVICES		
		None	Some only	Most/All	None	Some only	Most/All
1	The regional market(s)						
2	The national market						
3	Other EC countries						
4	North America						
5	Central/South America						
6	African continent						
7	Middle East						
8	Far East						
9	Asia						
10	Rest of the world						

Q3 How are your products and services sourced? Tick appropriately against each source used.

		PRODUCTS	SERVICES
1	Own design and manufacture		
2	Own human resource capabilities		
3	Franchises		
4	Direct purchase to fill range		
5	Licensing and manufacture/assembly		
6	Dealer agreement		
7	Distribution agreement		
8	Joint ventures with suppliers		
9	Other (Please describe)		

Q4 How are products and services distributed to end users? Tick appropriate box(es).

		PRODUCTS	SERVICES
1	Own direct sales force		
2	Own direct sales force for major accounts		
3	Subsidiaries/branches with own sales force		
4	Major distributors		
5	Original equipment manufacturers (OEMs)		
6	Dealers/Distributors		
7	Mail order through catalogue/direct mail offers		
8	Retailers		
9	Joint ventures with customers		
10	Franchises		
11	Vending machines		
12	Other (Please describe)		

Q5 Where distributors are used, how do you exercise control over the marketing mix?

	Aspect of marketing mix	Give distributor total freedom	Give distributor some flexibility within guidelines	Maintain total control
1	Target market segments			
2	Product/service specification			
3	Extent/quantity customer service			
4	Promotions			
5	Price			
6	Discounts			
7	Packaging			
8	Brand names			
9	Other (Please specify)			

Q6 How do you motivate distributors to perform? Which methods do you use?

		Relative importance			Success to date		
			Medium	High	Low	Medium	High
1	Exclusive territories						
2	Annual Over-riders/allowances						
3	Sales performance incentives						
4	Incentive awards						
5	Special training programmes						
6	Best service support in industry						
7	Others (Please specify)						

Q7 Which of the following complaints do you regularly hear from your distributors? Tick the relevant items listed below.

a	They do not know MY customers
b	They are only interested in volume
c	They do not provide sufficient help/information
d	They do not visit me enough
e	Only junior staff visit me, not the bosses
f	They ask for too many statistics and feedback
g	They are always changing pricing policy
h	They set out unrealistically high targets
i	They are poor on product training
j	They always squeeze me on margins
k	They could fire me any time
l	My contact is always changing

Q8 Which of the following complaints do you regularly make about your distributors? Tick the relevant items listed below.

a	They do not know my product
b	They do not push my product sufficiently
c	They are purely order takers
d	Their administration is inefficient
e	They fail to report/feedback information
f	They only provide erratic sales reports
g	They do not meet agreed performance standards
h	Their profit is too high compared to ours
i	They are a 'quick buck' outfit
j	They are not interested in service
k	They do not built long term customer relationships
l	They have become fat and lazy

Q9 When you select new distributors, how do you rank the following possible selection criteria?

		Relative importance		
		Low	Medium	High
1	Location in territory concerned			
2	Having good customer contact			
3	Having no competing lines			
4	Our lines would be complimentary			
5	Ability to give us priority support			
6	Financial soundness			
7	Extent of presence in the market			
8	Sales team/facilities			
9	Service team/facilities			
10	Support capability			
11	Condition of offices			
12	Condition of transport			
13	Condition of warehouse			
14	Attitude to advertising/promotion			
15	Is the distributor really interested in the product and its applications?			
16	Does the distributor need us?			
17	Other (Please specify)			

Source: V Iyer & R S Handscombe of EMSA/1992

APPENDIX 9
EMSTAR/MiSTAR Problem
Manager

Introduction

Marketing and distribution in any company has to keep pace with change that is largely brought about by competitive forces at work and by innovation, technology and communication. In the wake of such changes, every company faces a variety of problems and several issues may crop up. Such problems need solution and managers need to solve them.

EMSTAR/MiSTAR Problem Manager[1]

Problem-solving and decision-making are the principal responsibilities of management; they can also be the most complex ones. Many managers believe that the ability to solve problems is a skill which cannot be transmitted through training. However, systematic thinking and systems analysis provide highly valuable help to management in problem-solving. There is in fact a technique to problem-solving which most managers follow instinctively; this can be made conscious, systemized and taught. One such technique is the EMSTAR Problem Manager.

The skills in problem resolution can be extended to other activities; they can be used to create teams, bond customers and extend positive relationships to a strategic level. They can also be used as a catalyst in order to harness the latent potential in an organization, to identify tasks and resolve difficulties. The impact of a change is measurable as each activity can be self-managed and produces identifiable goals and results. There is a measurable financial payback on the majority of the projects. The resulting organizational culture is beneficial to all levels of management and staff who can all benefit from it and achieve satisfaction.

Objectives

The basic **EMSTAR** objectives may be summarized as follows (see also Fig. A9):

1. To enable teams and individuals to undertake personal and/or co-operative analysis of a problem situation, at a strategic, tactical or operational level and to identify the constraints or limitations within which such a problem has to be solved.
2. To identify root causes and issues which need resolution.
3. To explore alternative means of resolving the problem, together with an understanding of the risks and rewards, within the parameters of the business situation.
4. To enable the team to hold open discussions on all relevant aspects of the situation and to agree upon an appropriate course of action.

5. To complete the identified course of action.

The **EMSTAR** technique is designed to improve knowledge of and skills in:

- problem diagnosis
- identification of root causes and effects
- establishment of issues for resolution and alternative scenarios
- brainstorming techniques
- testing alternatives
- agreeing action programmes and responsibilities for actions to be undertaken
- review and completion.

Background to the application of EMSTAR Problem Manager

The changing economic scene creates a situation where, in most industries, volumes, margins and costs are constantly under pressure. All these factors limit the amount of flexibility of response to competitive pressures which is available to management. The development of a wider European market is creating increased opportunities but it has also brought in more competition. The new competitors often possess the advantage of owning strong international brands but they have to start forging new trade relationships. The EMSTAR process can help to protect existing relationships; at the same time, it is far more pro-active than a simple defence mechanism.

There are three key requirements for a business for it to compete in the market and prosper.

Strategic and tactical planning
Companies need clear, comprehensive strategies and tactical plans, which must also be well defined and achievable, with clear steps; the most important factor is the participation of the management and staff. Many companies lack a comprehensive strategy, apart from the business plan which is required by bankers or shareholders. It is unusual to find a business where the strategy is available to key managers and even rarer to find one where the strategy is accepted or even understood by the employees who are charged with its development. It is small wonder if all the available effort is not correctly focused! As a result, a significant amount of time and effort is spent on activities which do not contribute to the achievement of the objectives.

Culture
The implementation of any strategy requires a culture that can withstand change and respond to the competitive nature of the market-place and in which all human resources are utilized to their maximum potential. Company cultures are changing, but they are not always replaced with a satisfactory alternative which can be accepted by management, staff and the customers. Managers need to be able to merge the skills, culture and qualities into a co-operative, problem-solving and team working environment.

Strategic trade relationship
Third, it is of course essential to acquire customers and to retain and develop them. The opportunities to achieve these objectives through pricing, extra services and

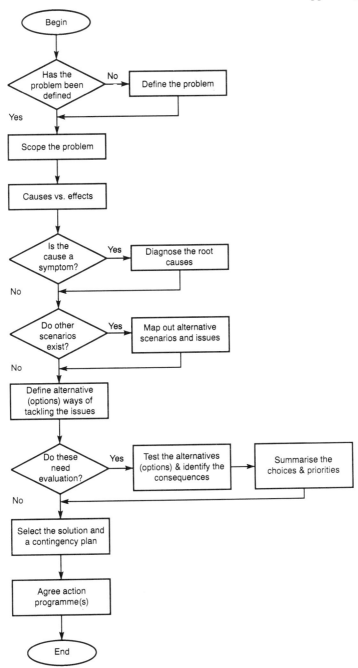

Figure A9 EMSTAR Problem Manager: route map to creative solutions.
© *Vinoo Iyer & EMSA (1992)*

unique responsiveness are becoming increasingly restricted. Tight margins and restricted flexibility associated with changing customer requirements and modern production methods, together with the increasing costs and logistical needs, are narrowing the available differential between competing goods and services.

Suppliers are increasingly selected and retained not only on the basis of the goods and services provided and their responsiveness but also on their 'relationship' with the trade customer and the end consumer. If this is to be a key differentiation, companies have to address the problem of how to achieve competitive advantage from these relationships. In order to win, the company has to be able to extend the relationship beyond the basic level of trade marketing and 'entertainment' to a strategic level.

Strategic trade relationship creates a position where all associated parties gain and the losers are the competitors who have to cope with additional barriers which have nothing to do with habit, price or service.

The technique(s) embodied in **EMSTAR/MiSTAR Problem Manager** assists a manager in the search for creative solutions.

[1] **EMSTAR and MiSTAR** are registered trade marks of Vinoo Iyer and EMSA (1992). The technique embodied in the **EMSTAR/MiSTAR Problem Manager** was created by Vinoo Iyer and his EMSA colleagues to help managers solve problems, in particular those experienced in the field of marketing and distribution.

APPENDIX 10
Articles 85 and 86 EEC Treaty

Article 85 – Agreements and Concerted Practices

1. "The following shall be prohibited as incompatible with the common market: all agreements between undertakings, decisions by associations of undertakings and concerted practices which may affect trade between Member States and which have as their object or effect the prevention, restriction or distortion of competition within the common market, and in particular those which:
   (a) directly or indirectly fix purchase or selling prices or any other trading conditions;
   (b) limit or control production, markets, technical development, or investment;
   (c) share markets or sources of supply;
   (d) apply dissimilar conditions to equivalent transactions with other trading parties, thereby placing them at a competitive disadvantage;
   (e) make the conclusion of contracts subject to acceptance by the other parties of supplementary obligations which, by their nature or according to commercial usage, have no connection with the subject of such contracts.

2. Any agreements or decisions prohibited pursuant to this Article shall be automatically void.

3. The provisions of paragraph 1 may, however, be declared inapplicable in the case of:
   ▶ any agreement or category of agreements between undertakings;
   ▶ any decision or category of decisions by associations of undertakings;
   ▶ any concerted practice or category of concerted practices;
   which contributes to improving the production or distribution of goods or to promoting technical or economic progress, while allowing consumers a fair share of the resulting benefit, and which does not:
   (a) impose on the undertakings concerned restrictions which are not indispensable to the attainment of these objectives;
   (b) afford such undertakings the possibility of eliminating competition in respect of a substantial part of the products in question."

Article 86 – Abuse of Dominant Position

"Any abuse by one or more undertakings of a dominant position within the common market or in a substantial part of it shall be prohibited as incompatible with the common market in so far as it may affect trade between Member States.

Such abuse may, in particular, consist in:

(a)   directly or indirectly imposing unfair purchase or selling prices or other unfair trading conditions;

(b)   limiting production, markets or technical development to the prejudice of consumers;

(c)   applying dissimilar conditions to equivalent transactions with other trading parties, thereby placing them at a competitive disadvantage;

(d)   making the conclusion contracts subject to acceptance by the other parties of supplementary obligations which, by their nature or according to commercial usage, have no connection with the subject of such contracts."

FURTHER READING

Anscombe Jonathan, *Separating leaders from the laggers*, Management Consultancy, February 1992

Armstrong Michael, *How To Be An Even Better Manager*, Kogan Page Ltd, London, 1988

Baker Michael J, *Marketing*, The MacMillan Press, London and Basingstoke, 1977

Christou Richard, *International Agency, Distribution and Licensing Agreements*, Longman Group UK Ltd, London, 1986

Cooper R G, *The dimensions of industrial new product success and failure*, Vol 43, Summer 1979

Davies Gary, *Managing Export Distribution*, William Heinemann Ltd, London, 1984

Handscombe, Richard S, *The Product Management Handbook*, McGraw-Hill Book Co, Maidenhead, 1989

Katz Bernard, *Managing Export Marketing*, Gower Publishing, Aldershot, 1987

Keegan Warren J, *Global Marketing Management*, Prentice-Hall International Inc., Englewood Cliffs N J, 1989

Kotler Philip, *Megamarketing*, Harvard Business Review, March–April 1986, Volume 64, pp. 117–124

Land Paul, *Where profits are a product of taste*, Financial Decisions, October 1988

McCall J B & Warrington, M B, *Marketing By Agreement*, John Wiley & Sons, Chichester, 1989

Myers James H, *Marketing*, McGraw–Hill Book Co., Singapore, 1986

Novick, Harold J, *Selling Through Independent Reps*, AMACOM, a division of American Management Association, New York, 1988

Peters T J & Waterman R H, *In Search Of Excellence*, Harper & Row, New York, 1982

Priest Andrew of Turner Kenneth Brown, *Agency agreements*, DTI Single Market News, Issue no 14, Spring 1992, p. 21

Quelch J A, Buzzell R D & Salama E R, *The Marketing Challenge of Europe 1992*, Addison–Wesley Publishing Company, Wokingham, 1990

Runyon, Kenneth E and Stewart, David W, *Consumer Behaviour*, Merill Publishing Company, a Bell & Howell Information Company, Columbus Ohio, 1987

Stephenson P R, Cron W L & Frazier G L, *Delegating pricing authority to the sales force: the effect on sales and profit performance*, Journal of Marketing, Spring 1979

Stern Louis W and El-Ansary Adel I, *Marketing Channels*, Prentice–Hall International Inc., Englewood Cliffs N J, 1988

Wellemin, John H, *Professional Service Management*, Chartwell–Bratt Ltd, Bromley, 1984

Wellemin, John H, *Customer Satisfaction Through Total Quality*, Chartwell–Bratt Ltd, Bromley, 1989

INDEX